PRAGUE

Research Manager
Dorothy McLeod

Managing Editor
Sarah Berlow

Editor
Mary Potter

Contents

Discover Prague

Prague is a city of magic. No, really, it is. Skip the tourist traps and everything that claims to be "authentic Czech culture," and open yourself to one of the most enchanting cities you'll ever experience. Prague is neither sterile West European capital nor Eastern European post-Communist wreck—it's caught somewhere in between daily reality and the realm of mortal legends. These cobblestone streets were once walked upon by Franz Kafka, the famous brooding author, and planned out by Charles IV, the ambitious Czech king, who dreamed up Prague the way it looks today (aside from the fast food restaurants, of course). And then there's the more recent specter of Communism, which left the entire country with a semi-permanent hangover and some peculiar sights, like a Malá Strana tower where the Communist secret police spied on foreign ambassadors and on Czech citizens with hilariously outdated equipment. But time moves forward as indicated by the giant metronome that ticks away where an enormous Stalin statue once stood. All this, and the hundreds of spires piercing the air, the roofs merging into one big sea of red, and the glistening Vltava River create the magic. Well, that and the beer that's cheaper than water, the hip cafes, and the art, from the subtlest of jazz melodies to the heaviest of modern sculptures. Sometimes all you will see are masses of tourists, but Prague's magic undoubtedly remains.

Budget Prague

If you're used to the dollar or the euro, boy did you come to the right place. If you stay in budget accommodations, take advantage of cheap food and beer, and stick to discounted sights and state-subsidized or free entertainment, you should be able to reap the full benefits of Prague's reasonable cost of living.

CHEAP EATS

With a little clever footwork you'll be avoiding the tourist traps of Old Town and sinking your teeth into some cheap *smažený sýr* (fried cheese) in no time. There is no shortage of wallet-friendly eats in Prague: the trick is discerning "authentic" (read: picture menus) from authentic (not an English-speaking soul in sight). When you tire of *knedlíky* (dumplings), meat, and potatoes, Prague offers an inexpensive grocery on just about every corner where you can stock up on cheap produce. And remember, in this city where a glass of water may cost you, the **pivo** (beer) is practically free.

▶ **RESTAURACE V CÍPU:** For a Czech meal in New Town that even the Czechs enjoy, head to V Cípu where fried cheese and some tank beer can be had for under 100Kč (p. 85).

▶ **LIBEŘSKÉ LAHŮDKY:** Stop into this bakery in New Town for a quick breakfast or lunch. The *chlebíčky* (open-faced sandwiches) are true works of art that cost no more than 19Kč (p. 85).

- ► **HAVELSKÁ KORUNA:** Lunch here (p. 93) is as authentic as it gets in Old Town. The dearth of English may be intimidating at first, but hop in line—all of the classic Czech entrees are under 80Kč.

- ► **APETIT:** Another cheap, locals-only joint (p. 96) in Old Town. Grab a tray, select a Czech meal, and take a seat next to some new friends.

- ► **BEAS VEGETARIAN DHABA:** In a city of meat and potatoes, BEAS (p. 93) is a vegetarian paradise with its fresh Indian buffet and free water.

Freebies

- ► **NEW EUROPE TOURS:** Czech out these free tours (p. 168) to get acquainted with Prague's major sights.

- ► **FREE MOVIES:** Cross Club (p. 131) has free film screenings every Wednesday.

- ► **PROPAGANDA PUB:** Live music and DJ sets most of the week at no cover charge. Get there early – the first 100 beers are just 12Kč (p. 122).

- ► **CLUB MECCA:** Experience legendary Holešovice nightlife at Club Mecca for no cover and just 39Kč per shot of vodka (p. 132).

- ► **MEETFACTORY:** Brush with the edge of contemporary art with free exhibits at the (in)famous David Černý's MeetFactory (p. 81) in Smichov.

BUDGET ACCOMMODATIONS

Don't worry about taking out a second mortgage to pay for your stay in Prague. As the city grows ever more popular with visitors from around the world, budget hostels spring up to accommodate them. Because Prague is small and its public transportation efficient, practically any neighborhood makes a convenient place to hang your hat. Like most European capitals, Prague is a zoo in summertime, so be sure to book ahead during the high season to take advantage of budget accommodations.

▶ **SIR TOBY'S HOSTEL:** Sir Toby's (p. 47) has plenty of character and common space. Wake up from a night out in Holešovice to Crepe and Cartoon Sundays with your hostelmates.

▶ **CZECH INN:** Check in to Czech Inn (p. 46), a "designer hostel" that doubles as an art gallery in Vinohrady.

▶ **HOSTEL ONE PRAGUE:** Rooms at Hostel One (p. 45) are more like mini-apartments. Come nightfall, the staff leads groups out to the pubs and bars that line the streets of Žižkov.

▶ **OLD PRAGUE HOSTEL:** If you're looking to stay close to the action in Old Town, this is the place (p. 38) to do it.

▶ **MOSAIC HOUSE:** With one of the comfortable rooms at the Czech Republic's first green hostel, Mosaic House (p. 33), you'll be right in the thick of it on Wenceslas Sq., near the sights of Old Town.

SIGHTSEEING ON THE CHEAP

Some of the best sightseeing in Prague won't cost you a crown. Just walk around and look up: you'll find everything from impeccably restored medieval churches to Art Nouveau wonders to Communist eyesores to dancing houses (we're not joking, check out the **Dancing House,** p. 53). When you do want to look inside, most sights offer **student discounts.**

Luckily for budget travelers, Prague is compact, and you could reach most sights by foot if you needed to. If you feel like splurging, the **trams** are probably the best way to get around; they go just about everywhere and, since they're above ground, they can double as a sightseeing tour. (Ride for 30min. for 18Kč or spring for a 5-day pass for 500Kč. See **Essentials,** p. 161.)

▶ **GET YOUR MUSEUM ON:** The **Alfons Mucha Museum** (p. 51), the **Franz Kafka Museum** (p. 69), and **DOX** (p. 78) all charge under 200Kč for admission.

▶ **L'CHAIM:** Josefov's synagogues may charge visitors as much as 300Kč, but some travelers report getting a free look at the **Old-New Synagogue** (p. 65) by attending services (F-Sa 8pm), which are technically open only to practicing members of the Jewish community.

▶ **PARK IT:** Prague has enough parks to keep you busy for days. Pack a cheap picnic and a couple of discreet Pilsners

and stake out a spot on the grass—for free. Czech out the view and the metronome at **Letenské sady** (p. 78), the grassy hills of **Riegrovy sady** (p. 77), the vine-covered **Havlíčkovy sady** (p. 77), or the hunting-ground-turned-"tree park" **Stromovka** (p. 79). For just 50Kč, you can also visit the **Charles University Botanical Gardens** (p. 57).

▶ **THE VIEW DON'T COST A THING:** Or if it does, it's just a small thing. Head to the **Petřínská Rozhledna** (100Kč; p. 67) at the top of Petřín Hill for a 360-degree view of the city; scale the heights of **Vyšehrad** (p. 77); take the tram up to **Strahov Monestary** (p. 74); or cough up the 120Kč to climb the **Žižkov Television Tower** (p. 76).

What To Do

ARTSY-FARTSY

Prague is one of those European capitals that practically gives away tickets to its major theater, music, and opera venues. **Rudolfinum** (p. 136) is the city's premier venue for classical music, while the student-rush program at **Státní Opera Praha** (p. 135) lets students see a fully staged opera for the price of a snack. The **Prague Spring Music Festival** (p. 139) brings the world's best soloists, small ensembles, symphony orchestras, and conductors to Prague annually.

DANCE THE NIGHT AWAY

Prague may not have quite the discotheque rep of some other European capitals, but there are still plenty of opportunities to embarrass yourself on the dance floor. No trip to Prague is complete without a trip to the legendary **Cross Club** (p. 131). The clientele is mostly Czech, so remember, *"pět piv, prosím"* ("five beers, please") and you should be good to go. In Vinohrady, **Radost FX** (p. 129) is a great place to dance to hip hop, house,

Student Superlatives

- **BEST USE OF A FORMER PUBLIC TOILET:** O2 Bar (p. 118) in Nové Město.

- **BEST PLACE TO KISS:** Below the ear. Just kidding – under the metronome in Letná Park (p. 78). Runner-up: Petřín's rose gardens.

- **BEST PLACE TO MEET CHARLES UNIVERSITY STUDENTS:** K4 Klub & Galerie (p. 123).

- **BEST-DECORATED CHURCH:** The Bone Church in Kutná Hora (p. 157).

- **MOST USELESS FORTIFICATION:** The Hunger Wall on Petřín Hill (p. 67).

- **BEST HANGOVER CURE:** A "Small Clear Head" from Lehká Hlava (p. 94).

- **BEST PLACE TO BUY BOOKS YOU CAN ACTUALLY READ:** Shakespeare & Sons (p. 142).

- **BEST ONE-EYED WAR HERO:** Jan Žižka. Czech out his statue on Vítkov Hill (p. 75).

- **GREATEST HERO WHO NEVER EXISTED:** Jára Cimrman. He has a museum in the basement of Petřín Tower (p. 67).

- **BEST MEXICAN FOOD:** Las Adelitas (p. 109).

and R and B under one of the most advanced light rigs that the city has to offer. For the quintessential study abroader experience, head to the enormous, industrial **Roxy** (p. 123). There's no cover, so you're guaranteed a packed dance floor. **ON** (p. 130), Prague's largest gay club, opens two large dance floors in addition to its usual disco and bar every weekend.

BEYOND TOURISM

Ready to learn more about Prague and give back to the community? Take classes on Czech culture, brush up on the basics of Czech, and volunteer or intern with local Czech organizations with a summer or semester with **CIEE** (p. 187). When you're too lazy to get out of bed in the morning, **Czech for Foreigners** (p. 192) brings lessons to you! If you're looking to volunteer, sign up for **Inex** (p. 193), where you can help clean up national forests or work at local community centers. If you're hungry for more, czech out **Beyond Tourism** (p. 188).

Planning Your Trip

Summer in Prague is the good life: think lounging on the grass on the banks of the Vltava, knocking back Pilsners late into the night at a pleasant beer garden, or picnicking in Letná Park overlooking the city. If you do visit in the summer, though, expect major tourist sights, streets, and squares in the Old Town to be a mob scene.

Visitors will need a warm coat and a dose of courage in winter; in return they can expect a magical, snow-covered city and a lively Christmas market in Old Town Sq.. As temperatures drop off and the days get shorter, the scene in the wine bars and cafes gains strength; so button up your parka, grab your hat and mittens, and venture out to find a hidden *hospoda*.

Travelers who come in the fall may get the best of both worlds: tourist hordes drop off and the weather holds steady (i.e. it's not freezing). You can still enjoy Prague's parks, and the grape harvest in Moravia means you can do it with a pleasant buzz thanks to the many wine festivals that take place throughout the city.

The Prague Spring comes around April, when the city finally starts to thaw. Travelers and residents can begin to venture outside in these months, taking advantage of the city's parks or cruising down the Vltava. Early May also brings the Prague Spring Music Festival, which means over 70 performances by world-renowned soloists, symphony orchestras, and small ensembles.

Icons

First things first: places and things that we absolutely love, sappily cherish, generally obsess over, and wholeheartedly endorse are denoted by the all-empowering 🖐 **Let's Go thumbs-up.** In addition, the icons scattered at the end of a listing can serve as visual cues to help you navigate each listing:

🖐	Let's Go recommends	☎	Phone numbers	⇉	Directions
i	Other hard info	$	Prices	⏰	Hours

NEIGHBORHOODS

Nové Město

Founded by Charles IV in 1348, Nové Město is not exactly "new." Its historical sights are a bit less known than those of the Old Town, but there's still a lot to see: the **New Town Hall** (where the Hussites famously chucked several town councilors out the window), **Our Lady of the Snow** (a dream cathedral whose construction was interrupted by the Hussite Wars), and **Saint Wenceslas Statue** (where Czechoslovak independence was proclaimed). Less touristy than the Old Town, Nové Město is home to nightlife and affordable restaurants as well as some of the most conveniently located hostels in the entire city. If you're skeptical of Staré Město's artificial charms, this is the perfect neighborhood to start searching for more authentic experiences.

The New Town is dominated by two enormous squares. **Wenceslas Square** (Václavské náměstí), a former horse market, is now occupied by Western-style shops, sausage hawkers, and the equestrian statue of St. Wenceslas, while **Charles Square** (Karlovo náměstí), a former cattle market, is today covered by a somewhat-unkempt park. **Národní třída** is a major street that separates the Old Town from the New; here you'll find the impressive **National Theater.** Fast-food joints litter **I.P. Pavlova,** a square on the border of Nové Město and Vinohrady.

Staré Město

No matter where you look, Staré Město is postcard material. Historical buildings are beautifully renovated, the pedestrian streets are covered in cobblestone, and churches appear around every corner. The downside? Foreigners flock by the hundreds of thousands, bringing out the ugly side of tourism: high prices, omnipresent tourist traps, and false claims of "authenticity." It is up to you—with help from *Let's Go*—to navigate the line between the beautiful and the fake, but don't take this task too seriously: after all, elbowing the crowds on Charles Bridge is pretty authentically Prague.

Old Town Square (Staroměstské náměstí) is the heart of Staré Město. Some of Prague's most famous landmarks—the **Astronomical Clock** and **Church of Our Lady Before Týn**—are located here. To the west is the iconic **Charles Bridge,** while the streets to the east lead to **Municipal House** and ⓜNáměstí Míru. To the north is Josefov, a small historic Jewish neighborhood completely enveloped by the river and Staré Město. Finally, streets to the south (Melantrichova, Jilská) connect Old Town Sq. with **Wenceslas Square** and **Národní Třída,** which mark the beginning of Nové Město. Trams and the Metro don't go directly through Staré Město but rather skirt its edges; walking is the preferred mode of transportation.

Josefov

Josefov is a historically Jewish district of Prague whose main attractions are five **synagogues** and the **Old Jewish Cemetery.** It may seem surprising that such a district survives in post-WWII Europe—in fact, during the Nazi occupation Hitler demarcated the area as a future museum of the soon-to-be extinct Jewish people. Aside from the surviving synagogues, most of the buildings in the area were demolished in the late 19th century and replaced with Art Nouveau architecture. The area is also famous for its connection to the writer **Franz Kafka,** who was born nearby, and whose name is now plastered on every other souvenir sold here. The synagogues here are certainly worth a visit, but the neighborhood is also one of the biggest tourist traps in Prague, with over-priced restaurants (think mussels and lobster), high-end fashion boutiques, and souvenir peddlers.

Malá Strana

Malá Strana, literally "Lesser Town," got the name because of its placement below the castle, but we see nothing "lesser" about it. Squeezed between Prague Castle and the Vltava, and stretching up Petřín Hill, Malá Strana is the stomping ground for more established, better-known artists. The area is full of interesting cafes and bars, and **Kampa Island,** a riverside park, calls out for you to lie on the grass. The other ace in Malá Strana's hole is **Petřín Hill,** the sprawling park that is home to Prague's fat cousin of the French Eiffel Tower.

To the north, Malá Strana merges smoothly into Hradčany, while to the south you'll find the neighborhood of **Smíchov,** best known for its large shopping mall and the Smíchov train station. **Malostranské náměstí** is Malá Strana's main square and **Újezd** is its main street, snaking from north to south along Petřín Park. Malá Strana's only Metro stop is **Malostranská** (on the A line), but it can also be conquered on foot or by **tram** (12, 20, 22).

Hradčany

A visit to Hradčany is a must—the neighborhood is home to the **Prague Castle,** which contains such well-known sights as **Saint Vitus Cathedral** and the **Golden Lane.** Outside of the castle, don't miss **Strahov Monastery's** collection of natural oddities (the remains of a dodo bird, a narwhal tusk, etc.) and **Loreta,** one of the most important pilgrimage destinations in the Czech Republic. Most of the surrounding establishments are unabashed tourist traps, but this doesn't detract from Hradčany's real charms—sloping cobblestone streets and some of the best panoramic views of Prague. Located just north of Malá Strana and west of **Letenské sady,** Hradčany is also a good place to start your hike up to Petřín Tower, or your dive down the hill toward Malá Strana's more affordable establishments. To get to Hradčany, take Metro A to **Malostranská** and then walk up the hill, or, better yet, take **tram 22,** which drops you off right above the castle.

Žižkov

In Žižkov there's no street that doesn't slope, no wall safe from graffiti, and no block without a pub or a bar. Known historically as a rough neighborhood, Žižkov also had a reputation as a bohemian (get it?) district, home to such writers as Jaroslav Hašek (author of *The Good Soldier Švejk*) and Jaroslav Seifert (a Nobel-winning poet). Today, the neighborhood's symbol is the **Žižkov TV Tower,** the tallest and ugliest structure in Prague. Though it's being slowly gentrified, Žižkov remains gritty and bustles with local nightlife.

At the northern border of Žižkov there's **Vítkov Hill** and the **statue of Jan Žižka,** the one-eyed Hussite general for whom the neighborhood is named. To the south Žižkov borders Riegrovy sady and Vinohrady, while to the east it includes two big cemeteries, including **New Jewish Cemetery,** where Franz Kafka is buried. **Trams** 5, 9, 11, and 26 are the best way of getting to and from Žižkov, as the nearest Metro station, **Jiřího z Poděbrad,** is in neighboring Vinohrady.

Vinohrady

Originally called Královské Vinohrady (Royal Vineyards) to commemorate King Charles IV's contribution to the founding of local viticulture, this relaxed residential neighborhood is a favorite among expats, students, and Prague's gay community. Aside from reigning over an abundance of parks and green spaces, Vinohrady is close to the **Vyšehrad** cultural monument, one of Prague's best known landmarks. You will also find the **Church of Saint Peter and Saint Paul** and the **Vyšehrad cemetery,** where some of the most prominent Czech artists are buried.

The western border of Vinohrady is roughly denoted by Ⓜ**I.P. Pavlova.** The neighborhood then stretches east along **Vinohradská,** all the way to Ⓜ**Želivského. Náměstí Míru** is located just a few blocks away from I.P. Pavlova, while **Jiřího z Poděbrad** is close to Žižkov. **Riegrovy sady** and Žižkov border Vinohrady to the north and **Havlíčkovy sady** is to the south. **Vyšehrad** is a separate district, just one Metro stop southwest of I.P. Pavlova. Walking in Vinohrady is an option, but if you want to save time, you can take advantage of the frequent tram service.

Holešovice

Holešovice used to be an industrial suburb, but today, thanks to steady gentrification, it's turning into one of Prague's most exciting neighborhoods. The industrial scale of the buildings here has lent itself well to arts spaces like **DOX** and **Veletržní Palác,** nightclubs like **Cross Club** and **SaSaZu,** and even hostels like **Prague Plus Hostel.** Home to other sprawling complexes such as the **Prague Market, Exhibition Ground,** and **Letenské sady,** Holešovice is the perfect escape from the cramped streets of Staré Město.

Situated north of Staré Město at a bend in the Vltava, Holešovice is split in two by railroad tracks. It's not as pedestrian-friendly a neighborhood as many others in Prague, so we recommend **trams** 1, 3, 5, 12, 14, 17, and 25 to get around. The two closest Metro stations are on the C line: **Vltavská** and **Nádraží Holešovice.**

Dejvice

There are few tourist sights in Dejvice and consequently, few tourists. This lively locals-only neighborhood has its own charms, and those spending more than a week or two in Prague should definitely take a walk around. Dejvice is organized around an enormous roundabout **(Vítězné náměstí),** and, in addition to being home to a university complex and two famous theaters (**Divadlo Semafor** and **Divadlo Spejbla & Hurvínka,** both on Dejvická), it has plenty of restaurants that won't charge you extra for being a foreigner. The neighborhood is close to both Letenské sady and Hradčany. Northwest of Dejvice, the sprawling natural reserve **Divoká Šárka** is Prague's best refuge for those tired of cobblestone.

Smíchov

Just across the river from Nové Město and Vyšehrad, Smíchov is not as appealing to tourists as the others—there are no old churches or historical buildings to speak of. Instead, it veers toward the modern: the area around Ⓜ**Anděl** is home to the mall **Nový Smíchov,** a few big bookstores, and two multiplex cinemas. To the south, you'll find **Smíchovské nádraží,** a train station that serves most Germany-bound trains and that is home to many a sketchy character. There is also some sightseeing to do—including the free contemporary art gallery, **MeetFactory** and the **Staropramen Brewery.** Metro B and numerous tram lines go to Smíchov.

SUGGESTED ITINERARIES

Cheap Date

We're talking grade-A indie romance starring Michael Serra.

   1. WE'RE ON A BOAT: Fancy boat cruises along the Vltava

Traffic Win or Traffic Fail?

We at *Let's Go* certainly love to pull readers' legs from time to time, but this story falls into the "You Can't Make This Stuff Up" category. In December 2010, in an effort to improve traffic safety (we still don't quite follow their logic on that one) while reducing costs, Prague and nearby towns placed cardboard cut-outs of female police officers along certain roads in lieu of costly traffic lights or even more expensive real people. Though cardboard, these officers are most certainly not flat, and they sport heels and miniskirts, no matter how cold the Prague winter gets. The plan quickly backfired, though: only two weeks after the "officers" were installed, their distracting presence had already led to an alleged doubling of the rate of accidents.

can cost as much as 750Kč for a 2hr. voyage. But all of the romance can be yours with a Metro pass and a little imagination. Basic, three-day, and five-day metro passes cover travel by ferry along the Vltava. So while the sun's still out, climb aboard and quote *Titanic* ironically... "king of the world," etc. (See **Essentials,** p. 161.)

2. SECRET GARDEN: Head over to the **Wallenstein Gardens** (p. 69) in Malá Strana for a quiet escape. Nothing says "let's make out on this park bench" like lush greenery and baby peacocks.

3. ROMANTIC DINNER: Relax post-makeout sesh with dinner at **Lehká Hlava** (Clear Mind, p. 94). Feed each other vegetarian delicacies and whisper sweet nothings.

4. THIS IS MY ARTISTIC SIDE: Let's face it: you'll never be able to afford the Met. Maintain the illusion that you are "cultured" without breaking the bank. Tickets to the **State Opera** (p. 135) or the **National Theater** (p. 135) go for as little as 50-100Kč. Impressing your boo has never been so cheap.

5. YOU WANT MORE? Get your second wind post-Opera and head over to **Roxy** (p. 123) for a sweaty dance floor, or cross the Vltava for a bit more class at **Jazz Dock** (p. 125) in

Malá Strana. Secretly riding solo on this "cheap date"? Call it a night with a luscious gelato at **Angelato** (p. 88).

Walking Tour: Cavorting With Kafka

Though Prague is only mentioned by name a few times in any of Kafka's works, the city left an indelible mark on the writer's psyche. A German-Jew, Kafka was doubly marginalized during a time when anti-foreign and anti-Semitic feelings were strong. Though he tried to leave Prague for Vienna and Berlin several times in his life, he always found himself drawn back to the city of his birth. Today's Prague is vastly different from Kafka's city, though you can still visit many of the places that played a role in the writer's development.

1. STATUE OF FRANZ KAFKA. Between the Spanish Synagogue (p. 64) and a nearby catholic church stands the only statue in Prague dedicated to its most alienated son (p. 66).

2. FRANZ KAFKA'S BIRTHPLACE. The downer-to-be was born on July 3, 1883, in an old tenement building on the corner of Kaprova and Maiselova streets in Staré Město (p. 57). Though the tenement has long since come down, there is a small sign on the side of the building marking the site.

3. DŮM U MINUTY. Kafka spent part of his childhood in the House on the Minute (Dům U Minuty) across from the famed Astronomical Clock (p. 58), which at that time still sported an anti-Semitic statue, complete with beard and horns, for its depiction of Greed.

4. NATIONAL GALLERY AT GOLTZ-KINSKY PALACE. Kafka attended an elite secondary school on the second floor of the Goltz-Kinsky Palace near Old Town Sq. The morning commute seems to have had a profound effect on young Kafka, as he mentions the routine more than once in his letters and journals.

5. FRANZ KAFKA MUSEUM. Across the river, the Franz Kafka museum (p. 69) attempts to tell Kafka's story largely through his relationship to Prague. The museum contains many of the writer's journals and letters as well as first editions of most of his works. The various audio-visual installations attempt to place you inside his psyche. If the haunting soundtrack and endless corridors of filing cabinets don't make you feel appropriately isolated and insignificant, then you might be too cheery for this walking tour.

6. PETŘÍN HILL. Petřín Hill (p. 67) was one of Kafka's favorite places to go as a teenager. It is also one of the only places in Prague ever mentioned by name in his works. His story, "Description of a Struggle" warns against scaling its slopes during winter, though the view from the top during a summer evening is still excellent.

7. CAFÉ LOUVRE. After the walk (or funicular ride) from Petřín, have a cup of coffee in this elegant cafe (p. 90). Kafka and his friends used to gather here every fortnight to debate current events and philosophy.

7. GRAND HOTEL EUROPA. From Narodní, make your way to the base of Wencelas Sq. and start walking toward the National Museum. Though the square has undergone many changes over the past century, the Grand Hotel Europa, with much of its original Art Nouveau decor preserved, remains one of its most identifiable landmarks. Kafka gave a reading of his recently completed story, "The Judgment" in the hotel's second-floor cafe.

Three-Day Weekend

Only have three days in Prague? Pity. But don't worry—we've got you covered with everything from the historical sights to the major museums to the best in Czech food and nightlife.

Day One: History

STARÉ MĚSTO: Your first mission is to knock out all of the major tourist sights in and around Old Town Sq.. Hit the **Astronomical Clock** (p. 58) on the hour to see a bunch of puppets pop their heads out of a window, swing through the **Church of Our Lady before Týn** (p. 59) to pay your respects to Tyco Brahe's remains, and then swing by the Art Deco

Municipal House (p. 59). Finally, make your way through the crowds out onto the historic **Charles Bridge** (p. 57). Remember, it's not always about paying to enter the sights of Staré Město; often just gazing at the magnificent facades is enough.

TYPICKÝ ČESKÝ OBĚD: That's "typical Czech lunch" to you non-Česky speakers. Grab some *smažený sýr* (fried cheese), *knedlíky* (dumplings), or *bramboraky* (potato pancakes) at a classic Czech restaurant in Old Town. We like **Havelská Koruna** (p. 93), **Lokál** (p. 94), or **Pivnice U Rudolfina** (p. 98).

JOSEFOV: Next up on the itinerary are the synagogues of Josefov. Prague's historically Jewish quarter was preserved by the Nazi's under Hitler's orders as a museum of the soon-to-be-extinct Jewish people. With a joint ticket (p. 62) you can visit **Pinkas, Klausen, Maisel,** and the **Spanish Synagogue.** Finish up with a wander through the **Old Jewish Cemetery,** which is also included in the combined admission.

RUDOLFINUM: Finish the night off with a little classical music in **Rudolfinum** (p. 136), which is home to the Czech Philharmonic Orchestra.

Day Two: Culture

ART MUSEUMS: Head to Holešovice in the morning to get a taste of the visual arts in the Czech Republic. Take your pick from the history of Central European art on display at **Veletržní Palác** (p. 79) or the contemporary scene at **DOX** (p. 78)—or, hit both!

LETENSKÉ SADY: Take a break from all that art with a stroll through Letenské sady or **Letná Park** (p. 78). Make your way to the metronome for a breathtaking view of Prague.

KAROLÍNY SVĚTLÉ: Head to this little street in New Town for a well-deserved drink. Tiny bars remain hidden from tourists all along this road. Start with hip **Duende** (p. 95) and explore from there.

DINNER: Grab dinner in New Town. Go Czech again with local favorite **Potrefená Husa** (p. 84) or **Restaurace V Cípu** (p. 85), or splurge at historic **Café Slavia** (p. 87) for great people-watching along the Vltava.

CLUBBIN': Return to Holešovice after dinner for the best of Prague's nightlife. Choose from the enormous maze of rooms that is **Cross Club** (p. 131), one of the district's newest additions **SaSaZu** (p. 132), or grab a few cheap shots of vodka and czech out the DJs and performers at **Club Mecca** (p. 132).

Day Three: The Castle

PRAGUE CASTLE (PRAŽSKÝ HRAD): It's time to slay the beast that is **Prague Castle** (p. 71). Hike up Nerudova or take the tram to the top, and take either the short or long tour. Arrive on the hour to see the changing of the guard.

SAINT VITUS CATHEDRAL (KATEDRÁLA SV. VÍTA): While you're up in Hradčany, don't miss this giant cathedral (p. 72) that took over six centuries to build. Tour the cathedral and then climb the Great South Tower for an incredible view of the city.

STRAHOVSKÝ KLÁŠTER (STRAHOV MONASTERY): Next, hit the Strahov Monastery (p. 74). In its library you'll find an 18th-century cabinet of curiosities with all kinds of wonders, but the real attraction is the vista.

WALLENSTEIN PALACE: Take a load of down the hill in Malá Strana at the **Wallenstein Palace and Gardens** (p. 69), which are home to immaculate hedges and reflecting pools, the Czech Senate, and a group of peacocks and owls.

Planning Your Trip

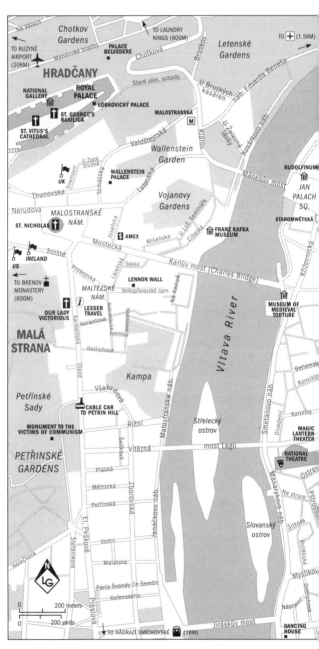

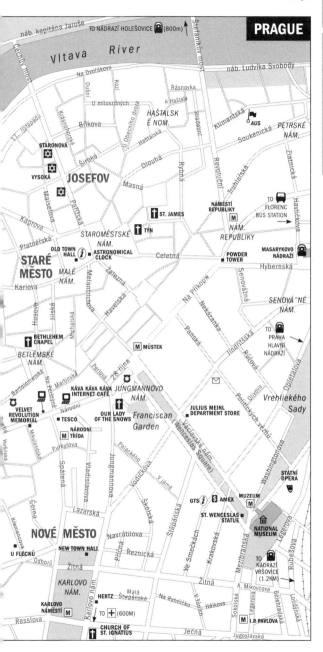

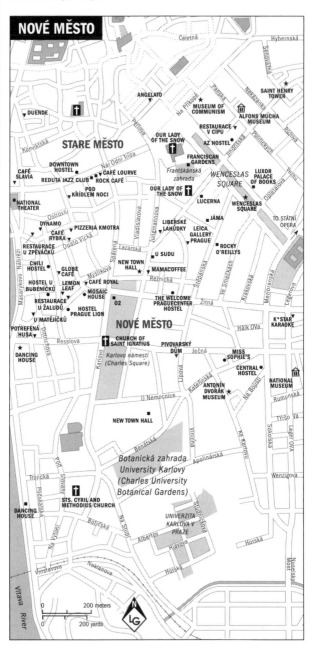

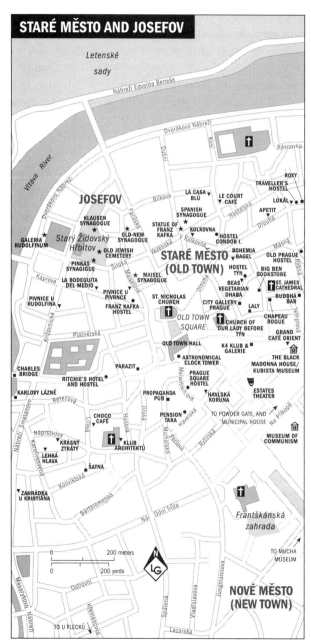

STARÉ MĚSTO AND JOSEFOV

Letenské sady

Nábřeží Edvarda Beneše

Vltava River

Dvořákovo Nábřeží

Dvořákovo Nábřeží

Dušní

Kosí

Rásnovka

ROXY

JOSEFOV

LA CASA BLÚ

LE COURT CAFÉ

TRAVELLER'S HOSTEL

Bílkova

Hastalská

LOKÁL

Bílkova

SPANISH SYNAGOGUE

Dlouhá

APETIT

KLAUSEN SYNAGOGUE

STATUE OF FRANZ KAFKA

KOLKOVNA

Vězeňská

Kolkovne

HOSTEL CONDOR I.

Masná

GALERIA RUDOLFINUM

Starý Židovský Hřbitov

OLD-NEW SYNAGOGUE

OLD JEWISH CEMETERY

BOHEMIA BAGEL

OLD PRAGUE HOSTEL

Pařížská

STARÉ MĚSTO (OLD TOWN)

Řbná

PINKAS SYNAGOGUE

Kaprova

Maiselova

Široká

MAISEL SYNAGOGUE

HOSTEL TÝN

BIG BEN BOOKSTORE

ST. JAMES CATHEDRAL

LA BODEGUITA DEL MEDIO

PIVNICE U PIVRNCE

BEAS VEGETARIAN DHABA

PIVNICE U RUDOLFINA

Dlouhá

BUDDHA BAR

ST. NICHOLAS CHURCH

FRANZ KAFKA HOSTEL

CITY GALLERY PRAGUE

LALY

Týnská

Platnérská

OLD TOWN SQUARE

CHURCH OF OUR LADY BEFORE TÝN

CHAPEAU ROUGE

GRAND CAFÉ ORIENT

CHARLES BRIDGE

Křižovnická

OLD TOWN HALL

K4 KLUB & GALERIE

THE BLACK MADONNA HOUSE/ KUBISTA MUSEUM

RITCHIE'S HOTEL AND HOSTEL

PARAZIT

ASTRONOMICAL CLOCK TOWER

Melantrichova

PRAGUE SQUARE HOSTEL

ESTATES THEATER

KARLOVY LÁZNĚ

Retezová

PROPAGANDA PUB

HAVLSKÁ KORUNA

Na Příkopě

TO POWDER GATE, AND MUNICIPAL HOUSE

Náprstkova

Nábřeží Smetanovo

Karoliny Světlé

Liliová

Husova

Jilská

CHOCO CAFÉ

PENSION TARA

Havelská

Michalská

Perlová

Rytířská

MUSEUM OF COMMUNISM

KRÁSNÝ ZTRÁTY

KLUB ARCHITEKTŮ

LEHKÁ HLAVA

ŠATNA

Konviktská

ZAHRÁDKA U KRISTIÁNA

Bartolomějská

Náprstkova

Nár. Odní třída

Frantškánská zahrada

0   200 meters

0   200 yards

N

TO MUCHA MUSEUM

Masarykovo

Ostrovní

Křemencova

TO U FLECKŮ

Spálená

Lazarská

Vladislavova

Jungmannova

NOVÉ MĚSTO (NEW TOWN)

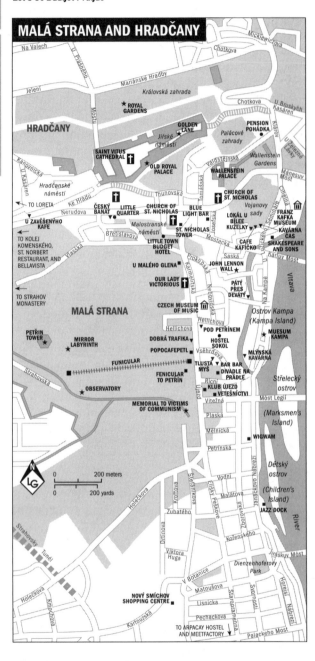

MALÁ STRANA AND HRADČANY

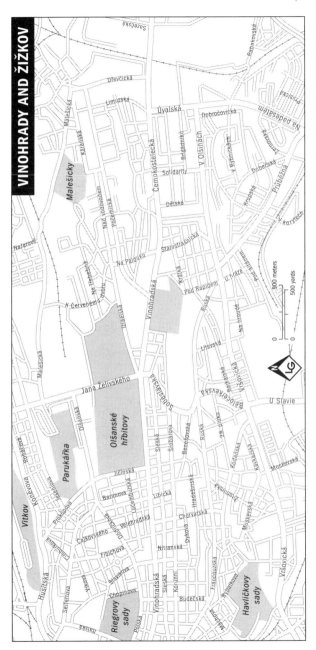

VINOHRADY AND ŽIŽKOV

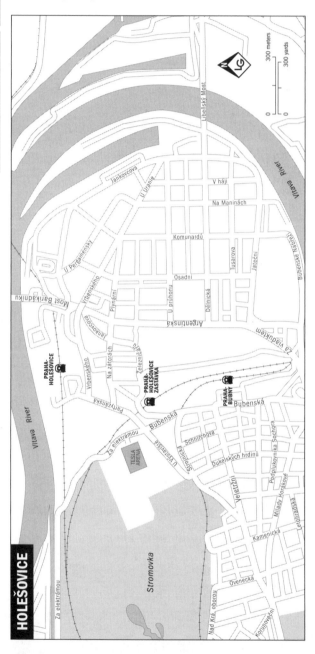

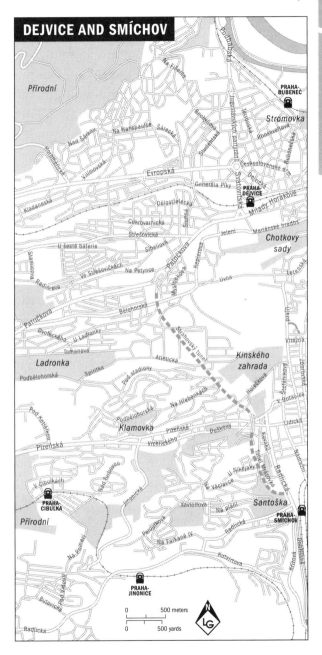

DEJVICE AND SMÍCHOV

Accommodations

Prague has accommodations to suit every budget. Thanks to the opening of some new "chic" hostels throughout the city (Mosaic House, Sir Toby's, Miss Sophie's, Czech Inn), travelers willing to pay a bit extra can find digs that almost feel like hotels, some with in-house restaurants and free Wi-Fi. There are many earthier options throughout the city, including a handful of cheaper party hostels. In general, Staré Město costs more and offers less, while Nové Město costs less and offers more. There are several great hostels in Holešovice, Vinohrady, and Malá Strana, but these may require a Metro or a tram ride to visit sights, which might be a bit out of the way for those staying only a few days in Prague. In addition to hostels, there's a network of student dorms that function as hostels during the summer (www.czechcampus.com). These may not give you the traditional hostel experience, but they tend to be cheaper than most hostels.

Finally, a note on prices: the prices included in this guide are approximate. Most Prague hostels price with an algorithm that takes into account the time of year, the day of the week, and hostel vacancy. No matter when you visit, the system rewards those who book in advance.

Budget Accommodations

Staying in Prague for cheap certainly isn't difficult. If you are especially, um, energy-efficient (read: lazy), Nové Město is a good option in the center of the action. If you're a true budgeteer, you'll find hostels outside the center in neighborhoods like Holešovice and Vinohrady to be cheaper and easily accessible by tram. Plus, if you stay away from touristy Staré Město, buying food nearby will also cost you less.

NOVÉ MĚSTO

Nové Město might be the best part of town to stay in. There's a cluster of reasonablypriced hostels around **Myslíkova.** Many mid-level hotels are also concentrated around **I.P. Pavlova,** but, if you're going to stay in Nové Město, we'd recommend staying a little closer to the center of town.

[icon] Mosaic House — HOTEL, HOSTEL $$

Odborů 4

☎246 008 324; www.mosaichouse.com

Staying at Mosaic House might be even more environmentally friendly than pitching a tent somewhere in Wenceslas Sq. The first of its kind in the Czech Republic, the hostel uses electricity solely from renewable sources and has a graywater recycling system. But the real difference between this and sleeping in a tent? The comfort. The four-star hotel rooms have a spillover effect on the sleek and private dorms. Another major plus is the restaurant downstairs; Belushi's has live music, comedy nights, and other events, in addition to serving generous portions of American food. (*Let's Go* does not recommend camping in Wenceslas Sq.)

▶ 🚇 B: Karlovo náměstí. From the station, head north along the western edge of the square. Take a left at Odborů at the northwest corner. ℹ Breakfast 150Kč. Towels included for hotel guests, with dorms 30Kč. Lockers included. Computer use 50Kč per hr. Women's dorm available. [$] Dorms 300-625Kč; doubles 1440Kč. ⏰ Reception 24hr.

Downtown Hostel — HOSTEL $$

Národní třída 19

☎224 240 570; www.hostel-downtown.cz

One of the best-located hostels in the city, Downtown Hostel straddles the border between Old and New Town, and is within spitting distance from tram and Metro stops. Among the hostel's highlights are its daily social events, which include cooking nights and free sightseeing tours. The rooms are simple and clean—if you're lucky, yours will have unusually tall windows that face the enormous anti-war graffiti across the street. The common room features a piano, and there's a guitar to borrow at reception—a jam session with other hostel guests is at your fingertips.

► 🚇 B: Národní třída. From the Metro walk up on Spálená, then turn left on Národní třída. The hostel is on the right. ℹ Breakfast 70Kč. Linens and towels included. Laundry 50Kč. Free Wi-Fi. $ Dorms 300-500Kč; doubles 1000-1800Kč. 10% discount for HI members. ⏰ Reception 24hr.

AZ Hostel

HOSTEL $

Jindřišská 5

☎224 241 664; www.hostel-az.cz

Well-located and quite cheap, AZ is best suited to those who don't ask for too much in terms of hostel culture. The common room may be forgettable, and there may not be that many extra perks (with the exception of complimentary tea and coffee), but the rooms are neatly painted and without bunk beds. Since the hostel lies just off Wenceslas Sq., staying here will afford you the additional pleasure of interacting with the sketchy men trying to lure you into their erotic clubs at night. (Always a perk.)

► 🚇 A or B: Můstek. From the station, walk up the square toward the National Museum, then make a left on Jindřišská. The hostel is on the left, inside a courtyard. ℹ Linens, towels, and lockers included. Laundry service 190Kč. Computer use 20Kč per 10min. Free Wi-Fi. Women-only dorm available. $ Dorms 320Kč; singles 950Kč; doubles 1000Kč. 10% discount for stays over 1 week. ⏰ Reception 24hr.

Miss Sophie's

HOSTEL, HOTEL $$

Melounová 3

☎293 303 530; www.miss-sophies.com

Miss Sophie's is a bit out of the way and on the pricier side, but it's not entirely out of the budget traveler's reach. Genuinely cool modern designs (including mural-sized original artwork) line the newly painted walls and the steel and glass showers are classier than what you'll find in most hotels. The polished wood floors, black bed frames, and intimate brick cellar (where one of Prague's most impressive hostel breakfasts is served) may be worth the few extra crowns and the tram ride to I.P. Pavlova.

► 🚇 C: I.P. Pavlova. From the Metro, walk west on Ječná, then take the 2nd left onto Melounová. *i* Breakfast 170Kč. Towels 30Kč. Free Wi-Fi. 2 computers available. $ Dorms 410-600Kč; private rooms 1150-2200Kč. 5% ISIC discount for online reservations. ⏰ Reception 24hr.

Chili Hostel

HOSTEL $

Pštrossova 7

☎603 119 113; www.chili.dj

Judging by the phone-book-length list of damage fines posted at the reception, this place can get rowdy. With its army of bunk beds and enormous underground lounge (with both pool and foosball tables), Chili is a real party hostel. Don't expect any luxury (the dorm rooms have barely any furniture); do expect international pregames in the common spaces.

▶ 🚇 B: Národní třída. From the Metro, walk west on Ostrovní and make a left on Pštrossova. The hostel is on the right on a street corner. *i* Linens, towels, and lockers included. Laundry 190Kč; free for stays of 5 days or more. Free Wi-Fi. Computers available. $ Dorms 200-480Kč; doubles 600-700Kč per person. ⏰ Reception 24hr.

Hostel Prague Lion

HOSTEL $$

Na Zbořenci 6

☎731 487 936; www.prague-lion.com

This little hostel may be called the lion, but roaring won't get you very far; with no common spaces, it's ideal for those who want quiet. The hostel is small and tends to fill up, so book at least a week in advance. If you're lucky enough to get a bed, you'll be able to enjoy the spacious, well-equipped rooms, some of which even have their own kitchen counters.

▶ 🚇 B: Karlovo náměstí. From the Metro, head down Resslova, then take the 1st right on Na Zderaze and another right on Na Zbořenci. *i* Linens and towels included. Free Wi-Fi and 1 computer available. Fridges and microwaves in all rooms. $ Doubles 1350-2200Kč; quads 1850-2700Kč. 4% fee for credit card payment. ⏰ Reception 24hr.

Hostel U Bubeníčků

GUESTHOUSE $

Myslíkova 8

☎224 922 357; www.ububenicku.com

This isn't your typical hostel—the only reception desk you'll find is the bar of the U Bubeníčků restaurant. Located above the restaurant, the fourth-floor hostel offers 38 budget beds and some apartments. Many of the typical hostel facilities are absent—no computers, no common room—but the place combines low rates and pleasant decor. The smells of roast pork and sauerkraut

downstairs are free of charge—should you decide to pursue them further, guests get a 10% discount at the restaurant.

▶ ⚑ B: Karlovo náměstí. From the Metro, take Resslova toward the river and take a right on Na Zderaze and a left on Myslíková. The guesthouse is on the left. *i* Breakfast 50-90Kč. Linens and lockers included. Towels 50Kč. Ⓢ Dorms 300Kč; doubles 490Kč per person. Ⓩ Reception 9am-midnight.

The Welcome Praguecenter Hostel   GUESTHOUSE $
Žitná 17

☎224 320 202; www.bed.cz

Possibly the worst-named hostel in the city, Welcome Praguecenter provides reasonably comfortable private rooms for dorm prices. Located on the second floor of an apartment building, this guesthouse has nine rooms featuring king-size beds, refrigerators, and safes. The lack of a common space or kitchen is the only downfall. Well, that and a lame name.

▶ ⚑ B: Karlovo náměstí. From the station, head away from the river down Žitná. The guesthouse is on the left. *i* Linens and towels included. Free Wi-Fi; computer use 20Kč per 10min. Reserve in advance. Ⓢ Private rooms 250-450Kč per person. Ⓩ Reception open 8am-8pm.

Hostel Centre   HOSTEL $$
Sokolská 29

☎224 247 412; www.hostel-centre.eu

Even though the name is more wishful thinking than reality, Hostel Centre still offers acceptable rooms at decent prices. The carpeting adds a level of hominess, and you can use the hostel's Playstation, for €2 per hour. Tram 22 or the Metro line C will take you wherever you need to go.

▶ ⚑ C: I.P. Pavlova. From the Metro, head 1 block toward the river on Jugoslávská and turn left on Sokolská. The hostel is on the right. *i* Breakfast 56Kč. Linens and towels included. Free Wi-Fi and computers available. Ⓢ Dorms 420-700Kč; doubles 750Kč. Ⓩ Reception 24hr.

STARÉ MĚSTO

Surprisingly, there's only a handful of hostels in Staré Město. The main draw of staying here is the location—roll out of bed in the morning and you'll land on the historic cobblestones. The Old Town is great for those staying in Prague for a day or two and who won't have time to explore the outer neighborhoods much.

Accommodations

Old Prague Hostel
HOSTEL $$

Benediktská 2

☎224 829 058; www.oldpraguehostel.com

Old Prague and its sister hostel, Prague Square, are perhaps the only hostels in Staré Město that really roll Western-style, despite the old-school buildings they occupy. Common rooms have flatscreen TVs and comfy couches, light breakfast (sandwiches, cereal) is included in the price, and receptionists tend to be young expats. Old Prague Hostel is marginally the better of the two—it feels more welcoming, thanks to some cheerful drawings on the walls. It's also a bit farther away from the rumble of the crowds in Old Town Sq., but still really close to everything in Staré Město.

▶ 🚇 B: Náměstí Republiky. From the station, walk down to Powder Tower, then turn right on Celetná. Turn right at an underpass that leads to Templová and take the first left on Štupartská. The hostel will be on the right. *i* Non-smoking. Breakfast, towels, linens, lockers, and adapters included. Wi-Fi available on the mezzanine and in the common area; free computer access. Key deposit 100Kč. [$] 8-bed dorms 270-450Kč; 4-bed 350-550Kč. Doubles 500-650Kč. Cash only. ⏰ Reception 24hr.

Prague Square Hostel
HOSTEL $$

Melantrichova 10

☎224 240 859; www.praguesquarehostel.com

In terms of services, Prague Square Hostel is identical to its twin, Old Prague Hostel. The only real difference is in location: the advantage of Prague Square Hostel is that it's right in the stream of people between Old Town and Wenceslas Squares, a bit closer to Nové Město. If you're bothered by the ruckus outside, the reception offers free earplugs.

▶ 🚇 A or B: Můstek. From the station, head north on na Můstku and continue on it as it turns into Melantrichova. The hostel will be on your right. *i* Non-smoking. Breakfast, adapters, towels, linens, and lockers included. Free computer access and Wi-Fi in common spaces. [$] 8-bed dorms 270-450Kč; 4-bed 350-550Kč. Doubles 500-650Kč. Cash only. ⏰ Reception 24hr.

Hostel Týn
HOSTEL $

Týnská 19

☎224 828 519; www.hosteltyn.com

Finding this hostel in the maze of Týn-related streets behind Church of Our Lady Before Týn can take a while, but it's worth it. The dorms are bunk-free, which offsets the lack of free breakfast. The underground common room and kitchen are virtually pleasant (helped by the fake window with LED tubes imitating sunlight) and a good place to socialize. The bad news is that the downstairs closes at 2am; the good news is that, depending on your charm, this time may be negotiable.

▶ ✦ B: Náměstí Republiky. From the station, head south to Powder Tower and continue on Celetná. Continue towards the river, then take a right at Štupartská and a left onto Týnská. Follow Týnská as it winds around. The hotel is in a courtyard on your right. *i* Non-smoking. Towels and lockers included. Free Wi-Fi in common spaces; free computer access. Ⓢ Dorms 300-400Kč; doubles 900-1200Kč; triples 1000-1400Kč. Cash only. ⏰ Reception 24hr.

Pension Tara   PENSION $
Havelská 15

☎224 228 083; www.pensiontara.net

If you're lucky, you'll score this pension's sole dorm, which features six beds in three separate rooms. You can also ask for one of their attic rooms, which are quiet and fun (and by fun we mean you have to step over wooden beams). It's not a hostel, so there's no kitchen, breakfast, or Wi-Fi, but as far as the whole sleeping thing goes, the rooms are nice enough.

▶ ✦ A or B: Můstek. From the station, head north on na Můstku and continue on it as it turns into Melantrichova, then take a left on Havelská. The pension will be on your right. *i* Linens and towels included. No Wi-Fi, but the reception has 1 Wi-Fi USB key that they lend to guests. Ⓢ Large dorms 300-400Kč; 4-bed rooms 450-550Kč; doubles 600-850Kč. ⏰ Reception 9am-8pm.

Ritchie's Hotel and Hostel   HOSTEL $$
Karlova 13

☎222 221 229; www.ritchieshostel.cz

Full of hidden steps, low ceilings, and staircases that twist and creak, this hostel is a bit like one of those colorful adventure playgrounds for kids. You might need to walk out on the balcony to go to the bathroom or to take a shower, or you might end up in a room with a 175cm (5 ft., 10 in.) ceiling. The upside: you're on Karlova, one of the busiest pedestrian streets in Prague, smack dab in the center of everything.

▶ ✦ A: Staroměstské. From the station, head down Křižovnická directly along the river. At the Charles bridge, turn left on Karlova. The hostel will be on the left, through a small gallery. *i* Lockers 30Kč per day. Breakfast 90Kč. Linens and towels included. Laundry

Accommodations

140Kč per load; no dryer. Women's dorms available. Ⓢ Large dorms 300-450Kč; 3-bed dorms 450-525Kč. Doubles 600-675Kč. ISIC holders get a 5% discount. Credit card use 3% fee. ⍉ Reception 24hr. Kitchen open 8am-1am.

Traveller's Hostel   HOSTEL $

Dlouhá 33

☎224 826 662; www.travellers.cz

It's a bit cheaper than other hostels in Staré Město, and we can see why—the walls could use a new paint job, the dorms have between 10 and 16 beds, bathrooms tend to be humid, and the third floor is a bit claustrophobic. The highlight is the big upstairs bar, where the foosball is free. If you stay for a week you get the seventh night free, but we'll leave it up to you to decide whether you really want to stay here for a week.

▶ ✢ C: Náměstí Republiky. From the station, walk north along Revoluční. Take a left at Dlouhá. The hostel will be on your right. *i* Smoking permitted only in dining room. Breakfast included. Absinthe bar 3rd fl. Computer access available in the front lobby. Free Wi-Fi on the 3rd floor. Key deposit 200Kč. Ⓢ Large dorms 270-350Kč; 4-bed dorms 330-500Kč. Singles 700-1390Kč. Doubles 400-800Kč. ISIC/IYHF card holders recieve 40Kč per night discount. ⍉ Reception 24hr.

JOSEFOV

Most accommodations in Josefov are the more-stars-than-through-a-telescope sort. There are no traditional hostels with dorms, but there are a few apartment-turned-hostels that are worth considering if you want to stay here on a budget.

Hostel Franz Kafka   HOSTEL $$$

Kaprova 13

☎222 316 800; www.czechhostelfranzkafka.com

With a magnificent total of four rooms, Franz Kafka Hostel may be one of the smallest hostels you'll come across in Prague. There are no dorms and the bigger rooms (up to eight bunk beds) are rented out only to groups. Bathrooms are shared. Longer stays are preferred; the minimum is three days.

▶ ✢ B: Staroměstská. From Old Town Sq. walk to St. Nicholas Church and turn left. Walk for a few meters down Kaprova; the hostel is on the right. *i* Free Wi-Fi. Linens and towels included. 3-day min. stay.

ⓢ Singles 800Kč; doubles 1100-1300Kč; quads 1560-1960Kč per person. Cash only. ⏰ Reception 9am-6pm, but times vary.

Hostel Condor I   HOSTEL $$$
Kozí 7
☎603 438 943; www.praguecondor.cz

A lot of things at this 12-room hostel are done on an unofficial basis. Reception is rarely open. If you have a small laundry load, they may do it for you for free. The owners of the building prohibit the use of the kitchen, so you can't cook, but you can order a 100Kč breakfast. The rooms are on the smaller side and rather bare, but the great location comes at a decent price. Confirm your arrival ahead of time.

▶ 🚇 B: Staroměstská. From Old Town Sq. walk past the Jan Hus statue on Dlouhá. At the roundabout, keep going straight on Kozí; the hostel is to the left. *i* Laundry 50Kč. No Wi-Fi, but internet cable available. Bike rental possible. ⓢ Singles 600-800Kč; doubles 1200-1400Kč. Cash only. ⏰ Call ahead to arrange check-in and check-out.

MALÁ STRANA

Not many people stay in Malá Strana, but those who do are rewarded by being farther from the drunken noise of Old Town and closer to Malá Strana's artsy cafes and green spaces.

Little Town Budget Hotel   HOTEL, HOSTEL $$
Malostranské náměstí 11
☎242 406 965; www.littletownhotel.cz

Officially a "budget hotel," Little Town still has dorms at manageable rates but adds in ensuite bathrooms and attached kitchens. This is perhaps the best-located budget accommodation this side of the Vltava—a short walk across the Charles Bridge lands you right in the Old Town. Plus, it's not the musty apartment building you're likely to find on the other bank, but a real Malá Strana house, with wood floors and a cobblestone courtyard.

▶ 🚇 A: Malostranská. From the Metro, walk down Letenská until you reach Malostranské náměstí. The hostel is in the southwest corner of the square, behind the church. *i* Linens and towels included. Free Wi-Fi; computers available. ⓢ Dorms 450Kč; singles 1500Kč; doubles 1600Kč. ⏰ Reception 24hr.

Hostel Sokol
HOSTEL $

Nosticova 2

☎257 007 397; www.hostelsokol.cz

Yet another unfortunate triumph of socialist architecture, Hostel Sokol serves primarily as housing for athletic teams in Prague for competitions but it will happily accommodate tourists when there's space. Their signature barracks-like 12-bed dorm has sparse white beds and linoleum floors, but the prices are some of the lowest in Prague. If you were hoping to get with well-toned jocks, this is the place.

▶ ✠ A: Malostranská. From the Metro, walk south or take tram 12, 20, or 22 to Hellichova. Turn left on Hellichova and continue to the end of the street as it curves left. Continue north on Nosticova, following signs for Hostel Sokol, and turn right into the courtyard. *i* Linens and towels included. Free Wi-Fi. Ⓢ Dorms 300-350Kč. Cash only. Ⓩ Reception 24hr.

Arpacay Hostel
HOSTEL $

Radlická 76

☎251 552 297; www.arpacayhostel.com

Not technically in Malá Strana, Arpacay is close to Smíchovské nádraží, which serves Germany-bound trains. For a hostel so close to the train station, Arpacay does a much better job than many of its competitors in the center. The dorms are spacious and neat, with noise-muffling double windows. Watch out for last-minute deals: if you book one or two weeks in advance, you can often save 20%. If you're worried about the length of the commute, tram 7 will get you to Karlovo náměstí in about 10min.

▶ ✠ B: Smíchovské nádraží. From the train station, turn left and walk until you reach a small park. Go into the park and turn left, walk up the stairs, and cross the train tracks. At the intersection, keep walking straight, and go up the hill on Radlická. Look for the Arpacay sign on the right. Alternatively, take tram 7, 12, 13, 14, or 20. *i* Breakfast, linens, towels, and locks included. Free Wi-Fi; computers available. Ⓢ Dorms 250-390Kč; doubles 430-650Kč. Ⓩ Reception 7am-midnight.

HRADČANY

Few budget travelers stay overnight in this hilly neighborhood, but where there's a will, there's a way. If you do stay here, you'll be close to Prague Castle, Malá Strana, and parks such as Letenské sady and Petřín.

Little Quarter
HOSTEL $

Nerudova 21

☎257 212 029; www.littlequarter.com

This is a hostel that you wouldn't expect to find in Hradčany—it's well-run and reasonably cheap. The dorms have no bunk beds. There's not much in the way of common spaces (just a small terrace and the reception room), but it's a great place to stay if you want to spend most of your time exploring the city. Tram 22, which stops down the road, can take you across the Vltava in a matter of minutes.

▶ 🚏 A: Malostranská. From the Metro, walk toward the bridge and take the first right onto Letenská. Continue as it curves, becomes Malostranské square, and then becomes Nerudova. The hostel is to the left. Trams 12, 20, and 22 stop nearby. *i* Breakfast 80Kč. Free Wi-Fi and computer use. Linens and lockers included. $ 10-bed dorms 240-290Kč; 5-bed 340-430Kč. Doubles 1300-1580Kč. ⏰ Reception 24hr.

Pension Pohádka
PENSION $$$$

Valdštejnská 288/4a

☎257 286 320; www.pensionpohadka.eu

If split between two romantically linked people, a room at this atmospheric little pension can be affordable. The five rooms have names like "President" or "Senator," and are equipped with air conditioning, luxurious beds, and, sometimes, a second floor. We recommend Pension Pohádka for couples on romantic retreats.

▶ 🚏 A: Malostranská. From the Metro, walk through the courtyard. The pension is across the street. *i* Breafast 100Kč. Free Wi-Fi. Minifridges in all rooms. $ 1 person 1162-1912Kč; 2 people 1550-2550Kč. Discounts for stays over 5 days. ⏰ Reception 8am-10pm.

Kolej Komenského
DORMITORY $$

Parléřova 6

☎220 388 400; www.kam.cuni.cz

Kolej Komenského is home to university students during the year and transforms into a hostel in the summer. While the summer rates might seem outrageous to Czech students, they run pretty much the going rate of hostel accommodations—single rooms are 550Kč. The more touristy area is just 5min. away by foot, and Kolej Komenského is close to tram 22. The facilities are adequate and popular with foreign students.

▶ 🚏 Tram 22: Pohořelec or 36: Hládkov. From the 22, walk past the Brahe/Kepler statue on Parléřova. Take the 2nd right, cross the tram tracks, and you'll arrive at the dorm. Ⓢ Singles 550Kč; doubles 880Kč. Cash only. Ⓩ Hostel reception M-F 7am-4pm. Building reception 24hr.

ŽIŽKOV

Predictably for the neighborhood, Žižkov's hostels are alternative, reasonably priced, and a bit wild. Staying here allows you to experience one of Prague's more authentic neighborhoods, just a tram ride away from Staré Město.

🖼 Hostel One Prague   HOSTEL $$

Cimburkova 8

☎222 221 423; www.hosteloneprague.cz

This cool hostel resides in a former residential building, so each room has its own bathroom, fridge, and kitchen counter (only the sinks are functional). Private rooms feel almost like little apartments (especially if they happen to have one of the 10 balconies), while the bigger dorms still offer some privacy. The cascading garden is a good place to grill. Every night, the staff organizes trips (no, not pub crawls—these trips are free) to some of Prague's best nightlife spots.

▶ 🚋 Trams 5, 9, or 26: Lipanská. Walk uphill on Seifertova past the big church, then turn right on Cimburkova. The hostel is on the right. *i* Linens included. Laundry 200Kč. Towels 20Kč. Free Wi-Fi. 8 computers available for use. Ⓢ Dorms 250-590Kč; private rooms 590-790Kč per person. Ⓩ Reception 7:30am-12:30am. Garden closes at 10pm.

Hostel Elf   HOSTEL $

Husitská 11

☎222 540 963; www.hostelelf.com

A true backpacker's hostel, Elf's walls are covered with all sorts of drawings and stenciled graffiti, supposedly the work of the staff. The common room and the bathrooms are on the smaller side, but all spatial constraints are made up for by Elf's colorful spirit. The staff grills three times per week, providing dinner to the guests at no extra charge.

▶ 🚋 Trams 5, 9, or 26: Husinecká. From the tram stop, follow Husinecká until you reach the square, then make a left at Orebitská, which will run into Husitská right in front of the hostel. *i* Credit card surcharge 3%. Breakfast, linens, and towels included. Free Wi-Fi, and computer use. Laundry 200Kč. Ⓢ Dorms 260-390Kč; doubles 380-730Kč. 5% student discounts for dorms. Ⓩ Reception 24hr.

Clown and Bard Hostel   HOSTEL $

Bořivojova 102

☎222 716 453; www.clownandbard.com

This party hostel is not for the squeamish—its interior can get very rough around the edges, with rusty stoves and scribbles on walls. But if you're here to party, this could be a place for you. The reception could easily be mistaken for a bar—there's foosball, plenty of wooden tables, and songs like "Keep on Rocking in the Free World" blast from the speakers. Plus it's right on Bořivojova, a street known in Žižkov for its bars.

▶ ⚑ Trams 5, 9, or 26: Husinecká. Walk uphill and take the 1st left on Krašová. Continue for 2 blocks, then turn right on Bořivojova. Enter through an underground bar. *i* Breakfast 50Kč. Linen and towels included. Free Wi-Fi and computer use. Ⓢ Dorms 250-300Kč; doubles 340-600Kč. Cash only. ⓩ Reception 24hr. Garden closes at 10pm.

VINOHRADY

There are many hotels scattered around Ⓜ**I.P. Pavlova,** but Vinohrady remains fairly residential otherwise. The walk from here to Staré Město can take quite a while (25min. from ⓂNáměstí Míru to Old Town Sq.); the Metro and frequent trams can save you some time.

Czech Inn   HOSTEL $$

Francouzská 76

☎267 267 600; www.czech-inn.com

Billing itself as a "designer hostel," Czech Inn tries hard to distinguish itself from the sweaty hostel world: it's clean, chic, and asks you to join its "social networks." The lobby and bar serve double duty as an art gallery, and every few weeks the hostel changes up the display and throws a gallery opening. Such appreciation for detail extends to the rooms, which have sleek single-sheet glass showers with polished concrete floors. To take advantage of all this elegance for little money, stay here during the week. Bonus points: if you end up staying here, make at least one joke about "Czeching Inn."

▶ ⚑ A: Náměstí Míru, or trams 4 or 22: Krymská. From the station, walk southeast along Francouzská. The hostel is on the right. *i* Breakfast 120Kč. Towels 30Kč with a 100Kč deposit. Wi-Fi and lockers included. Computer use 50Kč per hr. Non-smoking. Ⓢ Prices fluctuate wildly on a daily basis. Dorms from 285Kč; private rooms from 990Kč. Expect to pay more on weekends. ⏰ Reception 24hr.

Advantage Hostel HOSTEL $

Sokolská 11

☎224 914 062; www.advantagehostel.cz

The recently renovated Hostel Advantage has no major flaws, nor does it provide any particular thrills. Whether it's worth staying here or not depends mostly on the rates—visit the website to calculate the daily rate and then decide whether it will make a difference to stay this far from Old Town.

▶ 🚏 C: I.P. Pavlova. From the station, head 1 block toward the river on Jugoslávská, then turn left on Sokolská. The hostel is on the right. ℹ Breakfast, towels, linens, lockers included. Free WiFi and computer use. Women's dorms available. HI member. $ Dorms 300-450Kč; singles 1000-2200Kč; doubles 1300-2200Kč. ⏰ Reception 24hr.

HOLEŠOVICE

Holešovice is not the most central or pedestrian-friendly part of the town, so you'll probably need to use the tram or the Metro to get to the historic sights. On the other hand, staying in Holešovice will put you within walking distance of some of Prague's best nightlife.

✓ Sir Toby's Hostel HOSTEL $$

Dělnická 24

☎246 032 610; www.sirtobys.com

From rooms with outlandish names instead of numbers to events like Quiz Mondays, beer tastings, and Crepe and Cartoon Sundays, Sir Toby's does everything with a dose of personality. There's a pub in the brick cellar next to a modern kitchen and a few common rooms where you can cook, watch Czech movies, or have a home-cooked dinner of Czech and Afghan cuisine. The garden, which has a grill, is a good place to hang out on a sunny day. Before heading out, grab one of Sir Toby's custom maps of the area.

▶ 🚏 C: Vltavská. From the Metro, take tram 1, 3, 5, or 25 or walk along the tram tracks for 3 stops to Dělnická. Turn left onto Dělnická; the hostel is on the left. ℹ Breakfast 100Kč. Dinner 90-110Kč. Lockers included. Towels 15Kč with a 200Kč deposit; included with private rooms. Laundry 100Kč. Free Wi-Fi and computer use. $ Dorms 150-600Kč; doubles 700-1000Kč. 5% discount for ISIC holders who reserve online. ⏰ Reception 24hr.

Plus Prague   HOSTEL $$
Přívozní 1

☏220 510 046; www.plusprague.com

The reception area of this enormous hostel feels like an aiport—people arrive and depart, and things happen efficiently. All rooms have ensuite bathrooms, and one wing is women-only. A separate building houses the hostel's restaurant, which seems geared more toward larger groups, but in which even the solo traveler can enjoy a pool table, foosball, and a full-service bar and grill. Plus Prague is also one of the few hostels in Prague with a sauna and swimming pool. Before you leave the lobby, say hello to Boris the turtle, who isn't dead—"just sleeping."

▶ ⚡ C: Nadraží Holešovice. From the station, take tram 5 or 12, or walk along tram tracks on Plynární for 1 stop, to Ortenovo náměstí. At Hotel Plaza Alta take a left onto Přívozní. The hostel is on the left. *i* Washer 70Kč, dryer 100Kč. Towels 50 Kč. Full breakfast 100 Kč, cold breakfast 70Kč. Linens and lockers included. Free Wi-Fi and computers in the lobby. Ⓢ Dorms 190-500Kč, private rooms 400-700Kč per person. ⏰ Reception 24hr. Sauna open 8-10am and 4-10pm. Pool open 8am-10pm.

Hotel Extol Inn   HOTEL $$$
Přístavní 2

☏220 876 541; www.extolinn.cz

If you are set on staying in a private room, Extol Inn offers economy rooms for prices comparable to those you'll find at hostels. We're not going to extol the economical amenities—you'll be barred from most of the free services that are offered to guests in more expensive rooms, including wheelchair access, and you might share a bathroom with one other room—but the set rates mean that staying here might be cheaper than a hostel during the high season.

▶ ⚡ C: Vltavská. From the station, take tram 1, 3, 5, 25 or walk along the tram tracks for 3 stops to Dělnická. Keep walking an additional block, then take a left onto Přístavní. *i* Breakfast included. Free Wi-Fi. Computer use 2Kč per min. Ⓢ Singles 820Kč; doubles 1400Kč; triples 1900Kč. ⏰ Reception 24hr.

A&O Hostel   HOSTEL $$
U Výstaviště 1

☏220 870 252; www.aohostels.com

This hostel may not be as generous with its facilities as others (linens aren't included, and there are no laundry facilities or lockers), but it's very close to the Holešovice train station. On the upside, all rooms have tiny TVs, and there's a dungeon-like bar downstairs where you can buy drinks and play with the Wii. We're still deciding whether the strip club that's located right behind this hostel is a good or a bad thing.

▶ 🚏 C: Nadraží Holešovice. From the station, walk along tram tracks on Vrbenského and Partyzánska in the direction of Výstaviště (Prague Exhibition Ground); the hostel is on a raised street behind the overpass. ℹ Breakfast 100Kč. Linens 80Kč. Safes available at the front desk. Wi-Fi and computer use available. $ Dorms 250-500Kč; private rooms 450-800Kč per person. 10% discount for ISIC card holders. ⏰ Reception 24hr.

Dirty Mouth?

You may be surprised to be walking through the historic streets of Prague, overwhelmed by your romantic European notions, only to hear people saying "f*** you" to each other. But don't worry, the city isn't filled with crude or angry Czechs, just a bunch of tourists, like you, who don't know the language. What the natives are really saying is *"fakt jo,"* pronounced fahkt yo. It's a common phrase that means "really?" or "for real?" The Bohemians are pretty nice after all.

Sights

If you visit Prague during the summer months, you will be viewing the historical sights around Prague Castle and Old Town Sq. with thousands of other people trying to cram into the same tightly packed spaces as you. The tours of many of the historic buildings are often long and dry. It will be loud. It will be unpleasant. You might get your wallet stolen. It doesn't have to be like this. You'll miss the crowds and save a lot of money if you do your Old Town sightseeing at night. You won't get to see the interiors of the buildings, but for most part that's no great loss. The entire Old Town, and especially the Charles Bridge—virtually impassable during the day—are lit up beautifully at night. Once you get away from Old Town Sq., your options start to open up. Žižkov has its share of large structures, including the TV Tower and the Jan Žižka Statue. In Malá Strana, a panoramic view of the city awaits from the top of Petřín Tower.

Aside from historic sights, it's worth spending a little extra to visit Prague's art museums, which are some of its best treasures. The largest art museum around is the fantastic Veletržní Palác in Holešovice. For more contemporary art, head a little further into Holešovice to DOX. If you need another reason to hit this hip 'hood, Letenské sady (Letná Park) is a great place to relax, and the Metronome has one of the best (free) views of the city.

Budget Sights

Fortunately for you, oh budget-traveler, many of Prague's best sights may be seen simply by walking down the street. And, as far as we know, you won't be charged for walking (though do watch out for pickpockets). From churches to walls with John Lennon's face on them to picturesque streets and gardens, Prague's free sights are enough to keep you entertained for several days. Additionally, look out for one of the zillion festivals that pop up all over Prague year-round (see www.praguewelcome.cz for a full list).

NOVÉ MĚSTO

🖼 Alfons Mucha Museum   MUSEUM
Panská 7
☎224 216 415; www.mucha.cz

A national hero, artist Alfons Mucha rose to fame overnight when he designed a poster on short notice for the French actress Sarah Bernhardt. These days, you can find copies of his work anywhere (you know, semi-nude women in flowing robes, surrounded by flowers and such), but the Alfons Mucha Museum offers a more in-depth look at Mucha's career. From original banknotes that Mucha designed for the First Czecho-slovak Republic to photos of the painter Paul Gaugin playing Mucha's piano to Mucha's childhood drawings, the exhibits paint an intimate portrait of the artist. Don't miss his sketch of a window design for St. Vitus Cathedral (then see the window for yourself in Hradčany). The souvenir shop sells all kinds of reproductions (300-500Kč), so you can take home some Mucha of your very own.

▶ ⚰ A or B: Můstek. Walk up Wenceslas Sq. toward the St. Wenceslas statue. Turn left on Jindřišská and left again on Panská. Ⓢ 90Kč, students 60Kč. Ⓩ Open daily 10am-6pm.

Wenceslas Square (Václavské náměstí)   SQUARE
Once a horse market, Václavské náměstí now sells every-thing but. American-style department stores and historic hotels compete for attention with vendors peddling up to six different types of sausage. The square is dominated by the **National Museum,** which closed for a five-year

Good Square Wenceslas

You wouldn't know it from the traffic, McDonalds, and souvenir shops, but enormous **Wenceslas Square** has quite an eventful history. Here are just some of the square's noteworthy events:

- **1348:** Holy Roman Emperor Charles IV founds the New Town of Prague, including this, the "Horse Market" square.

- **1680:** An equestrian statue of St. Wenceslas (not the statue that is there now) is erected in the middle of the Horse Market square; the saint informally lends his name to the square.

- **June 12, 1848:** A mass is held in protest of the Hapsburgs' military response to calls for liberal constitutional reform. A week of fighting in the streets ensues.

- **1848:** To commemorate the unsuccessful revolutionary uprisings, the square is officially renamed for Wenceslas, the 10th-century duke and patron saint of Bohemia.

- **1912:** The currently standing equestrian statue of St. Wenceslas is installed. Nationalism follows. Other sculptures in the square include a stack of cars and Superman flying face-first into the pavement.

- **October 28, 1918:** The First Czechoslovak Republic declares itself an independent nation. Independence is brief.

- **January 16, 1969:** Student Jan Palach protests the Soviet invasion of Czechoslovakia by lighting himself on fire. Today, a monument commemorates the heroic act.

- **March 28, 1969:** Czechoslovakia defeats its Soviet occupiers in ice hockey. And there is much rejoicing (in Wenceslas Sq., of course).

- **November 17-December 19, 1989:** "Velvet Revolution" demonstrations fill the square. Neither the Czechs nor the velvet is crushed—a turning point in the history of each.

- **Today:** Make your own history! (No tanks or fires, though, please.)

renovation in July 2011, and which will hopefully be less of a snoozefest when it reopens. Some of the exhibits have been moved to the modern building next door (Vinohradská 1, www.nm.cz Ⓢ 100Kč, students 70Kč.), so, if you're intent on looking at Czech archaeological finds, rock samples, and stuffed animals, they're all yours. Don't miss the **statue** of St. Wenceslas, where the proclamation of Czechoslovakia's independence was read in 1918. Artist David Černý's hilarious parody of this statue can be found inside the Lucerna complex on Vodičková.

▶ ⚇ A or B: Můstek; A or C: Muzeum.

Dancing House   LANDMARK
Rašínovo nábřeží 80

Now in its mid-teens, the Dancing House is one of Prague's most recognizable buildings. Designed by Frank Gehry and Vlado Milunić, it was originally dubbed "Fred and Ginger" after the famous dancing duo. The Dancing House was built in an empty lot left after the Bombing of Prague—an aerial raid by the US Army Air Forces in 1945 that was supposedly the result of a navigational error. It doesn't quite fit in with the crusty Baroque and Art Nouveau crowd nearby, and its construction sparked a heated debate about architecture in Prague. The top floor of the Dancing House is home to an upscale French restaurant, but you can get in for the price of a drink when the restaurant closes to let in customers from the downstairs cafe (4-6pm).

▶ ⚇ B: Karlovo náměstí. From the Metro, walk down Resslova toward the river. The building is on the left. Ⓢ Coffee 45-70Kč. Beer 40-90Kč.

Saint Henry Tower (Jindřišská věž)   TOWER
Jindřišská ulice
☎224 232 429; www.jindrisskavez.cz

Dating back to 1455, this tower was ingeniously converted so that most of its floors serve different roles—from the bottom up: whiskey bar (fl. 0-1), gallery (fl. 2-4), toilets (fl. 5), museum (fl. 6), restaurant (fl. 7-9), and observation deck (fl. 10). The price of a ticket allows you to see everything inside, so take the elevator to the top and then descend. The view from the top is rather average, the gallery space is encroached upon by a liquor store, and the exhibition on Prague's 120 towers takes itself a little too seriously, but it's worth peeking inside the posh restaurant, where patrons compete for space with the tower's scaffolding system and a 16th-century bell.

▶ ♯ A or B: Můstek. From the Metro, walk up Wenceslas Sq. toward the St. Wenceslas statue. Turn left on Jindřišská and continue to the end of the street. Ⓢ 80Kč, students 55Kč. Cash only. ⏰ Open daily Apr-Sept 10am-7pm. Oct-Mar 10am-6pm.

New Town Hall (Novoměstská radnice)   LANDMARK
Karlovo náměstí 1/23
☎224 948 225; www.nrpraha.cz

This town hall is more interesting for its history than its architecture—it was here that the First Defenestration of Prague took place in 1419, when a mob of Hussites stormed the town hall and tossed some 15 councilors and other dignitaries out the window. Later on, the building functioned as a prison, and executions took place in the town hall's courtyard as recently as during the Nazi occupation. Today you can climb the tower's 221 steps to the top and check out photo exhibits as you go.

▶ ♯ B: Karlovo náměstí. From the Metro, look for the giant tower on the northern end of the square. Ⓢ 30Kč. Cash only. ⏰ Open Apr-Oct Tu-Su 10am-6pm.

Our Lady of the Snow
(Kostel Panny Marie Sněžné)   CHURCH
Jungmannovo náměstí 18
www.pms.ofm.cz

Our Lady of the Snow is one of the most oddly shaped churches in Central Europe. Charles IV commissioned it the day after his coronation, hoping to end up with a monster cathedral that would overshadow even St. Vitus. Unfortunately, the Hussite Wars interrupted construction, and the church was severely damaged. When Dominican monks reconstructed it, they had to abandon the original design. Only one nave and the impressively large ceilings remained from Charles IV's plan. Before you leave, check out the tiny St. Michael's chapel (on the right when you enter), where services take place in winter, since the disproportionately tall church isn't heated.

▶ ♯ A or B: Můstek. From the Metro, walk down 28. října, then turn left on Jungmannovo náměstí. The entrance to the church is behind the statue of the poet J. Jungmann. ⏰ Open daily 6:30am-7pm. Services Su 9, 10:15, 11:30am, 6pm.

Franciscan Gardens   GARDEN

With clipped evergreen hedges and plenty of trees, this hidden oasis between Our Lady of the Snow and bustling Wenceslas Sq. may surprise if you happen upon it by chance. Massive, strange, lightbulb-like street lamps line the walk, but, unfortunately, the park closes before you can see them in their full glory. The picturesque cottage in the middle of the roses is actually a secondhand clothing store.

▶ ⚑ A or B: Můstek. Enter through the arch to the left of Jungmannova and Národní, behind the statue. ⏰ Open daily Apr-Aug 7am-10pm; Sept-Oct 7am-8pm; Oct-Apr 8am-7pm.

Emauzy Monastery   MONASTERY
Vyšehradská 49
☎ 324 917 662; www.emauzy.cz

Founded by (who else?) Charles IV, Emauzy Monastery avoided being burned down by the Hussites thanks to its connection to the martyr Jan Hus, who studied here. Instead, it was turned into the first and only Hussite monastery, which lasted long after the Hussite Wars ended. Some centuries later, the monastery served as home to Johannes Kepler, the

Prague's Quirkiest Museums

When you tire of castles, churches, and pretty houses, check out some of these funky Czech museums:

· **Museum of Communism.** The best things about this museum are its promotional posters, featuring a fanged but otherwise adorable matryoshka doll.

· **Sex Machines Museum.** The name says it all. The collection (Melantrichova 18) covers the gamut from 16th-century chastity belts to pornographic films allegedly made for King Alfonso XIII of Spain.

· **Kepler Museum.** Rumor has it that the people in charge of this bizarre, clearly counterfactual museum (Karlova 4) of untruth believe the Earth revolves around the sun!

· **Franz Kafka Museum.** If the authorities decide to allow you to visit this museum, you will wake up one morning to find two men in your hotel room who will let you know when you are scheduled to arrive. **Do not be late.**

Sights

scientist who explained planetary motion. If you don't want to pay for a ticket, you can come see the impressive chapel during mass (daily 10am and 6pm). Outside of religious services, Emauzy is your typical monastery—empty, decrepit, and echoing.

▶ ⚑ B: Karlovo náměstí. From the park, follow the signs to the monastery down Vyšehradská. Ⓢ 50kč. ⏰ Open M-F 11am-5pm, closes earlier in winter. Mass daily 10am, 6pm.

Museum of Communism   MUSEUM
Na Příkopě 10
☎224 212 966; www.museumofcommunism.com

If your understanding of communism is limited to Borat's "my sister is number four prostitute in all of Kazakhstan," this is a good opportunity to branch out. Recreations of some of the typical architectural spaces (a grocery store, an interrogation room, etc.) and a number of artifacts from the communist era make this museum amusing for some and terrifying for others. The only gripe on our side is the disproportionately high admission price, but hey, it's capitalism.

▶ ⚑ A or B: Můstek. From the Metro, head down Na Příkopě, then turn right inside a courtyard. Enter through a casino door. The museum is on the 2nd floor. Ⓢ 180Kč, students 140Kč. ⏰ Open daily 9am-9pm.

Antonín Dvořák Museum   MUSEUM
Ke Karlovu 20
☎224 918 013; www.nm.cz

Also called "Michnův Letohrádek", this nobleman's villa served as a restaurant and a cattle market before becoming the museum that it is today. The exhibit is on the smaller side, but contains quite a few of Antonín Dvořák's worldly possessions, which range from his graduation gown from Cambridge University (he received an honorary degree) to his musical instruments to his flask and eyeglasses. The upper floor's walls are covered with 18th-century paintings, the only remaining feature of the villa's original decor.

▶ ⚑ C: I.P. Pavlova. From the station, head west on Ječná and take the 1st left onto Kateřinská. Then take the 1st left on Ke Karlovu; the museum is on the left. Ⓢ 50Kč, students 25Kč. Concerts 575Kč. Cash only. ⏰ Open Tu-W 10am-1:30pm and 2-5pm, Th 11am-1:30pm and 2-7pm, F-Su 10am-1:30pm and 2-5pm.

Charles University Botanical Gardens GARDEN

Na Slupi 16

☎221 951 879; www.bz-uk.cz

Founded in 1898, the Charles University Botanical Gardens contain some 3000 species of plants in a several-acre garden. Admission to the garden is free, but you'll need a ticket to enter the greenhouses, which house temporary plant exhibitions (cacti, orchids, etc.) and a few caged parrots.

▶ 🚇 B: Karlovo náměstí. From the Metro, follow Vyšehradská south until it becomes Na Slupi. Alternatively, take tram 18 or 24 to Botanická záhrada. $ 50Kč, students 25Kč. ⏰ Gardens open daily Apr-Aug 10am-7:30pm; Sept-Oct 10am-6pm; Nov-Jan 10am-4pm; Feb-Mar 10am-5pm. Greenhouses close 1hr. earlier.

Church of Saint Ignatius CHURCH

Ječná 2

☎221 990 200; www.jesuit.cz

Notice the figure of St. Ignatius on the peak of this Baroque Jesuit church—in its heyday, it was considered semi-heretical, as clerical rules stated that a full-body halo could only be used for Christ himself. The Jesuit order was so strong, though, that it could afford to break this rule without consequence. The church is the third largest Jesuit complex in all of Europe. The sculptures on the altar are the work of Matěj Václav Jäckel, who is best known for the statues on the Charles Bridge.

▶ 🚇 B: Karlovo náměstí. From the Metro, head away from the river toward Ječná. The church is on the corner. ⏰ Open daily 6am-noon and 3:30-6:30pm. Services daily 6:15, 7:30am, 5:30pm. Mass Su 7, 9, 11am, 5:30pm.

Sights

STARÉ MĚSTO

👍 Charles Bridge BRIDGE

Probably the most famous sight in all of Prague, Charles Bridge is always packed, and for good reasons. Charles IV commissioned the bridge (if you haven't figured it out already, Charles IV is responsible for everything cool in Prague), and he laid the first stone on July 9, 1357 at exactly 5:31am. Can you guess why? (See answer below.) Although the bridge was originally decorated with a single crucifix, 30 statues were added between 1600 and 1800, including such shady characters as St. Augustine and Lamenting Christ. Weather damage forced the city to remove the original statues, which are now displayed at the National Gallery (see **Holešovice**) and Vyšehrad (see **Vinohrady**). The bridge also features the **Old Town Bridge Tower** *(Staroměstská mostecká věž)*, which offers a bird's eye view of the city below. If you don't cross the bridge around sunset at least once, you haven't really been to Prague.

▶ ⚑ A: Malostranská or Staroměstská. *i* Here's the answer: if you write down the date and time of when the first stone was laid, you get the chiasmus 1-3-5-7-9-7-5-3-1. (A Dan Brown novel is waiting to be written.) Ⓢ Tower 70Kč, students 50Kč. ⏰ Open daily Nov-Dec 10am-8pm; Apr-Oct 10am-10pm; Dec-Mar 10am-6pm.

Astronomical Clock Tower and Old Town Hall (Staroměstská Radnice)   LANDMARK

Staroměstské náměstí

☏724 911 556; www.praguetowers.com

It is said that after the city council hired the clockmaker Hanuš to build this world-famous clock, they gouged out his eyes so he could never repeat his work (talk about worker's comp issues). In reality, Hanuš wasn't even the builder—the astronomical clock was the work of another clockmaker, Mikuláš of Kadaň. At the ripe age of 600 years (the big birthday bash was in 2010), this mysterious machine still tracks movements of the sun, the moon, and much, much more. On the hour, there's always a little show: 12 apostles poke their heads out, a rooster crows, and the crowd of tourists below goes bananas. If you want to go all meta, take a photo of all the gaping tourists; if you want to go meta-meta, take a photo of people taking photos of people... the possibilities are endless. For an amazing view of the city, head to the top of the tower. There's also a tour of the Old Town Hall, which includes a behind-the-scenes view of the apostle clock (if you come on the hour, you'll see the apostles move) and a walk through the original Romanesque basement. The basement served as the original ground floor before the king raised the level of Old Town by some 5m to protect it from flooding.

▶ ⚑ A: Staroměstská. Southwest corner of Old Town Sq. Ⓢ Exhibition hall 100Kč, students 80Kč. Tower 100Kč/50Kč. Cash only. ⏰ Hall open M 11am-6pm, Tu-Su 9am-6pm (last tour at 5pm). Tower open M 11am-10pm, Tu-Su 9am-10pm.

Church of Our Lady Before Týn (Matky Boží před Týnem) CHURCH

Staroměstské náměstí

www.tyn.cz

Our Lady Before Týn dominates the skyline of Old Town Sq. with two enormous spires sticking out among the surrounding Baroque buildings. This 14th-century church contains the remains of the astronomer **Tycho Brahe,** who revolutionized the way the movement of planets was understood and who allegedly peed himself to death: as the popular story goes, in 1601 Brahe was at Emperor Rudolf's for dinner, and, in the name of decorum, he refused to leave the dinner table to relieve himself, until his bladder burst. Today, science suggests that the real reason for his death might have been mercury poisoning, but who cares about science? Maybe we'll know for sure when the results of the latest analysis come in—in 2010, scientists closed the church down, opened Brahe's tomb, and studied his remains.

▶ ⚕ A: Staroměstská. It's the giant twin towers in Old Town Sq. Ⓢ Free. ⏰ Open Tu-Sa 10am-1pm and 3-5pm, Su 10:30am-noon.

Municipal House (Obecní Dům) CONCERT HALL

Naměstí Republiky 5

☎222 002 101; www.obecnidum.cz

Standing on the grounds where Czech kings used to reside, Municipal House is the site of two important events in Czech history. It was here that Czechoslovakia declared independence in 1918 and that the Communist Party held the first meetings with Václav Havel and other leaders of *Občanské fórum* (Civic forum, a pro-democracy movement) in 1989. But Municipal House is not only historically significant—it's also beautiful. Built in the Art Nouveau style in 1912, this state house features works from more than 20 of the country's top artists; every detail, from the shape of the door handles to the patterns on the banisters, is the careful work of some Art Noveau master. Daily guided tours take visitors through **Smetana Hall,** where the Czech Philharmonic plays, and the **Mayor's Hall,** decorated by Czech artist Alfons Mucha. There's also a separate exhibition that features just one object: a replica (!) of the Crown of St. Wenceslas, a jewel-studded national treasure (the original is locked away in St. Vitus Cathedral). If you don't feel like paying for a tour, you can stop by **Kavárna Obecní Dům** located on the ground floor. It's a bit expensive, but ordering a coffee (58Kč) will allow you to linger under its eight enormous chandeliers in the impressive Art Nouveau interior.

▶ 🚇 B: Náměstí Republiky. From Old Town Sq., walk east on Celetná all the way to Náměstí Republiky; Municipal House is on the left. *i* Tours in Czech and English. Tickets must be purchased on the day of your visit at the ticket office located in the basement of the Municipal House. $ Guided tours 270Kč, students 230Kč. Crown of St. Wenceslas (Svatováclavská Koruna) exhibit 120Kč, students 60Kč. ⏰ Open daily 10am-7pm. Tour times vary by week and month; check the online calendar for details.

Saint James Cathedral (Kostol Svatého Jakuba Většího) CHURCH

Malá Štupartská 6

This spectacular church is the subject of several gory legends. According to one, a thief tried to steal the necklace off of a Virgin Mary statue. As you can imagine, the statue came to life, grabbed the thief's arm, and refused to let go. He had to cut off his arm and, to this day, a mummified arm hangs in the church. Another one: during the funeral of Václav Vratislav z Mitrovic, a nobleman and writer, the body was placed into one of the cathedral's most beautiful tombs. For days after he was buried, terrible noises sounded from the tomb, so the priests sprinkled holy water on it. After some time, the noises subsided. It was only years later, during the burial of Vratislav's son, that the tomb was reopened and the coffin discovered to be broken with scratch marks everywhere. Coincidentally, a few years before his death, Vratislav had dreamt that he would be buried alive.

▶ 🚇 From Old Town Sq. head down Týnska (pass Our Lady Before Týn on the left), continuing straight through the courtyards as it turns into Týn. The courtyard lets out at Malá Štupartská, where you should take a left. $ Free. ⏰ Open M-Th 9:30am-noon, F 2-4pm, Sa 9:30am-noon and 2-4pm, Su 2-4pm.

Estates Theater (Stavovské Divadlo) THEATER

Železná 11

☎224 228 503; www.stavovskedivadlo.cz

The Estates Theater is famous for its connection with Wolfgang Amadeus Mozart. It was here that Mozart's *Marriage of Figaro* first became a smash success following a rather lukewarm premiere in Vienna. Perhaps thanks to this turnaround, Mozart premiered his next opera, *Don Giovanni,* in this same theater in 1787—be sure to check out the haunting statue commemorating the premiere outside the theater. More recently, the Oscar-winning film *Amadeus* (directed by Czech emigré Miloš

Sights

Forman in 1984) features a scene in which Mozart conducts inside the Estates Theater. But Mozart isn't the theater's only claim to fame—it was here that the song *"Kde Domov Můj?"* first played publicly as part of the opera *Fidlovačka*. Why is that important, you ask? It happens to be the anthem of the Czech Republic. Popular ballets, dramas, and operas still play nightly in the Estates, and since the theater offers no public tours, the moderate ticket price is definitely worth the experience.

▶ A or B: Můstek. From Old Town Sq., walk south on Železná. The theater is on the left. $ Tickets 300-1200Kč. ⏰ Performances usually at 7pm.

The Black Madonna House (Dům Černé Matky Boží) MUSEUM

Ovocný trh 19

☎224 301 003; www.ngprague.cz

The Black Madonna House is the best standing example of Cubist architecture—a uniquely Czech trend that tried to apply the rules of Cubism to the third dimension. Designed by Josef Gočár, one of the godfathers of Cubist architecture, the building now contains a permanent exhibit devoted to this Bohemian movement. The paintings can be a bit underwhelming for the layman, but one might find some appreciation for the displays of Cubist furniture. Consumers will also enjoy the gift shop downstairs. Finally, check out the fully restored Cubist **Grand Café Orient** (see **Food**) located on the second floor.

▶ B: Náměstí Republiky. From Old Town Sq., walk east on Celetná. The museum is on the left, where Celetná forks with Ovocný trh. $ 100Kč, students 50Kč. ⏰ Open Tu-Su 10am-6pm.

Powder Gate (Prašná Brána) TOWER

Na Příkopě

www.praguetowers.com

Six hundred years ago, *Horská brána* or "Mountain Tower" stood on this site, protecting the city and marking the start of royal coronation ceremonies. When New Town (Nové Město) became a part of the city proper, the tower lost its function and became known as the "Shabby Tower." The tower was torn down and in its place an essentially symbolic monument, the Powder Gate, was erected. While the tower served as a gunpowder storage center for a while, these days it just kind of chills and lets cars tickle its belly as they drive underneath. Climb to the top for a great view of the city and a small exhibit.

▶ B: Naměstí Republiky. From Old Town Sq., walk east on Celetná until you reach the tower. $ 70Kč, students 50Kč. ⏰ Open daily Apr-Sept 10am-10pm, Oct 10am-8pm, Nov-Feb 10am-6pm, Mar 10am-8pm.

Saint Nicholas Church (Kostol Svatého Mikuláše) CHURCH

Staroměstské náměstí

☎224 190 994

Saint Nicholas Church (not to be confused with the far more impressive church of the same name in Malá Strana) might not be the most famous of the lot, but the "chandelier" hanging in its center might be the city's coolest. Given as a gift to Prague in 1787 by Tsar Nicholas II, this ornament is an enormous replica of the royal crown worn by Russian tsars. The church was under the control of Benedictine monks for most of its existence, and a plaque on the former Benedictine monastery attached to the building marks the site of Franz Kafka's birth. Today, you can enjoy classical music concerts here, if that's the kind of thing you enjoy.

▶ ⛎ A: Staroměstská. Northwest corner of Old Town Sq. $ Entry free. Concerts 350-490Kč, students 200-300Kč. Cash only. ⏰ Open Tu-Sa 10am-4pm, Su noon-4pm. Concerts daily 5 and 8pm.

JOSEFOV

A **joint ticket** grants admission to all synagogues (aside from Staronová Synagoga) and the Old Jewish Cemetery. (*i* Audio tours for the entire circuit can be purchased inside Pinkas Synagogue for 250Kč, students 200Kč. $ 300Kč, students 200Kč. ⏰ Open in summer M-F 9am-6pm, Su 9am-6pm; in winter M-F 9am-4:30pm, Su 9am-4:30pm.) There are at least five ticket offices, so if a particular line seems to be advancing at a glacial pace, skip to the next one. (The least busy and fastest location seems to be inside the antique shop at Maiselova 15.) Aside from the Jewish sites, there are some other places worth visiting: Rudolfinum, Klášter Sv. Anežky České, and the Franz Kafka statue.

Pinkas Synagogue (Pinkasova Synagoga) SYNAGOGUE

Široká 23/3

☎222 317 191; www.jewishmuseum.cz

The walls of this otherwise bare 500-year-old synagogue are covered with the names, birth dates, and death dates of almost 80,000 Czech Jews who were murdered at Terezín and other concentration camps during the Holocaust. The names were

The Makings of a Monster

Derived from Jewish lore, one traditional Prague legend is the mysterious golem, a strange, human-like monster. Sorry, *LOTR* fans, this golem isn't a manic 500-year old hobbit searching for the precious ring. Rather, according to legend, rabbis attempted to create golems in order to protect Jews.

As the tale goes, conjuring a golem was not as simple as making morning coffee. The rabbi had to dress in white to show his pureness, and get his hands on soil which no man had ever dug in before, usually from the banks of a river. While kneading the soil with spring water and imagining his creation, he had to meditate, utter complex Hebrew incantations, and say the ancient 42-letter name of God—all without mispronouncing anything, which would result in the speaker's instant death.

One of the most famous golem stories takes place in Prague. The story goes that Rabbi Loew created the last successful golem during WWII to protect the Jews from persecution—a noble effort, but instead the creature became increasingly powerful and began destroying the city. Rabbi Loew put his monster to sleep, and it is said that he still slumbers in Prague's Old New Synagogue. Visitors may still worship, but the attic stairs are inaccessible—they probably don't want anyone getting any bright ideas and waking up the ol' mud monster.

originally added in the 1950s, but, following the Seven-Day War in 1967, the Communist regime closed the synagogue under the pretext of prolonged renovation and had the walls whitewashed. It was only after Václav Havel was elected president that the names could be painstakingly reinscribed between 1992 and 1996. The second floor contains the haunting drawings and collages done by children during their time in Terezín, all made under the guidance of an imprisoned drawing teacher.

▶ ✡ B: Staroměstská. 1 block north of the Metro at the southern border of the Old Jewish Cemetery.

Sights

Old Jewish Cemetery
(Starý Židovský Hřbitov)   CEMETERY
U starého hřbitova 243/3a
☎222 317 191; www.jewishmuseum.cz

This cemetery may remind one of a shark's mouth—the eroded

and broken tombstones jut out at unexpected angles, one over another. Between the 14th and 18th centuries, the graves were dug in layers, and over time the earth settled so that stones from the lower layers were pushed to the surface, forcing many of the newer stones out of position. Rabbi Loew, the supposed creator of the mythical 🏛**Golem,** is buried by the wall opposite the exit. Notice the little stones on the tombstones—traditionally, these are used instead of flowers. Outside the exit is the **Ceremonial Hall,** a two-floor museum on the history of Jewish burials.

▶ ♯ Enter through Pinkas Synagogue. Ⓢ Camera permit 40Kč.

Spanish Synagogue (Španělská Synagoga) SYNAGOGUE
Vězeňská 141/1

☎222 317 191; www.jewishmuseum.cz

The Spanish Synagogue is the most richly decorated of the synagogues in Josefov. Built in the Moorish-Byzantine style, the synagogue is covered from floor to ceiling with elaborate geometric patterns in red, green, and gold, and topped off with a cupola. The synagogue houses an interesting exhibit on the history of the Czech Jews from the Jewish Enlightenment onward, chronicling their attempts at full emancipation (before the rule of Joseph II, Jews had to pay special taxes for their "protection," wear yellow hats and Stars of David, and live in the ghetto). There's also an impressive set of silver Torah crowns and pointers. The synagogue also hosts classical music concerts throughout the year.

▶ ♯ On the corner of Široká and Dušní, close to the statue of Franz Kafka.

Klausen Synagogue (Klausová Synagoga) SYNAGOGUE
U starého hřbitova 243/3a

☎222 317 191; www.jewishmuseum.cz

The Klausen Synagogue was originally built in 1573, burned down a while later, rebuilt in 1604, and then reconstructed in the 1880s. The exhibits inside are dedicated to the cultural aspects of Jewish life, with artifacts like Torah pointers, skull caps, menorahs, and velvet valances. Don't miss the special Halizah shoe on the second floor—according to the Old Testament, a widow had to marry a brother of her dead husband if her marriage was childless. The only way to get out of that obligation was to take this shoe off the brother's foot in front of witnesses.

▶ ♯ Adjacent to the Old Jewish Cemetery.

Maisel Synagogue (Maiselova Synagoga)   SYNAGOGUE
Maiselova 63/10

☎222 317 191; www.jewishmuseum.cz

Like most old things in Prague, the Maisel Synagogue has been partially destroyed and subsequently rebuilt several times. Today it contains artifacts from the history of Judaism in Bohemia and Moravia up until the Jewish Enlightenment. Some of the more interesting objects include the tombstone of Avigdor Kara as well as the robes of a 16th-century Jewish martyr who was burned at the stake by the Inquisition.

▶ ✠ On Maiselova, 1 block south of Široká.

Old-New Synagogue (Staronová Synagoga)   SYNAGOGUE
Maiselova

☎222 318 664; www.synagogue.cz

This is the oldest operating synagogue in all of Europe and one of the earliest Gothic structures in Prague. The usual explanation for its oxymoronic name is that it was called the "New" synagogue when it was built in 1270, then took its present name when newer synagogues were built. Yet, a rumor persists that the name "Old-New" *(Alt-Neu)* is a mistranslation of the Hebrew "Al-Tenai," meaning "on condition," implying that the stones would be returned when the temple in Jerusalem was rebuilt. There are a few legends attached to the place. First, the remains of Golem are said to be hidden in the synagogue's attic. Second, the synagogue is supposedly protected from fire by angels (this would account for its longevity). Unfortunately, it doesn't seem to have been protected from water—a line drawn on a wall inside shows how high the water was during floods in 2002. Inside there's also a replica of the flag flown by the congregation in 1496, when Ladislaus Jagiellon first allowed the Jews to fly their own city flag. The Old-New Synagogue is still the center of Prague's Jewish community. Just south of the Old-New synagogue is the **Jewish Town Hall,** which is not accessible to the public, but whose clock tower has a clock that ticks counter-clockwise.

▶ ✠ Between Maiselova and Pařížská, north of the cemetery. *i* Men must cover their heads. Yarmulkes free. Services reserved for practicing members of the Jewish community. Ⓢ 200Kč, students 140Kč. ◷ Open Apri-Oct M-F 9:30am-6pm, Su 9:30am-6pm; Nov-Mar M-F 9:30am-5pm, Su 9:30am-5pm.

Sights

If I Could Turn Back Time

If a clock turns counterclockwise, is it still, in a sense, going clockwise? This question is posed, if not answered, by a clock on Prague's **Jewish Town Hall,** next to the Old New Synagogue. There are two clocks on this building: the higher one's face has Roman numerals and turns clockwise; the lower's has Hebrew numerals (the digits are indicated by letters of the Hebrew alphabet) and turns counterclockwise, since Hebrew is read from right to left. But unless you're used to calculating minutes past hours, it'll probably be easier to stick to the conventional clock above.

Statue of Franz Kafka   STATUE
Dušní

One of the more original sculptures from among Prague's lot, the statue portrays Franz Kafka sitting astride an enormous suit. Loosely alluding to Kafka's early story "Description of a Struggle," the statue has become a local landmark. For more Kafka-related places, check out the plaque close to St. Nicholas's Church that marks the building where Kafka was born, the blue house at Golden Lane 22 where Kafka lived for a year, and any souvenir shop, where Kafka lives on as an integral symbol of Prague's tourism industry.

▶ ⚑ On the square where Široká and Dušní intersect, close to the Spanish Synagogue.

Galerie Rudolfinum   GALLERY, CONCERT HALL
Alšovo nábřeží 12
☎227 059 205; www.galerierudolfinum.cz

The Neo-Renaissance Rudolfinum hosts both classical musical concerts (it's the home of the Czech Philharmonic Orchestra) and fascinating contemporary art exhibitions. The likes of Damien Hirst and Cindy Sherman have exhibited here in the past, and there's more to come. Rudolfinum is located at **Náměstí Jana Palacha,** named after a student who set himself on fire in 1969 in protest of the Soviet occupation of Czechoslovakia. Also notice the statue of **Antonín Dvořák,** the famous Czech composer who conducted the first concert at Rudolfinum.

▶ ⚑ B: Staroměstská. It's the imposing building dominating the square near the Metro. The gallery entrance is on the left side of the building. ⓢ Ticket

Sights

50-190Kč. Cash only. ⏰ Open Tu-W 10am-6pm, Th 10am-8pm, F-Su 10am-6pm.

MALÁ STRANA

👍 Petřín Tower (Petřínská Rozhledna) TOWER

Petřín Hill

If the Petřín lookout tower seems like a shameless knockoff of the Eiffel Tower, that's because it is. The Eiffel Tower debuted at the 1889 World's Fair, and this shorter, fatter cousin popped up two years later at the Czech Jubilee Exposition. It's at the top of **Petřín Hill,** and, from the lookout 299 steps up, you can see a 360-degree panorama of the Czech countryside. If you're lazy and have money, you can pay extra to take the elevator (50Kč). Even if you don't go up on the tower, be sure to stop in at the free **Jára Cimrman museum** that's in the basement. Cimrman was a brilliant inventor, dramatist, composer, philosopher, and self-taught midwife. Oh, also, he didn't exist. Invented by two playwrights, Cimrman's life is the biggest inside joke of Czech culture. The objects in the museum might not strike foreigners as outrageously funny, but approach them with an open mind, and you'll learn something about the Czech sense of humor.

▶ 🚏 Walk up Petřín hill or take the funicular from Újezd (26Kč). After getting off the funicular, turn right and continue along the wall until you see the tower. There's also a path that leads here from Strahov Monastery. $ 100Kč, students 50Kč. Lift 50Kč. Museum free. Cash only. ⏰ Open daily 10am-10pm.

Petřín Area OBSERVATORY, MAZE, MONUMENT

Petřín Hill

The hilltop has a number of sites worth checking out. Housed in a tiny château near the tower, the **mirror labyrinth** (built for the 1891 Jubilee Exposition) must have been all the rage back in the day, but it's a little underwhelming in our cynical age. The **gardens** have hundreds of varieties of roses and merit a brief stroll. The **observatory** behind the funicular station houses three telescopes and temporary exhibits on space exploration. On your way down, check out the medieval **Hunger Wall,** the perpendicular wall going from the base to the top of the hill. Built by Charles IV, it could just have easily been named "useless public project" (it is said Charles had it built to give work to the city's poor). When you get back down, stop by the **Memorial**

to the Victims of Communism, a haunting monument near the Újezd tram station.

▶ 🪧 A: Malostranská. Walk southwest toward the hill. Or, take the funicular from Újezd. The alpine tram runs daily every 10-15min. 9am-11:30pm and accepts standard 26Kč public transportation tickets. $ Observatory 55Kč, students 40Kč. Mirror labyrinth 70Kč, students 50Kč. Cash only. ⏰ Observatory open Apr-Aug Tu-F 2-7pm and 9-11pm, Sa-Su 11am-7pm and 9-11pm; shorter hours in winter. Mirror labyrinth open daily 10am-10pm.

Church of Saint Nicholas — CHURCH

Malostranské náměstí 1

☎257 534 215; www.psalterium.cz

If you've spent any time in Europe, you've likely seen a church or two (or 50) by now. But this ain't no ordinary house of the Lord. Boldly colored celestial scenes play out on an enormous fresco that spans the length of the towering ceiling. Floating above it all, like the magical cherry on this holy sundae, sits the behemoth dome. Built by a father-son team in the 17th century, St. Nicholas is considered to be the most beautiful example of High Baroque architecture in Central Europe and was influential in defining the style throughout the continent. Don't forget to climb upstairs and see the 19th-century graffiti on the wooden handrail.

▶ 🪧 A: Malostranská. Follow Letenská to Malostranské náměstí. $ 70Kč, students 35Kč. Free entry for prayer daily 8:30-9am. Cash only. ⏰ Open daily Apr-Oct 9am-4:45pm; Nov-Mar 9am-3:45pm.

John Lennon Wall — MONUMENT

Velkopřevorské náměstí

Western songs were banned during the Communist years, so when someone painted John Lennon's face on this wall after the iconic singer was shot in 1980, it was an act of defiance against the regime. Since then, the wall has been an ever-changing community work of art—graffiti is layered over more graffiti, almost all celebrating peace, freedom, and other things Mr. Lennon stands for. The original drawing is long gone, but there will always be at least one Lennon face for you to pose with. Better yet, draw your own.

▶ 🪧 From the Charles Bridge, take a left on Lázeňská soon after the bridge ends. Stay on it as it curves around into Velkopřevorské náměstí. $ Free. ⏰ Open 24hr.

Church of Our Lady Victorious CHURCH

Karmelitská 14

☎237 532 018

This place might seem insigificant when you first enter, but there's more to it than meets the eye. On the right side, notice the wax figurine of the infant Jesus, which is said to have protected the church during the 30 Years' War and which supposedly possesses healing powers. This figurine is known internationally, and a small museum behind the altar displays costumes made for the figurine by friends from around the world, including Empress Maria Theresa. Continue wandering in the area near the souvenir shop, and you'll discover a startling collection of African wood sculptures, brought back from the Carmelite Order's missions. Every week, there are masses in five languages.

► 🚇 A: Malostranská. Follow Letenská through Malostranské náměstí and continue south onto Karmelitská. The church will be on the right. $ Free. ⏰ Church open daily 8:30am-7pm. Museum open M-Sa 9:30am-5:30pm, Su 1-6pm. English mass Th 5pm, Su noon.

Wallenstein Palace and Gardens PALACE

Valdštejnské náměstí 4

☎257 075 707; www.senat.cz

Originally built in 1626 as a castle for nobleman Albrecht Wallenstein, this immaculate compound now serves as the seat of the Czech Senate. Keep your eyes peeled for live peacocks wandering among the hedge rows and reflecting pools. And don't worry: that albino peacock isn't possessed by Satan, he was just born that way. Some sad-looking owls chill in the aviary next to the "stalactite wall," where a disorienting array of concrete affects the interior of a cavern. If the statues of Hercules killing all manner of mythical beasts aren't enough to impress you, come back on the weekends, when the castle's interior is open to tourists.

► 🚇 A: Malostranská. $ Free. ⏰ Gardens open June-Sept M-F 7:30am-7pm, Sa-Su 10am-7pm; Oct M-F 7:30am-6pm, Sa-Su 10am-6pm; Apr-May M-F 7:30am-6pm, Sa-Su 10am-6pm. Palace open Sa-Su 10am-5pm.

Franz Kafka Museum MUSEUM

Cihelná 2b

☎221 451 400; www.kafkamuseum.cz

In an attempt to be as disorienting as Kafka's writing, this museum goes crazy with shadowy video projections, sounds of dripping water, and dramatic lighting. There are spiderweb tunnels, rooms of mirrors, and, to be fair, at least one cool staircase. We can't decide whether the whole thing is kitschy or powerful—we'll leave it up to you to judge. The actual exhibit is a bit less dramatic; it's mostly facsimiles of Kafka's written documents and some old photographs. If you want to fuel the Kafka souvenir industry even more, buy a map that marks 34 places in Prague that have something to do with the man—seems like Mr. K was all over the place. Note David Černý's sculpture of pissing statues near the entrance to the museum. Recognize the shape of that pool? It's the Czech Republic.

▶ ✠ A: Malostranská. Go down Klárov along the river, veering left at the fork between U Lužické Semináře and Cihelná. The museum is on the left. Ⓢ 180Kč, students 120Kč. ⏰ Open daily 10am-6pm.

Saint Nicholas Tower   TOWER

Malostranské náměstí 29

☎724 323 375; www.abl.cz

During Communist rule, the secret police used the belfry of this tower to spy on Western diplomats and targeted Czechs. Today, said spy work is the subject of a mildly interesting exhibit, which includes old newspaper clippings (seems like the secret police loved soccer) and the TV that helped the agents pass time. (Their office was 299 steps up, so they probably didn't have much fun otherwise.) The climb up is lined by an exhibit on the tower, which was used as a fire tower before it burned down. In the days of yore, the bell was rung on cloudy days—the sound was believed to prevent rain.

▶ ✠ A: Malostranská. Follow Letenská to Malostranské náměstí. The tower entrance is at the back of the church. Ⓢ 100Kč, students 50Kč. Cash only. ⏰ Open daily Apr-Sept 10am-10pm; Oct 10am-8pm; Nov-Feb 10am-6pm; Mar 10am-8pm.

Museum Kampa   MUSEUM

U Sovových mlýnů 2

☎257 286 147; www.museumkampa.cz

The cost of admission may be a bit high, but modern art enthusiasts should not miss this riverside museum. The collection focuses on sculptures and paintings by Central European artists, most of whom were persecuted under Communism. At the end, climb the stairs to the observation deck, which has a great view over the Vltava (and feels as though it's about to keel over into it).

▶ ✠ A: Malostranská. From the Metro, walk south along the river to Kampa

Island. The museum is on the east side of the island at the edge of the river. Look for a giant chair or 3 enormous black babies. $ 280Kč, students 140Kč. ⏰ Open daily 10am-6pm.

HRADČANY

Around Prague Castle

The following sights are only a small sampling of what the castle complex has to offer. **Saint George's Basilica** dates back to 920 CE and is also part of a **short tour** of the area. Next door, **Saint George's Convent** now functions as a museum of 19th-century Bohemian art and sculpture. The **Powder Tower** houses a small exhibit on the castle guards. Admission to the latter two comes with the **long tour** ticket.

★ Prague Castle (Pražský Hrad) CASTLE

☎224 372 423; www.hrad.cz

One of the largest castles in the world, Prague Castle has been the seat of the Bohemian government since its construction over a millennium ago. It was home to such legendary kings as Charles IV and Rudolph II as well as the first Czechoslovak president, Tomáš Garrigue Masaryk. During WWII, Reinhard Heydrich, the Nazi-appointed protector of the city and notorious "Butcher of Prague," used the castle as his headquarters. It is said that whoever unlawfully wore the crown jewels would die within a year—Heydrich supposedly wore the jewels and, as predicted, was assassinated less than a year later. Arrive on the hour to catch the changing of the guard—the ceremony at noon also includes fanfare. Bonus points: make one of the guards on duty move without breaking the law. We can't seem to do it, but there must be a way.

▶ 🚏 Tram 22: Pražský hrad. From the stop, go down U Prašného Mostu past the Royal Gardens and into the Second Courtyard. Alternatively, hike up Nerudova. *i* Ticket office and info center located opposite St. Vitus Cathedral, inside the castle walls. "Short tour" covers admission to everything important, "long tour" includes other–rather uninteresting–sights. These are not guided tours. Tickets are valid for 2 consecutive days. $ Short tour 250Kč, students 125Kč. Long tour 350Kč, students 175 Kč. ⏰ Ticket office and historical monuments open daily Apr-Oct 9am-5pm; Nov-Mar 9am-4pm. Castle grounds open daily Apr-Oct 5am-midnight; Nov-Mar 6am-11pm.

🔲 Saint Vitus Cathedral (Katedrála sv. Víta)   CHURCH

Saint Vitus Cathedral is an architectural masterpiece, complete with three magnificent towers and more flying buttresses than it knows what to do with (no wonder it took almost 600 years to complete). Part of the cathedral is accessible without a ticket, but the inner part is cordoned off for ticket holders. Don't miss the Wenceslas Chapel (Svatováclavská kaple), which has walls lined with precious stones and paintings. Despite their old look, the window mosaics were all made in the 1940s, and some even contain sponsorship messages (including those for an insurance company). Some of the most important Czech kings are buried here, including Charles IV (plus his four wives), Jiří z Poděbrad, and Wenceslas IV. The silver tomb next to the altar belongs to St. John Nepomuk, who supposedly had his tongue torn out and was then thrown off the Charles Bridge because he refused to tell Wenceslas IV what his wife had confessed. The Bohemian crown jewels are kept in a room with seven locks, the keys to which are kept in the hands of seven different Czech leaders, both secular and religious. There's also a reliquary (not accessible to the public) that contains the skulls of various saints and some brain matter of John Nepomuk. For a great view, climb the 287 steps of the Great South Tower.

▶ 🏃 Enter the Great South Tower from outside the cathedral. Ⓢ Tower 150Kč.

Old Royal Palace (Starý královský palác)   PALACE

The Old Royal Palace, to the right of the cathedral, is one of the few Czech castles where visitors can wander largely unattended—probably because it's mostly empty. The lengthy Vladislav Hall is the largest Gothic hall in the Czech Republic; it once hosted coronations and indoor jousting competitions. Upstairs is the Chancellery of Bohemia, in which a Protestant assembly found two Catholic governors guilty of religious persecution and threw them out the window in the **Second Defenestration of Prague** in 1618.

Golden Lane and Dalibor Tower   STREET, TOWER

The authorities' decision to make the formerly free Golden Lane accessible only with a paid ticket caused an uproar among Czech citizens a few years ago. This legendary street with hobbit-size houses once belonged to the castle's artillerymen and artisans. Franz Kafka spent a year living in the

Spooky Stories

Prague is all fairy-tale charm by day, but at night (especially with your beer goggles on), the city transforms into a land of demons, ghosts, and nagging ghost wives. Learn which nooks and crannies to avoid (or perhaps seek out) so you don't accidentally come across any ghouls, witches, or ghosts.

- **OLD TOWN SQUARE.** Look for the 27 crosses on the ground commemorating the rebel leaders executed in Prague in 1621 as part of the 30 Years' War. The rebels are said to haunt the square, coming out annually to check that all is well with the astronomical clock.

- **LILIOVÁ STREET.** If you are on Liliová St. between midnight and 1am, strain your ears to block out the sounds of clanking beer mugs and rowdy Czech drinking songs from the surrounding taverns and you might just hear the pleas of the horse rider of Templar. Only the brave attempt to release him from his ghostly prison. Only the bravest attempt to look him in the eye, as he holds his head casually at his side in a saddle bag.

- **PRAGUE CASTLE.** If you just can't get enough of family bickering, head to the royal crypt of Prague Castle, where the four wives of Emperor Charles IV are buried. Late at night, it is said they rise from their graves to quibble over Charles' body, who evidently remains a studmuffin, even at the age of 700.

- **THE VLTAVA.** The Vltava is thought to be inhabited by water nymphs who appear in the form of tiny men with coats and pipes. They pop up at night to offer advice to passersby, but don't be fooled by their impish cuteness: these nymphs will trick you into crashing your boat and sinking to the murky depths.

Sights

blue house (#22); today it's a disappointing gift shop. Other highlights include the former house of a psychic (killed by the Gestapo for predicting "an early end to the war") and a few houses showcasing traditional crafts. At the end of the street you'll come to the base of Dalibor Tower, a former prison whose most famous resident was the knight Dalibor. Dalibor is the subject of the imprecise Czech adage "Necessity taught Dalibor how to play the fiddle"—indeed, the only "fiddle" that Dalibor encountered in the prison was the torture instrument designed to get prisoners to confess, by stretching them like horsehair on a fiddle bow. The tower exhibits a variety of torture and execution implements, including cages, "Spanish boots" (designed to crush legs and feet), and an executioner's axe.

▶ To the right of the Basilica, follow Jiřská halfway down and take a left on Zlatá ulička, or "Golden Lane."

Royal Summer Palace and Royal Gardens PALACE, GARDENS

The Italian-designed palace was built in the 16th century to provide entertainment for royals. Near the summer palace, the Singing Fountain uses a vibrating bronze plate to create its rhythmic, enchanting sound, though you have to squat down awkwardly to actually hear it. The surrounding Royal Gardens contain dozens of species of trees and shrubbery and make for a relaxing stroll. The garden is also home to an assortment of birds of prey that a falconer displays daily, usually between noon and 5pm.

▶ The gardens are located outside the castle complex. Exit through the 2nd courtyard, walk across the moat, and turn right. $ Free. ⏰ Open daily June-July 10am-9pm; Aug 10am-8pm; Sept 10am-7pm; Oct 10am-6pm; Apr 10am-6pm; May 10am-7pm.

Other Sights

Strahov Monastery (Strahovský klášter) MONASTERY

Strahovské nádvoří 1

☎233 107 711; www.strahovskyklaster.cz

There are two ticketed parts of the monastery: the gallery and the library. We like the library more—it contains thousands of volumes of philosophical, astronomical, mathematical, and historical knowledge, though your admission only entitles you to look from behind a barrier. Even more interesting is the library's antechamber, home to an 18th-century cabinet of curiosities, the predecessor of the modern museum. There you'll find a dried hammerhead shark, two elephant trunks (or dried whale penises, depending on whom you ask), a crocodile, a narwhal tusk (originally people believed this came from a unicorn), a Tatar bow, Hussite weaponry, bucketloads of boring shells, and the grotesque remains of a dodo bird. Compared to this, the gallery section may seem a bit boring, with its exhibit related to the history of Strahov Monastery and another floor dedicated to Czech paintings from between the 14th and 19th centuries. The remains of St. Norbert can be seen here in a glass coffin.

▶ ⚔ Tram 22: Pohořelec. From the tram, walk south and up the street, then take a sharp left onto Strahovské nádvoří. Ⓢ Library 80Kč, students 50Kč. Gallery 80Kč, students 40Kč. Photo or video permit 100Kč. Cash only. ⚿ Library open daily 9am-noon and 1-5pm. Gallery open daily 9am-noon and 12:30-5pm.

Loreta   CHAPEL
Loretánské námĕsti 7
☎220 516 740; www.loreta.cz

Loreta is one of the most important Christian sites in the Czech Republic and is the traditional starting point of pilgrimages. The central Santa Casa contains a statue of the Lady of Loreta, holding what is purported to be a piece of Mary's house at Bethlehem. Perhaps the most impressive part is the collection of treasures on the second floor, which includes diamond and pearl mitres, coral-decorated bowls, jewel-encrusted religious texts, and some astonishing monstrances.

▶ ⚔ Tram 22: Pohořelec. From the tram stop, walk south, turn left on Pohořelec, then left on Loretánské námĕsti. Ⓢ 110Kč, students 90Kč. Photo permit 100Kč. Audio tour 150Kč. Cash only. ⚿ Open daily in summer 9am-12:15pm and 1-5pm; in winter 9am-12:15pm and 1-4pm.

ŽIŽKOV

🏛 Jan Žižka Statue and Vítkov Hill   MONUMENT, MUSEUM
U Památniku 1900
☎224 497 111; www.nm.cz

On top of the hill, you'll find the statue of **Jan Žižka,** the one-eyed Hussite general who gave Žižkov its name. Appropriate to Žižka's stellar reputation (he was a brilliant tactician who supposedly never lost a battle), the statue is the largest equestrian statue in the world. The monument also honors those who fell in WWI and WWII—behind the statue you can find a hall dedicated to the memory of "the unknown soldier" (which is actually two soldiers who died in 1917 and 1944). After 1948, the monument became an important meeting place for the Communist Party and also the mausoleum of Klement Gottwald, the first Czechoslovak socialist president. A ticket to the **museum** allows you to see the presidential salon, mosaics by Max Švabinský, the view from the roof, and the eerie underground laboratory where the Communist leader's preserved body was kept for seven years before it started to go black and had to be cremated. On your way down from the monument, stop by the **Army Museum,** which features artifacts from WWII as well as a stuffed Rottweiler.

▶ ♯ Tram 5, 9, or 26: Husinecká. From the tram, follow Husinecká until you reach the square, then make a left at Orebitská, which will merge into Husitská. Walk down Husitská, then make a sharp right and climb the hill. Ⓢ 110Kč, students 60Kč. Camera 80Kč. Army Museum free. Cash only. Ⓩ Open W-Su 10am-6pm. Army Museum open Tu-Su 10am-6pm.

Žižkov Television Tower   TOWER
Mahlerovy sady 1
☎724 251 286; www.praguerocket.com

From a distance, the Žižkov TV Tower looks like a Soviet launch missile that never left Earth. The tower was initially met with some hostility during its construction in the mid-1980s, in part because some feared that the tower would hurt infants living around the area with its radio transmissions. After more than 20 years, the tower remains an eyesore, but it's become one of Prague's best-known landmarks. In 2000, controversial Czech artist David Černý cast nine figures of babies—perhaps in reference to that earlier paranoia—and attached them to the tower, where they've been ever since. The tower hosts a restaurant and three observation decks, allowing for impressive views of the city (don't worry, there's an elevator). In the square next to the tower, there's a historic **Jewish cemetery** that was partly destroyed by the tower's construction.

▶ ♯ A: Jiřího z Poděbrad. From the Metro, cross diagonally through the park and then take Milešovská toward the tower. Ⓢ 120Kč, students 90Kč. Cemetery 60Kč. Cash only. Ⓩ Observation deck open daily 10am-10pm. Cemetery open M and W 11am-3pm, F 9am-1pm.

Church of Saint Procopius   CHURCH
Čajkovského 36
☎775 609 952

In 1881, Žižkov became an independent city. Amid jubilation over their newfound autonomy, the residents of Žižkov realized that they did not have a Catholic place of worship big enough to accommodate the population of the new city. This neo-Gothic church was completed 13 years later.

▶ ♯ Trams 5, 9, or 26, Lipanská. Head west 2 blocks on Seifertova.

VINOHRADY

Aside from Vyšehrad, Vinohrady is also home to some of Prague's nicer parks and greenery. **Riegrovy sady** is a hilly park north of Náměstí Míru with grassy slopes from which you can see the Castle and much of Prague. Do as the young locals do: buy a plastic cup of beer from one of the nearby beer gardens, sit on the grass, and take in the view. The vine-covered **Havlíčkovy sady,** to the southeast of Náměstí Míru, is a posher setting: visit its wine bar, **Viniční Altán,** where you can sample many varieties of wine. (www.vinicni-altan.cz $ Wine from 30Kč. ⏰ Open daily 11am-11pm.)

Vyšehrad MONUMENT

V Pevnosti 5B

☎241 410 348; www.praha-vysehrad.cz

Overlooking the beautiful Vltava, Vyšehrad served as the royal residence of Czech kings until 1140, when they moved to Hradčany. It was supposedly founded by Princess Libuše, who foresaw the greatness of Prague before it became, well, great. Today, the complex contains a number of interesting sites. There's the towering **Church of Saint Peter and Saint Paul,** whose two spires can be seen from much of Prague. Next to the church is the beautiful **Vyšehrad cemetery,** where some of the most prominent Czech artists—writers, painters, poets—are buried. Among those in attendance are writer Karel Čapek (who coined the term "robot"), painter Alphonse Mucha (the pioneer of Art Nouveau), and composer Antonín Dvořák. There's also a snoozefest of an archeological exhibition in the **Gothic Cellar,** while the **Vyšehrad Gallery** exhibits work by Czech painters. If you're interested in seeing six of the statues that were originally part of the Charles Bridge, you can go on a short guided tour of **casemates and Gorlice.** Finally, make sure you check out the view of the city from Vyšehrad's fortifications—it's one of the best in Prague.

▶ 🚇 C: Vyšehrad. From the Metro, head toward "Kongresové Centrum" and walk across this conference complex, keeping right. At the end turn right and head down a staircase, then turn left and cross a parking lot. To your right you'll see a cobblestone road that leads to Vyšehrad. *i* Guided tours of the casemate leave every hr. 10am-5pm. $ Park admission free. English map and guide 35Kč. Church of St. Peter and St. Paul 30Kč. Casemate 50Kč. Vyšehrad gallery 20Kč. Gothic cellar 50Kč. Cash only. ⏰ Exhibitions open daily Nov-Mar 9:30am-5pm; Apr-Oct 9:30am-6pm. St. Peter and St. Paul open Tu-Th 9am-noon and 1-5pm, F 9am-noon.

HOLEŠOVICE

DOX MUSEUM

Poupětova 1

☎774 145 434; www.doxprague.org

Along with NOD (an art space affiliated with the Roxy club in Staré Město), DOX is at the leading edge of Prague's contemporary art scene. With exhibits of both domestic and international artists, DOX houses up to eight exhibitions at a time. For about a year, it was home to David Černý's controversial *Entropa,* which depicted each member country of the EU as a stereotype of itself (ire came mostly from Bulgaria, shown as a squatting toilet). We can't predict what show will be up when you visit, but it's sure to be crazy interesting.

▶ C: Nádraží Holešovice. Take tram 5 or 12 or walk along the tram tracks to Ortenovo náměstí. From there, continue along the tracks on Komunardů and take the 1st right. DOX is to the right. $ 180Kč; students 90Kč; art history, art, design, or architecture students 40Kč. ⏰ Open M 10am-6pm, W-F 11am-7pm, Sa-Su 10am-6pm.

Letná Park (Letenské Sady) PARK

A stroll through this sprawling, wooded park with unparalleled views of Vltava will make your day. Don't miss the gigantic **Metronome** that overlooks the city—it was installed in 1991, on the spot where a statue of Joseph Stalin once stood. Today the area is full of skaters doing things their moms probably wouldn't approve of. Toward the east side of the park you can find a sometimes-functioning carousel, the oldest in Europe. There are also a few cheap beer gardens where you can enjoy a cold one while looking over Prague's rooftops. Finally, there's the famous **Hanavský Pavilon** (Letenské sady 173 ☎233 323 641; www.hanavskypavilon.cz $ Small beer 60Kč.), an expensive restaurant in a beautiful Art Nouveau château that was constructed for the Jubilee Exhibition in 1891.

▶ B: Hradčanská. From the station, walk to the other side of the building, and head southeast. You'll run into the enormous park. Or take Metro C to Vltavská and head west.

Veletržní Palác / National Gallery
(Národní Galerie)   MUSEUM

Dukelských hrdinů 47

☎224 301 111; www.ngprague.cz

One of the coolest National Galleries (the others house mostly older art), Veletržní Palác is Prague's MoMA: there are five enormous floors packed with modern art, both Czech and international. The permanent collection contains the likes of Gustav Klimt, Edvard Munch, Vincent van Gogh, Pablo Picasso, Alfons Mucha, and many more.

▶ ⚑ C: Nádraží Holešovice. From the station take tram 12, 14, or 17 or walk along the tram tracks (passing the Exhibition Ground) for 2 stops, to Veletržní. The museum is at the tram stop. Ⓢ 250Kč, students 120Kč. Audio tour 30Kč. ⓩ Open Tu-Su 10am-6pm.

Prague Exhibition Ground   LANDMARK

Unless there's a big concert or an exhibition going on, visiting this place feels like going to an abandoned amusement park. It was built for the 1891 Jubilee Exhibition and still contains some of the "modern" wonders exhibited there. There's the ghostly Art Nouveau **Exhibition Palace,** whose left wing burned down some years ago and was replaced by a temporary replica. Behind the palace is the reconstructed **Křížiková Fontána** (☎723 665 694; www.krizikovafontana.cz ⓩ Ticket counter open daily 7:15-10:15pm, performances usually start at 8pm.), a fountain that combines light shows with popular tunes ranging from opera to Metallica. In front of the palace, the **Lapidary of National Museum** (Ⓢ 50Kč. ⓩ Open W 10am-4pm, Th-Su noon-6pm.) houses some of the original statues from the Charles Bridge, along with other historical exhibits. Officially, the **Marold's Panorama** (Ⓢ25Kč. ⓩ Open Tu-F 1-5pm, Sa-Su 10am-5pm.) is the biggest panoramic painting in Central Europe, but unofficially it looks like the interior of some bird pavilion in a zoo. East of the Exhibition Ground, **Stromovka,** a bigger park than Letenské sady, is great for some unstructured lolling around.

▶ ⚑ C: Nádraží Holešovice. From the Metro, take tram 5, 12, 14, or 17 or walk along the tracks to the next stop, Výstaviště.

Prague Zoo   ZOO

U Trojského Zámku 3

☎296 112 111; www.zoopraha.cz

Looking at exotic animals might not seem like the thing to do in Prague, but, in fact, Prague's leafy zoo is a popular refuge

Sights

for many locals. Among the zoo's highlights are the critically endangered Przewalski's horse and Komodo **dragons.** Before you enter, check out the "walk of fame" near the entrance—star-shaped tiles contain footprints of rhinos, chimps, tigers, and other tenants.

▶ 🚏 C: Nádraží Holešovice. From the Metro, take bus #112. The zoo is a 10min. ride. $ 150Kč, students 100Kč. ⏰ Open daily Jun-Aug 9am-7pm; Sept-Oct 9am-6pm; Nov-Jan 9am-4pm; Feb-Mar 9am-5pm; Apr-May 9am-6pm.

DEJVICE

The Bába Ruin (Zřícenina Bába) RUIN

Nad Paťankou

Bába looks like a significant ruin, but it isn't. It's the remnant of an 18th-century wine press (or a chapel, nobody knows for sure) that was renovated to look like a castle ruin in 1858. Nevertheless, the hill where it's located offers a great view of the Vltava and Dejvice, which is perhaps the reason for Bába's popularity as a wedding site. The Bába Ruin remains undiscovered by tourists, so if you're done with all the traditional sightseeing, it might make for a short and refreshing hike.

▶ 🚏 A: Dejvická. There are many ways to get here. On foot, it's 3km north from the Dejvice roundabout. Public transport can take you closer—buses #116 and #160 leave from the roundabout (get off at Ve Struhách, and then follow Pod Paťankou, Paťanka, and Nad Paťankou up the hill; the whole trip is about 2km), while bus #131 leaves from Hradčanská and stops much closer to the ruin. From the bus stop, walk down the stairs and continue to the end of Nad Paťankou.

Divoká Šárka PARK

This beautiful nature reserve is where Prague's locals take a break from people like you. Spread over some 25 hectares, it's the largest green area in the city, occupying the valley of the Šárka river. The reserve boasts an abundance of forest paths, grassy fields, steep hills, and a **swimming pool** (☎603 723 501; www.koupaliste-sarka.webnode.cz), which is 10min. from the tram stop by foot.

▶ 🚏 Take trams 8 or 36 to the final stop, Divoká Šárka, which is about 5km west of the Dejvice roundabout. $ Pool 60Kč. ⏰ Open in summer daily 10am-6pm.

SMÍCHOV

MeetFactory
GALLERY

Ke Sklárně 15

☎251 551 796; www.meetfactory.cz

If you enjoyed any of David Černý's works around Prague (Žižkov babies, Lucerna horse, pissing statues at Kafka Museum), you might be interested in visiting his pet project, MeetFactory. Founded in 2001 as a space for cultural dialogue, this converted glass factory hosts all kinds of events, from concerts to exhibitions to film screenings. It's a bit out of the way, down below the Smíchov train station, but it's just 'cause it's alt.

▶ ⚓ B: Anděl. From the Metro, take tram 12, 14, or 20 5 stops to Lihovar. Continue walking south along the tram tracks and cross the bridge over the railroad tracks. Turn right and continue until you reach MeetFactory. Ⓢ Exhibits free. Theater 150Kč, students 100Kč. Film screenings 60Kč, in summer free. Concert tickets vary. Cash only. ⏰ Hours depend on events; generally open M-F 1-8pm, Sa-Su 3-8pm.

Staropramen Brewery
BREWERY

Nádražní 84

☎257 191 111; www.pivovary-staropramen.cz

Staropramen is the second largest beer producer in the Czech Republic and this brewery, established in 1868, churns out hundreds of thousands bottles every day. The tour, which includes

Let There Be Beer

When they say that beer is sacred to the Czech people, they mean it almost literally. The first documented beer in the Czech Republic was brewed by the Benedictine monks in the Brevnov Monastery in the year 993 CE (they may have been preparing kegs for a huge millennium rager). The beer was fermented in huge caves underneath the monastery and then served to those notoriously fun-loving monk bros in the main abbey. The Czech people clearly liked the taste, and since 993 CE beer has evolved to be the much loved drink of the entire country. To this day, many monasteries in the Czech Republic brew their own ale; one popular lager, Klaster, translates to "monastery." It seems God may be on this liquid's side.

Sights

a beer tasting, guides you through a few of the giant copper vats that process malt and introduces visitors to the brewing process.

▶ B: Anděl. Exit the Metro station and take a right. The brewery is a few blocks down Nádražní on the left. $ Tour and tasting 199Kč. Cash only. ⏰ At the time of writing, the tours were being re-designed and put on hold, but they should be back up in 2012.

Bertramka MUSEUM

Mozartova 69

www.mozartovaobec.cz

Wolfgang Amadeus Mozart once lived in this villa, and it was here that he finished writing his famous opera, *Don Giovanni*. The exhibition inside is small and rather boring—you'll probably learn more about the ownership struggles that have plagued this little house for decades than about Mozart himself. Here's the shortened version: during the early years of Communism, the state took the house from its original owner (Mozartova Obec), and didn't return it until 2009. But the house was empty when it was returned—the original exhibits were taken to the National Museum in Malá Strana, which is why Bertramka now exhibits mostly borrowed artifacts.

▶ B: Anděl. Exit the Metro station and turn left. Then take the 1st left onto Plzeňská. Continue past the overpass and take the 1st left onto Mozartova. Bertramka is up a small hill at the end of Mozartova. $ 50Kč. Cash only. ⏰ Open daily 10am-6pm.

Food

Czech food tends to be simple, hearty, and meat-heavy. Ironically, the most iconic Czech meal is the fried cheese (*hermelín* or *eidam*), which rose to prominence thanks to Communism, when meat was in short supply. Among other staples are pork knee, goulash with dumplings, and schnitzel (basically a chicken fried steak). Consistent deliciousness comes at the price of variety. Most restaurants share practically the same menu; after a while you'll probably be looking to diversify. American and Mexican food is common, especially in bars and expat restaurants, while Chinese and Thai restaurants are also pretty easy to come by. The cheapest way to eat in Prague is to buy your own groceries. For groceries, head to chain supermarkets (Albert, Billa, Tesco) or small, usually Vietnamese-run corner stores.

No explanation of Czech cuisine is complete without a description of beer, the only liquid substance Czechs seem to consume. Czechs drink beer with every meal, and in restaurants, it's cheaper than non-alcoholic beverages (including water). There's a whole army of dishes that are eaten mainly with beer, including pickled sausages, cheese, or cabbage; "head cheese" (meat in aspic); and deep-fried bread. If you need a break from beer, try Kofola, the Communist answer to Coca Cola.

The best deals in town are the daily lunch menus, which are usually served between 11am-3pm, and cost somewhere between 80-110Kč. The menus are often in Czech, but since they

Budget Food

Though the food you'll find in Prague's restaurants is delicious, there may be cheaper deliciousness awaiting you just out the door. Street food in Prague mostly consists of **sausage,** which comes with mustard on dark bread and sometimes a beer. If you ever get tired of sausage, head for the grocery store. Bring your own bag to avoid paying for one at supermarket chains like **Albert** or **Billa,** or check the little Vietnamese corner stores you'll find in every neighborhood.

serve the same dishes in most Czech restaurants, it shouldn't be hard to learn the words for the basic dishes. The locals eat small breakfasts, usually just some cheese and bread, but the abundance of tourists has made English and American breakfasts a standard option. Dinner with a mug of beer should come in at below 200Kč, though some items (steaks, pork knees) will generally cost you more.

In addition to restaurants, Prague boasts hundreds of cafebars, small atmospheric establishments that serve double duty as cafes during the day and bars at night. They usually have extensive coffee options as well as a full bar and a small food menu.

NOVÉ MĚSTO

The food in Nové Město is generally more affordable than in the Old Town to the north. The best place to buy groceries is **Tesco** on Národní Třída.

🐦 Potrefená Husa   CZECH $$
Resslova 1
☎224 918 691; www.staropramen.cz/husa

Launched by the Staropramen brewery to "improve the beer culture in Czech Republic" (which is kind of like somebody aiming to improve the cocaine culture in Colombia), Potrefená Husa is a classy chain restaurant where locals come if they want an above-average meal. The barbecued ribs (185Kč) are an unforgettable experience, especially when paired with a garlic baguette. From the designer flourishes that adorn the brick cellar to the music on the stereo to the food itself, everything is slightly more interesting here than at a typical Czech restaurant.

▶ ⚏ B: Karlovo náměstí. From the station, head down Resslova, toward the river. The restaurant will be on the right. $ Entrees 145-285Kč. Desserts 35-89Kč. Beer 25-37Kč. ⏰ Open M-W 11am-midnight, Th-Sa 11am-1am, Su 11am-11pm.

Libeřské Lahůdky — BAKERY $

Vodičkova 9

☎222 540 828; www.liberskelahudky.cz

With its amazing variety of small sandwiches, cakes, cold salads, baguettes, donuts, and more, Libeřské Lahůdky is the perfect place to get your breakfast or midday snack. The *chlebíčky* (open-faced sandwiches) are artistic creations that come in many variations, all at surprisingly low prices (16-19Kč). If you're unsure about which one of the traditional Czech cakes you'd like, there are also bite-sized versions (8Kč) that allow you to make an informed decision. There's no seating, but you can eat your food standing at the counters or take it with you to the streets.

▶ 🚇 B: Karlovo náměstí. From the Metro, head north past the New Town Hall, staying right on Vodičkova when it forks. The restaurant is on the left. $ Baguettes 35-45Kč. Cakes 12-36Kč. Cash only. ⏰ Open M-F 7am-7pm, Sa-Su 8am-6pm.

Restaurace V Cípu — CZECH $$

V Cípu

☎607 177 107; www.restauracevcipu.cz

Even though it's right in the center of the city, this little restaurant remains a secret to most foreigners. With wooden benches and some rustic decorations, V Cípu feels unpretentious and inviting. Locals come here for cheap Czech classics and for Zlatopramen tank beer, which you can't get anywhere else in the country. Try the excellent fried cheese (75-80Kč) or the duck (94Kč).

▶ 🚇 A or B: Můstek. From the Metro, walk northeast on Na Příkopě and take the 1st right onto Panská. Take the 1st right onto V Cípu, opposite the Alfons Mucha Museum. $ Meat entrees 118-153Kč. Lunch menu 73-94Kč. Beer 18-32Kč. ⏰ Open M-Sa 11am-midnight, Su 11am-11pm.

Globe Café — AMERICAN $$

Pštrossova 6

☎224 934 203; www.globebookstore.cz

Part bookstore, part cafe, part cultural center, Globe is one of the best-known American outposts in Prague. Even though the American expat community has dwindled considerably in recent years and the clientele is starting to lean toward locals, Globe still offers some cultural comfort: up to 10,000 English-language books, refillable drip coffee (45Kč), and a menu of burgers, sandwiches, and other Western food. Cultural events (free film screenings, author readings, live music) take place almost every night, and, during happy hour (daily 5-7pm), chicken wings go for 7Kč a piece.

▶ B: Karlovo náměstí. From the Metro, take Resslova toward the river and then turn right on Na Zderaze, which becomes Pštrossova; the cafe is on the right. $ Sandwiches and burgers 140-180Kč. Desserts 65-80Kč. Beer 20-40Kč. Internet access 60Kč per hr. ⏰ Open M-Th 9:30am-midnight, F-Sa 9:30am-1am (or later), Su 9:30am-midnight. Bookstore open daily 9:30am-11pm.

Pizzeria Kmotra

PIZZA $$

V Jirchářích 12

☎224 934 100; www.kmotra.cz

Kmotra ("the godmother") is known for its quality pizza and low prices. Supposedly the oldest pizzeria in Prague, Kmotra sports a cozy downstairs cellar with floating lamps and wooden

Czech These Out

Looking for a quick snack before heading to one of Prague's historic sites or a night on the town? Don't overlook this delectable street fare:

- **Trdelník Rolled Pastries:** These pastries are sold fresh all over Prague in Staré Město and Malá Strana. They're hot, fluffy, and sprinkled with sugar—perfect for those seeking a sugar high.
- **svařené víno:** This cold-weather beverage is made from red wine mixed with mulling spices. Sweeten it with sugar or honey.
- **sausages:** You'll find plenty of sausage carts in areas like Wenceslas Sq. Much like the hot dog, an American favorite, these snacks are filling and easy to take on-the-go.
- **fried cheese sandwich:** This delicious treat may look like a chickwich, but those are actually thick slices of cheese that have been breaded and fried in that bun. The sandwich is usually topped with mayonnaise.

tables. There are 36 kinds of pizza, all of which come with thin crusts and generous toppings. If you're after slightly less traditional toppings, try Špenátová II, which is topped with spinach, bacon, and a sizzling egg.

▶ ☼ B: Národní třída. From the Metro, head down Ostrovní towards the river. Take the 2nd left at Voršilská. Ⓢ Pizzas 109-155Kč. Pasta 89-150Kč. ⏰ Open daily 11am-midnight.

Café Slavia
CAFE $$

Smetanovo nábřeží 2

☎224 218 493; www.cafeslavia.cz

Perhaps the best-known cafe in all of Prague, Slavia was historically the haunt of artists, intellectuals, and dissidents, including Václav Havel. Today it's a bustling tourist attraction, but completely worth the slightly above-average prices. In a prime people-watching and Vltava-gazing setting, Slavia sends you back in time with nightly piano music, an Art Deco interior, and waiters in bowties. And the biggest surprise? The food is actually great. Try something from the seasonal menus built around a single ingredient (asparagus, strawberries, etc.).

▶ ☼ B: Národní třída. From the Metro, walk north on Spálená and then turn left on Národní. The restaurant is at the end of the street, across from the National Theater. Ⓢ Czech dishes 139-189Kč. Desserts 45-109Kč. Coffee 39-70Kč. ⏰ Open M-F 8am-midnight, Sa-Su 9am-midnight.

Mamacoffee
COFFEE $

Vodičkova 6

☎773 337 309; www.mamacoffee.cz

Mamacoffee is the best coffee place in Prague. In fact, if you're not satisfied, this *Let's Go* researcher will eat a paper coffee cup. The organic, fair trade beans come from all corners of the world and the entire process (from three spoonfuls of coffee beans to a steaming cup) takes place before your eyes. Have your cup to go, or enjoy it while checking your email using the Wi-Fi upstairs.

▶ ☼ B: Karlovo náměstí. From the Metro, head north past the New Town Hall. Stay to the right on Vodičkova when it forks; the cafe is on the right. *i* 2nd location in Vinohrady. Ⓢ Coffee 35-67Kč. ⏰ Open M-F 8am-10pm, Sa-Su 10am-10pm.

Lemon Leaf
THAI $$

Myslíkova 14

☎224 919 056; www.lemon.cz

Classy Lemon Leaf serves delicious Thai food at affordable

Food

prices, especially on weekdays during lunchtime (11am-3pm) and during happy hours (3:30-6pm, 20% discount on all meals). If you approve of these, you might also be interested in coming for the weekend all-you-can-eat brunch (noon-3:30pm), which at 249Kč is a bit more costly but gives you a choice of several appetizers and entrees. The spacious interiors and the tables outside are equally alluring.

▶ ⚑ B: Karlovo náměstí. From the square, take Resslova toward the river and make a right onto Na Zderaze. Continue to the intersection of Na Zderaze and Myslíkova. Ⓢ Curries 159-189Kč. Entrees 139-199Kč. Lunch menu 89-149Kč. ⏰ Open M-Th 11am-11pm, F 11am-midnight, Sa noon-midnight, Su noon-11pm.

Angelato   ICE CREAM $
Rytířská 27
☎224 235 123; www.angelato.cz

Word on the street is that this is the best ice cream place in all of Prague. We're inclined to agree—the taste is smooth, creamy, and downright surprising. Intrigued? Then don't take our word for it; go find out for yourself. Ice cream heaven is only 30Kč away.

▶ ⚑ A or B: Můstek. From the Metro, walk up Na Můstku toward the Old Town. The shop is on the left. Ⓢ 1 scoop 30Kč; 2 scoops 55Kč. Cash only. ⏰ Open daily 11am-10pm.

Pivovarský Dům   CZECH $$$
Ječná 15
☎296 216 666; www.gastroinfo.cz/pivodum

Sure, it's a touristy place, but for good reason. To begin with, there's a microbrewery that makes eight different kinds of flavored beers (among them nettle, cherry, coffee, and banana) which you can drink individually (40Kč) or in a sampler (130Kč). Beer comes in regular sizes as well as in 4L towers that dominate the dining rooms. Food is served in enormous portions, and the football-sized pork knee (205Kč per kg) could be hazardous if it fell from any kind of height. Look for little beer icons on the menu—they denote dishes made with beer.

▶ ⚑ B: Karlovo náměstí. From the Metro, take Ječná east away from the river; Pivovarský Dům is on the right at the corner of Ječná and Štěpánská. Ⓢ Czech dishes 155-295Kč. Entrees 105-385Kč. Small beer 40Kč. ⏰ Open daily 11am-11:30pm.

Leica Gallery Prague
CAFE $

Školská 28

☎222 211 567; www.lgp.cz

Artsy travelers should stop in to this photography-themed gallery and cafe. The gallery in the back exhibits the work of international and local photographers and offers a new show every month. The cafe itself displays photographs, too, in addition to selling an impressive variety of monographs and magazines. As for food, the selection is small—three kinds of sandwiches and some quick bites. Try one of the exotic lemonades, which come in nettle, hemp, rooibos, and elderberry flavors.

▶ ♯ B: Karlovo náměstí. From the Metro, head away from the river down Žitná. Školská is the 2nd left. Ⓢ Soup 38Kč. Sandwiches 59-67Kč. Coffee 39-50Kč. Gallery admission varies, but usually 70Kč, students 40Kč, and art students 30Kč. Cash only. ☒ Open M-F 11am-9pm, Sa-Su 2-10pm.

Pod Křídlem Noci
CZECH $$$

Národní 10

☎224 951 741; www.podkridlemnoci.cz

This innovative restaurant has two faces: the modern, green-chaired cafe that's visible to the outside world and the hidden second room, where people gather to eat in absolute darkness two times per week. Should you choose the second option, you'll need a reservation, and you'll have to remove all light-producing objects before you enter. The entire experience costs 790Kč, and includes one of the four set menus and a live performance (all in total darkness). This option is recommended for ugly dates. If, on the other hand, you actually find your date attractive, dine in the properly lit cafe downstairs, which serves a handful of meat entrees and some old-school Czech desserts at surprisingly reasonable prices.

▶ ♯ B: Národní třída. From the Metro, walk north on Spálená, turn left on Národní, and head toward the river. Take the 3rd left onto Voršilská. The restaurant is on the left (despite its address on Národní). Ⓢ Entrees 129-245Kč. Set menu 790Kč. ☒ Open M 11am-4pm, Tu-F 11am-11pm.

Café Rybka
CAFE $

Opatovická 7

☎224 931 265; rybkapub.cz

Antique typewriters hang on the book-lined walls of this smoky, cheap cafe. You'll have to compete for table space with Czech hipsters (both young and middle-aged), who'll be feeding on

Food

toast (25-45Kč), or, more likely, on beer and cigarettes. When the cafe closes at 10pm, patrons usually move to the cafe's sister; just down the street, the bar Malá Ryba offers everything at the same prices, and stays open 'til 2am.

▶ B: Národní třída. From the Metro, walk down Ostrovní toward the river. Take the 1st left at Opatovická and follow it around the curve. The cafe is on the right. $ Breakfast 40-45Kč. Coffee 28-40Kč. Beer 17-35Kč. Cash only. ⏰ Open M-F 9:15am-10pm, Sa-Su 10am-10pm.

U Matějíčků CZECH $$

Náplavní 5

☎224 917 136; www.umatejicku.cz

U Matějíčků does solid Czech favorites right. For an introduction to Czech beer pairings, go for the "Big Board full of Goodies" (199Kč), which includes spicy sausage, head cheese, smoked pork neck, hot peppers, pickled onions, and Hermelin, Edam, and *olomoucké tvarůžky* cheeses. The lunch menu (79-99Kč) is also cheap and filling.

▶ B: Karlovo náměstí. From the Metro, head toward Resslova. Take the 2nd right onto Dittrichova; the restaurant is on the left at the fork. $ Entrees 109-249Kč. Beer 15-32Kč. ⏰ Open daily 11am-11pm.

Café Louvre CAFE $$

Národní třída 22

☎224 930 949; www.cafelouvre.cz

This smart Parisian bistro has brought French sophistication to Prague since 1902, serving figures like Kafka, Einstein, and Karel Čapek. It had too much class for its own good, though: during the Communist coup in 1948 its furniture was flung out the windows (defenestrated!). The cafe wasn't renovated until after the '89 revolution. Welcome back, capitalism. Stop by for a breakfast plate (109-149Kč), or for something small later in the day (quiche 129Kč). Any of the mouthwatering cakes on display (46-69Kč) will go well with Louvre's coffee and the view overlooking Národní třída.

▶ B: Národní třída. From the Metro, head north on Spálená and turn left onto Národní třída. The cafe is to the left. $ Entrees 129-319Kč. Coffee 39-55Kč. ⏰ Open M-F 8am-11:30pm, Sa-Su 9am-11:30pm.

Zvonice FRENCH $$$$

Jindřišská věž

☎224 220 009; www.restaurantzvonice.cz

Visitors to this intimate restaurant inside historic St. Henry

Tower have to share space with the tower's wooden scaffolding and an old bell. It's definitely a splurge, but the setting is unparalleled—perfect for a candlelit dinner, interrupted only by the shaking of the tower when the bells chime. The entrees feature mostly venison and other meat, all prepared in expensive-sounding ways (450-790Kč). If you'd like to make alcohol the focus of your night, try the downstairs **Whiskeria,** which offers some 400 kinds of whiskey at prices that are both student- and billionaire-friendly, depending on what you choose from the enormous menu.

▶ ⚑ A or B: Můstek. From Wenceslas Sq., walk down Jindřišská. Zvonice is the giant tower at the end of the street. *i* Reservations recommended. Dress to impress. Whiskeria ☎224 248 645; www.whiskeria.cz. ⓢ Expect to pay 1000Kč for the full dinner experience. Lunch menu 290Kč. 🕐 Open daily 11:30am-midnight. Kitchen closes 10pm. Whiskeria open daily 10am-midnight.

Restaurace U Zpěváčků   CZECH, ITALIAN $$
Na struze 7
☎224 930 493; www.restauraceuzpevacku.com

This place has been a hangout of opera singers, a meeting place for political dissidents, and a drug lair (not all at once). Today, it's an unpretentious restaurant that serves Czech and Italian dishes. The fried cheese with fries and tartar sauce (122Kč) is always a safe bet, while the big selection of spaghetti, risotto, and gnocchi will do if it's Italian cuisine you're after.

▶ ⚑ B: Národní třída. Head toward the river down Ostrovní. Turn left onto Pštrossova and then take the 1st slight right. The restaurant is on the right. ⓢ Entrees 124-198Kč. Beer 21-68Kč. 🕐 Open M-F 10am-2am, Sa-Su 11am-2am.

Restaurace U Žaludů   CZECH $
Na Zbořenci 5
☎776 327 118; www.lunchtime.cz/u-zaludu

Don't search for this restaurant in any other travel guide—it's the kind of place where old Czech men hang out, drink beer, smoke cigarettes, and turn and stare if somebody unknown shows up. We are listing it as an interesting cultural experience, so if you're feeling too pampered by the tourist establishments, stop by. The ridiculously cheap food is served only at lunch, but the ridiculously cheap beer flows non-stop.

▶ ⚑ B: Karlovo náměstí. From the station, head toward Resslova. Take the 1st right onto Na Zderaze and right onto Na Zbořenci. *i* Czech menus only. Ⓢ Meals 69-79Kč. Beer 14-24Kč. Shots 25-50Kč. Cash only. 🕐 Open M-F 10:30am-11pm, Sa-Su 11am-11pm.

Dynamo   FUSION $$
Pštrossova 29
☎224 932 020; www.dynamorestaurace.cz

Dynamo prides itself on being the kind of restaurant where you can't get fried cheese—the menu aims to surprise with such combinations as quesadilla with aubergine chutney, or spaghetti with arugula and anchovies. There are only three traditional Czech meals on the menu, and their price tags (190-225Kč) make the other cuisines more appealing. The lime-green interior may have been edgy back in '99 when the restaurant opened; today it comes off as a bit run-down. The walls sport some Andy Warhol pieces, one of them signed.

▶ 🚊 B: Národní třída. From the Metro, walk down Ostrovní toward the river and take the 3rd left on Pštrossova; Dynamo is on the right. Ⓢ Entrees 150-255Kč. Desserts 60-135Kč. Beer 37Kč. 🕐 Open daily 11:30am-midnight.

Café Royal   CAFE $$
Myslíkova 24
☎224 913 037; www.lunchtime.cz/royal-cafe

The real deal at this vaguely colonial cafe is the lunch specials (84-105Kč). There are always five options to choose from, all with a daily soup (which may arrive before you order, if you come here often enough). Coffee and an apple strudel with vanilla ice cream can be added to your lunch for just 55Kč. The lunch menus are in Czech, but the waitresses will happily translate. On sunny days, the terrace is a great place to lounge and watch passersby.

▶ 🚊 B: Karlovo náměstí. From the Metro, walk north and turn left onto Odborů. Continue until it runs into Myslíkova. The cafe is on the right. Ⓢ Chicken dishes 109-145Kč. Desserts 25-65Kč. 🕐 Open M-F 11am-midnight, Sa-Su noon-midnight. Lunch M-F 11am-3pm.

STARÉ MĚSTO

The rule of thumb for dining out in Staré Město is to follow the locals. Due to the density of tourism, there are a lot of tourist traps more than willing to serve food for twice the price you'd pay in a more residential neighborhood. There are a few grocery stores (Žabka, Albert), but the best place to shop for food is **Tesco MY** (Národní 26 🕐 Open M-Sa 8am-9pm, Su 9am-8pm.), which has low prices and a large selection.

[icon] Havelská Koruna

CZECH $

Havelská 21

☎224 228 769

As authentic as anything you might find in Staré Město, Havelská Koruna may be a bit intimidating at first: if you're standing in the lunch line, you'd better have your order from the Czech-language menu ready. But it's hard to go wrong; this is real food for real people. If you're in the market for an enormous dessert, try one of their sweet meals, like *šišky s mákem* (potato dumplings with poppy seeds) or *buchtičky s krémem* (buns in custard). The seating area is very cozy; during lunch hour you may even need to share space with some new friends.

▶ 🚇 A or B: Můstek. From the station, head north on na Můstku and continue as it turns into Melantrichova. Take a right on Havelská. The restaurant will be on the left. $ Sides 13-26Kč. Soups 21-33Kč. Entrees 35-79Kč. Cash only. ⏰ Open daily 10am-8pm.

[icon] Grand Café Orient

CAFE $$

Ovocný trh 19

☎224 224 240; www.grandcafeorient.cz

Grand Café Orient is supposedly the world's only Cubist cafe. It is located on the second floor of **Black Madonna House** (see **Sights**), and it originally closed after just 10 years in business when the winds of fashion changed. Luckily, the cafe reopened 80 years later when the taste for Cubist architecture returned. Come here after your visit to the Cubist museum (or skip the museum portion altogether) and have a delicious spinach crepe (95Kč) or one of the other light meals on the menu. Bonus points: guess the shape of their special dessert, "cubist cake."

▶ 🚇 B: Náměstí Republiky. From Old Town Sq., walk toward Church of Our Lady Before Týn. Keep the church on your right and continue down Celetná. The cafe is at the fork of Celetná and Ovocný trh, on the 2nd floor, through the museum entrance. $ Crepes 95-140Kč. Desserts 25-60Kč. Coffee 45-85Kč. Cash only. ⏰ Open M-F 9am-10pm, Sa-Su 10am-10pm.

Beas Vegetarian Dhaba

INDIAN, VEGETARIAN $

Týnská 19

☎608 035 727; www.beas-dhaba.cz

This vegetarian buffet is about as good a deal as you can get in the Old Town. It's cheap, tasty, and while most restaurants here try to rip you off on your teeny-tiny beverage, the water at Beas is free. The selection changes daily, but you can always count on basmati rice, two kinds of *daal,* samosas, and a daily special.

▶ ✦ B: Náměstí Republiky. From Old Town Sq., walk toward Church of Our Lady Before Týn, pass it on the left, and continue down Týnska. After you pass the church, keep to the left on Týnska—don't go straight. Turn left into a small courtyard; Beas Vegetarian Dhaba is next to Hostel Týn. *i* Other locations at Vlastislavova 24 (Ⓜ Národní Třída), Sokolovská 93 (Ⓜ Křížikova), Bělehradská 90 (Ⓜ I.P. Pavlova). Ⓢ Self-service food 16Kč per 100g. Lassi 22Kč. Coffee 24-32Kč. ◴ Open M-F 11am-8pm, Sa noon-8pm, Su noon-6pm.

Lokál
CZECH $$

Dlouhá 33

☎ 222 316 265; www.ambi.cz

Let this place be your introduction to a uniquely Czech way of treating beer—the "tank system." The beer skips pasteurization and is instead stored in giant tanks—not kegs—where it remains cut off from oxygen. The beer's first meeting with air is when it's poured. The menu, which changes daily, comprises traditional Czech dishes served inside a single arched hallway that's as long as a street block and echoes with conversation. Lokál is packed with locals, so it's a good idea to make a reservation.

▶ ✦ B: Náměstí Republiky. From Old Town Sq., head northeast past the Jan Hus statue, and continue on Dlouhá. Lokál is on the left. Ⓢ Sides 35-45Kč. Buffet appetizers 39-89Kč. Entrees 99-159Kč. Beer 29-39Kč. ◴ Open M-F 11am-1am, Sa noon-1am, Su noon-10pm. Kitchen open M-F 11am-9:45pm, Sa noon-9:45pm, Su noon-8:45pm.

Lehká Hlava
VEGETARIAN $$

Boršov 2

☎ 222 220 665; www.lehkahlava.cz

Even alpha-wolf carnivores should consider this cozy restaurant whose name means "Clear Mind." The interior was created by a number of Czech designers, and each room has a different feel (there's one that looks like a starry night sky), but the atmosphere remains relaxed throughout. Unlike many vegetarian restaurants, this one delivers big plates of great food: try the eggplant quesadilla (145Kč), a blasphemy by Mexican standards but tasty nevertheless. For dessert, go for millet carrot cake covered in chocolate (70Kč), or, if you're low on energy, have some of the Brazilian guarana juice, which has three times the caffeine of coffee (50-75Kč).

▶ ✦ A: Staroměstská. From Old Town Sq., head west and turn left at the river. Continue on Křižovnické as it becomes Smetanovo nábřeží, then make a quick left fork onto Karoliny Světlé. Then, make a left onto Boršov (it's a tiny street). *i* Reservations recommended. Ⓢ Sides 25-45Kč. Salads 125-145Kč. Entrees 140-175Kč. Desserts 70-80Kč. ⏲ Open M-F 11:30am-11:30pm, Sa-Su noon-11:30pm. Lunch menu until 3:30pm. Between 3:30-5pm, only drinks, cold appetizers, and desserts. Brunch served 1st Su of the month 10:30am-2pm.

Duende

CAFE, BAR $

Karolíny Světlé 30
☎775 186 077; www.barduende.cz

One of the many small bars that cluster around this area, Duende has plenty of personality—so much that it could be mistaken for a junk shop. Buoys hang next to leaping tigers, old guitars, and Christian posters...you get the picture. The small round tables are perfect for friendly conversations—if you have nobody to talk to, try to engage one of the artsy student types brooding over her diary. Drinks are cheap, and there's a small menu of snacks (35-99Kč).

▶ ⊹ B: Národní třída. Walk up on Spálená and turn left on Národní třída. Turn right at Karolíny Světlé, and continue as it curves to the left and to the right. Duende is on the right after the street narrows. Ⓢ Beer 20-35Kč. Coffee 30-55Kč. Cash only. ⏲ Open M-F 1pm-midnight, Sa 3pm-midnight, Su 4pm-midnight.

Krásný Ztráty

CAFE $

Náprstkova 10
☎775 755 142

"Beautiful Losses" is where it's at, at least if you ask local art students, intellectuals, and similar loafers. You'll rarely see someone over 40 here, and the place is clearly geared toward the younger crowds. Photography exhibits hang on the walls and the cafe frequently hosts cultural events. Food is light and reasonably cheap. Try the chicken quesadilla (95Kč), or if you happen to be around late at night, get the "midnight Hermelín" cheese (35-69Kč). If it's a busy night and you want to be really cool, grab some chairs from inside and sit outside, smoke heavily, and perch your beer on the windowsill.

▶ ⊹ A: Staroměstská. From Old Town Sq., set out in the direction of Charles Bridge, but continue south on Jilská. When you reach the intersection with Skořepka, take a right and continue to Betlémské Náměstí. Continue as it turns into Náprstkova. The cafe is on the left. Ⓢ Breakfast 85-95Kč. Coffee 29-66Kč. Beer 20-39Kč. ⏲ Open M-F 9am-1am. Sa-Su noon-1am.

Choco Café

CHOCOLATE $

Liliová 4

☎222 222 519; www.choco-cafe.cz

As the name implies, these guys take their chocolate seriously. Hot chocolate is made on the spot using melted chocolate chips instead of some packaged mixture. Choose from an array of flavors that includes ginger, sea salt, and chili, or get the evening started by spiking your chocolate with rum, egg nog, or whiskey. We also highly recommend their desserts; the tiramisu (60Kč) is massive. This space was a postcard museum before Choco Café came along—be sure to scope out the hilariously old-fashioned collection on the walls.

▶ ⚐ A: Staroměstská. From Old Town Sq., set out in the direction of Charles Bridge, but continue south on Jilská. When you reach the intersection with Skořepka, take a right, and continue to Betlémské Náměstí. Pass the church and take a right on Liliová. The cafe is on the right. $ Bruschetta 78-93Kč. Cakes 60Kč. Hot chocolate 55-75Kč. ⏰ Open M-Sa 10am-10pm, Su 10am-8pm.

Apetit

CAFETERIA $

Dlouhá 23

☎222 329 853; www.apetitpraha.cz

Apetit embodies the way Czechs and tourists are seen as two different species by most restaurants in Staré Město. There are actually two parts of Apetit: a no-nonsense eatery serving hungry locals upstairs and a gussied-up restaurant downstairs, serving dishes that contain shark, swordfish, and the like at exorbitant prices. Choose the former, which may be one of the cheapest places to eat in Staré Město. Grab a tray, take some silverware, wait in the cafeteria-style lunch line, and use sign language to indicate which of the traditional Czech meals you'd like. It's normal to sit at the same table with strangers in the cramped dining area: just say *dobrý den* (hello) as you join and *na shledanou* (goodbye) when you leave.

▶ ⚐ B: Náměstí Republiky. From Old Town Sq., head northeast past the Jan Hus statue, and continue on Dlouhá. Apetit is on the left. $ Lunch menu 72Kč. Entrees with soda 89-92Kč. Beer 17-25Kč. Cash only. ⏰ Open M-F 9am-8pm, Sa-Su 10am-8pm.

Bohemia Bagel

AMERICAN $

Masná 2

☎224 812 560; www.bohemiabagel.cz

Other (less touristy) locations at Lázeňská 19, Dukelských Hrdinu 48

Designed for homesick Americans, the Bohemia Bagel chain brings bagels, free coffee refills (49Kč), Ben & Jerry's ice cream, democracy, and more to the Old Continent. Breakfast is served all day, but the restaurant delivers solid lunch options too: burgers, sandwiches, and grilled meat. And, if you need to send an email home or tweet about how *crazy* Europe is, Bohemia Bagel also serves internet.

▶ ⇆ A: Staroměstská. From Old Town Sq., head northeast past the Jan Hus statue, and continue on Dlouhá. At the roundabout, take a right on Masná. $ Bagels 25-80Kč. Sandwiches 95-130Kč. Coffee 35-50Kč. Computers 2Kč per min. Wi-Fi 1Kč per min. Cash only. ⏰ Open daily 8am-9:30pm.

La Casa Blů

LATIN AMERICAN $$

Kozí 15

☎221 818 270; www.lacasablu.cz

Burritos and quesadillas are on the menu, but calling La Casa Blů a Mexican restaurant would do this cool hang-out an injustice. The Latin American chefs also prepare South American sandwiches, plus there's Chilean wine on the menu. A generous happy hour until 6pm includes some cheap meals (tacos 116Kč) and drinks (beer 19-26Kč). La Casa Blů also serves as the local ambassador for Latin culture: the walls are covered with the work of Latin artists, and Latin musicians perform here regularly. La Casa Blů was also the filming site for parts of the Czech cult film Samotáři (*Loners,* 2000)—you can't get much cooler.

▶ ⇆ B: Náměstí Republiky. From Old Town Sq., head northeast and continue on Dlouhá. At the roundabout, take a left on Kozí. $ Burritos 168Kč. Quesadillas 148-168Kč. Beer 21-43Kč. ⏰ Open M-F 11am-midnight or later, Su 2pm-late.

Klub Architektů

INTERNATIONAL $$

Betlémské náměstí 5A

☎224 248 878; www.klubarchitektu.com

If you're in the market for a candlelit dinner in a cavernous setting, this is the place. The cuisine bills itself as "international," but don't expect anything too exotic—it's mostly good old Czech pub entrees in fancier sauces. Given the sophisticated ambiance, the prices are surprisingly reasonable; there's many a dump that will try to sell you this fare for the same price. Oh, and if the ridiculously low-hanging lamp happens to be poking your "beef medallion with apples in cream sauce and mashed potatoes" (185Kč), just ask the waiter to raise the light fixture.

▶ B: Národní třída. From Old Town Sq., set out in the direction of Charles Bridge, but stay south on Jilská. Take a right at the intersection with Skořepka, continue to Betlémské náměstí, and then turn right into a courtyard (it's next to Betlémska Church). The restaurant is down a staircase. $ Sides 30-40Kč. Entrees 145-185Kč. Desserts 55-80Kč. ⏰ Open daily 11:30am-midnight.

Zahrádka U Kristiána — BEER GARDEN $

Smetanovo nábřeží 5

This bare-bones assemblage of tables and sunshades has only about three items on the menu: sausage (65Kč), Hermelín (80Kč), and "chicken steak" (180Kč), all grilled on a tiny grill in plain sight. If this sounds tempting, walk down the steps to the river, sit on one of the benches, and enjoy the view. (The view goes well with a beer.)

▶ A: Staroměstská. From Old Town Sq., head toward the river and when you reach it, turn left on Křižovnická. Continue as it becomes Smetanovo nábřeží. The outdoor terrace will be close to the river on your right, close to the river, down some stairs. $ Food 65-180Kč. Beer 32-42Kč. Cash only. ⏰ Officially open Apr-Sept daily 11am-10pm, but closing time depends on demand and weather.

Pivnice U Rudolfina — CZECH $$

Křižovnická 10

☎222 328 758

You need to know what you're looking for to find it, because the tiny street-level floor doesn't hint at the size of this smoky underground pub. It's quintessentially Czech—there are no English menus and waiters aren't very well-equipped linguistically—but you'll do good to pop in for a traditional Czech meal or for a beer (served from the tank).

▶ A: Staroměstská. From Old Town Sq., head toward the river and, when you reach it, turn right on Křižovnická. $ Meat entrees 99-199Kč. Beer 25-38Kč. Cash only. ⏰ Open daily 10:30am-11pm. Lunch menu until 2pm.

JOSEFOV

Josefov is full of tourist traps that are to be avoided at all costs. If you do find yourself sightseeing around lunchtime, there are some very cheap lunch menus, even at the more expensive restaurants. Ask about these deals before you sit down.

Kolkovna CZECH $$$

V Kolkovně 8

☎224 819 701; www.kolkovna-restaurant.cz

If there's one restaurant in Josefov that's worth the price, it's Kolkovna—not that it's very expensive in the first place. The focus is on grilled meat and skewers, but chances are that whatever dish you order will be tasty and generously portioned. Locals come here for the tank beer, and you should consider yourself lucky if you're able to get a table without a reservation at dinner time. Try the lunch menu first (95Kč)—even lunches here tend to be more creative than elsewhere.

▶ B: Staroměstská. In the square with the Franz Kafka statue. To get here from Old Town Sq., head north on Dlouhá and turn left on Dušní. $ Czech specialties 169-345Kč. Beer 36-43Kč. ⏰ Open daily 11am-midnight.

Le Court Café/Galerie CAFE $

Haštalská 1

There's no food served at Le Court, unless we're talking about food for the soul, in which case there's plenty—the indoor part of the cafe serves as a gallery that hosts a new contemporary art exhibit every month. The real place to be, however, is the courtyard, with its wobbly wooden tables and cozy nooks. Decorated with rampant ivy and other greenery, the courtyard is a great place to discuss anything and everything over a beer, coffee, or hot chocolate.

▶ A: Staroměstská. From Old Town Sq., walk up Dlouhá and, after the roundabout, continue straight on Kozí. The cafe is inside a courtyard in the building that says "Galerie." $ Beer 35-40Kč. Coffee 35-50Kč. Cash only. ⏰ Open daily 10am-10pm.

La Bodeguita del Medio CUBAN $$$

Kaprova 5

☎224 813 922; www.bodeguita.cz

Few places in the neighborhood are as hopping as this Cuban restaurant-bar (it doesn't hurt La Bodeguita's odds that most of the neighborhood is a cemetery). Live Latin music flows as freely as the mojitos and margaritas. While most of the meat entrees are on the pricier side, it's possible to keep within the budget by getting one of their soups (85Kč) and perhaps combining it with an appetizer. This is also the place to buy Cuban cigars.

▶ ✦ A: Staroměstská. About 25m east of the Metro on Kaprova. *i* Latin music and dancing most nights. Ⓢ Creole dishes 250-380Kč. Grilled meat dishes 310-440Kč. Beer 60-95Kč. ◷ Open M 9am-2am, Tu-Sa 9am-4am, Su 9am-2am.

Pivnice U Pivrnce   CZECH $

Maiselova 3

☎222 329 404; www.upivrnce.cz

This could well be the cheapest place in Josefov, offering ordinary, unadorned Czech cuisine. U Pivrnce seems to compete with all the classy tourist traps of the neighborhood by doing the exact opposite—by which we mean not having any class at all. The walls are decorated with vulgar, misogynistic cartoons by a well-known local cartoonist. But even this is Czech authenticity—far more so than what you'd find in the prettied up establishments nearby.

▶ ✦ A: Staroměstská. From the Old Town Sq., walk past the Church of St. Nicholas and onto Maiselova. U Pivrnce is on the left. Ⓢ Czech entrees 95-114Kč. Desserts 35-75Kč. Beer 15-35Kč. ◷ Open daily 11am-midnight.

MALÁ STRANA

Restaurants in Malá Strana tend to be pricey, but there are a few good finds. Thanks to the high proportion of artistic types, the neighborhood has plenty of marvelous cafes. There are no supermarkets in Malá Strana because the neighborhood's aesthetic is under official protection, but to the south there's **Nový Smíchov,** a big shopping mall near ĆAnděl.

🖾 Bar Bar   INTERNATIONAL, BAR $$

Všehrdova 17

☎257 312 246; www.bar-bar.cz

Bar Bar's blend of local flavor and exotic influences, and its balance of excitement and comfort, would make it a find in any neighborhood. Hiding just off the main street in Malá Strana, this gem has an original menu featuring mostly international dishes, such as souvlaki (174Kč) and fried, cheese-filled jalapeños (79Kč). But the house specialty is the crepes, both sweet (79-85Kč) and savory (125-139Kč). Bar Bar is also—surprise!—a bar, so don't hesitate to come by at night for drinks, all in the company of brooding poets and painters.

▶ 🚏 A: Malostranská. From the station, walk south or take a tram 12, 20, or 22 to Hellichova. Continue walking south on Újezd, then turn left on Všehrdova. The restaurant is on the right. $ Entrees 139-195Kč. Desserts 95-125Kč. Beer 23-38Kč. Cocktails 90-175Kč. ⏰ Open M-Th noon-midnight, F-Sa noon-2am, Su noon-midnight.

Dobrá Trafika

CAFE, WINE BAR $

Újezd 37

☎257 320 188; www.dobratrafika.cz

If you go through the unremarkable store in front, you'll discover an excellent cafe, popular with artists, musicians, and other tea-drinking types. Speaking of tea, this place has a four-page menu dedicated to the stuff, in addition to coffee from 20 different countries and the rare Primátor beer on tap. If you're hungry, try the weirdest pita bread you've ever seen: fillings range from banana (29Kč) to Georgian eggplant (78Kč). There's also a small wine bar downstairs.

▶ 🚏 A: Malostranská. From the Metro, walk south or take tram 12, 20, or 22 to Hellichova. Continue walking south on Újezd; the specialty store is to the right. $ Pitas 29-78Kč. Coffee 35Kč. Beer 29-32Kč. Cash only. ⏰ Open M-F 7:30am-11pm, Sa-Su 9am-11pm.

Tlustá Myš

CZECH $$

Všehrdova 19

☎605 282 506; www.tlustamys.cz

Tlustá Myš ("Fat Mouse"), next door to Bar Bar, has similarly awesome food and prices. The main difference between the two is that Fat Mouse focuses on Czech cuisine and feels down-to-earth, with wooden tables and brick walls. Grilled sausages (55Kč) are cheaper here than at a street vendor, and can be ordered from a menu decorated with cute mice drawings (the real reason to come here). We recommend the steak California (chicken cutlet with cheese and peaches), which, name aside, is a traditional Czech meal.

▶ 🚏 A: Malostranská. From the Metro, walk south or take tram 12, 20, or 22 to Hellichova. Continue walking south on Újezd and turn left onto Všehrdova. The restaurant is on the right. $ Entrees 119-165Kč. Desserts 49-59Kč. Beer 20-34Kč. 20% discount daily noon-2pm. Cash only. ⏰ Open M-Sa noon-midnight, Su noon-10pm.

Pod Petřínem

CZECH $$

Hellichova 5

☎257 224 408; www.pivnicepodpetrinem.cz

This low-key Czech pub is as cheap as it looks. There are just a few menu items: goulash (85Kč), chicken with rice (95Kč), and pork knee (165Kč), in addition to a set of alternating lunch dishes. There's no English menu, but the staff will kindly translate. Frankly, we were surprised to find such a no-nonsense pub in the middle of Malá Strana.

▶ ⚑ A: Malostranská. From the Metro, walk south or take tram 12, 20, or 22 to Hellichova. The restaurant is at the intersection of Újezd and Hellichova. Ⓢ Entrees 85-165Kč. Lunch menu 99Kč. Beer 16-36Kč. ☺ Open daily 11am-12:30am.

Lokál U Bílé Kuželky

CZECH $$

Míšeňská 12

☎257 212 014; www.ambi.cz

Decorated like its Old Town cousin, Lokál changes its menu of reasonably priced Czech dishes daily. Aside from normal beer, Lokál also offers *šnyt,* a sort of half beer—most of the glass is occupied by beer foam, which keeps the liquid below fresh and unoxidized. It's the perfect lunchtime solution to the age-old dilemma "have another beer or not?"

▶ ⚑ A: Malostranská. From the Metro, head south along the river on Klárov past the Kafka Museum. Take a right at Míšeňská; the restaurant is on the right. Ⓢ Lunch menu 89-115Kč. Dinner entrees 159-205Kč. Beer 29-38Kč. ☺ Open daily 11:30am-midnight.

Mlýnská Kavárna

CAFE $

Všehrdova 14

☎608 444 490

Students love this watermill cafe on Kampa Island, with a functioning water wheel and a terrace that's perfect for sunny days. The food pickings are rather slim, but the daily soup and one of the beer pairings will stave hunger off.

▶ ⚑ A: Malostranská. From the Metro, head south along the river to Kampa. The cafe is at the southwest corner of the island; look for a giant water wheel. The cafe's address is on Všehrdova, but the entrance is from Kampa Island. Ⓢ Food 24-59Kč. Beer 21-36Kč. Coffee 34-74Kč. Cash only. ☺ Open daily noon-midnight.

Pátý Přes Devátý (5/9 Café)   CAFE, BAR $
Nosticova 8

☎736 425 011; www.59cafebar.cz

This new cafe is rapidly ascending the popularity ladder among Malá Strana locals. The best feature is the cozy terrace, which sits right above the Vltava (or rather, above the tiny rivulet that separates Kampa from Malá Strana). There are toasts and other snacks, but the drinks are the main event.

▶ ⚥ A: Malostranská. From the Metro, head south along the river, all the way to Kampa. When you reach the island's park, take the 1st right just after the small statue. The cafe is behind the bridge. Ⓢ Toasts 59Kč. Beer 18-37Kč. Coffee 39-60Kč. ⌚ Open daily 11am-11pm.

Wigwam   INTERNATIONAL $$
Zborovská 54

☎257 311 707; www.cafebarwigwam.cz

The menu at the ambiguously ethnic Wigwam oscillates between Czech experiments, like the pork neck burger (149Kč); American non-experiments, like the classic hamburger (149Kč); and curveball Asian dishes, like the *mat saman* curry (170Kč). The blue cheese nachos (90Kč) are enough to start any party—any cheese party, that is.

▶ ⚥ A: Malostranská. From the Metro, walk south or take tram 12, 20, or 22 to Újezd. From the tram stop, walk toward the river until you reach Zborovská and turn right. The restaurant is on the left. Ⓢ Entrees 80-195Kč. Beer 20-40Kč. Cocktails 60-90Kč. ⌚ Open M-F 11am-1am, Sa noon-1am, Su noon-10pm.

Cafe Kafíčko   CAFE $
Míšeňská 10

☎724 151 795

A quiet stop in the middle of tourist town, Cafe Kafíčko is also one of the first nonsmoking cafes in all of Prague. Its coffee comes from 12 different countries, is made from whole beans on the spot, and is *not* served in a paper cup (due to some principled belief about how coffee deserves time and attention). Other than a selection of breakfast items, food is mostly limited to dessert (15-55Kč).

▶ ⚥ A: Malostranská. From the Metro, head south along the river on Klárov past the Kafka Museum. Take a right at Míšeňská; the restaurant is on the right. Ⓢ Coffee 42-68Kč. Cash only. ⌚ Open daily 10am-10pm.

Food

Kavárna Čas

SNACKS $

Míšeňská 2

☎721 959 903

Kavárna Čas wouldn't be very remarkable if it didn't offer delicious and cheap snacks in this overpriced neighborhood. Toasted cheese sandwiches (45Kč) come with ketchup, and strudel pastries (40-65Kč) are filled with bologna, sausage, or cabbage. The menu has photos of the "Golden Voice of Prague," Karel Gott, visiting the cafe. If you don't know who Karel Gott is, that's one more thing to YouTube tonight.

▶ 🚏 A: Malostranská. From the Metro, head south along the river on Klárov past the Kafka Museum. Take a right at Míšeňská; the restaurant is on the right. $ Toasts 30-60Kč. Beer 20-30Kč. Coffee 20-50Kč. Cash only. ⏰ Open daily 10am-8pm.

HRADČANY

When it comes to most restaurants in Hradčany, we'll quote Admiral Ackbar: "It's a (tourist) trap!" For a cheap bite to eat, try the fast food hole-in-the-wall near the intersection of Pohořelec and Úvoz ($ Hot dogs 25Kč. Cheeseburgers 50Kč.), or the **Žabka** market across the street.

👍 U Zavěšenýho Kafe

CZECH $$

Úvoz 6

☎605 294 595; www.uzavesenyhokafe.com

Unlike so many of the touristy establishments nearby, this restaurant has a strong base of local patrons—in fact, an entire wall is covered by snapshots of customers wearing "U Zavěšenýho Kafe" T-shirts in exotic travel destinations. The portions are huge, and the cozy dining area is segmented into a number of smaller rooms. The inner courtyard is a great place to sit on both sunny and rainy days. Check out the abacus counter near the entrance—it shows the number of coffees that have been purchased in advance by local patrons for the benefit of people without the money to pay. Please don't abuse the honor system.

▶ 🚏 Tram 22: Malostranské náměstí. From the tram stop, walk uphill on Nerudova and continue as it becomes Úvoz. The restaurant is on the right. $ Entrees 85-175Kč. Desserts 22-65Kč. Cash only. ⏰ Open daily 10am-11pm.

Český Banát   CZECH, ROMANIAN $$
Nerudova 21

☎721 029 205; http://czrestaurace.ceskybanat.cz

Probably the cheapest restaurant on the block, Český Banát is bare but neat and very welcoming. The owner is Romanian, and it's one of the few places in Prague where you can try cuisine from that corner of the world. To get started, try the *čorba* soup with meat dumplings (55Kč). On your way out, pick up some of the traditional, sugar-covered pastries sold at the entrance.

▶ 🚊 Tram 22: Malostranské náměstí. From the stop, walk uphill on Nerudova. The restaurant is on the left side, next to Little Quarter hostel. Ⓢ Entrees 89-129Kč. Sweets 69-115Kč. Lunch menus 89-109Kč. Cash only. 🕗 Open M-Th 9am-9pm, F-Sa 9am-2am, Su 9am-9pm.

Bellavista   CZECH $$$
Strahovské nádvoří 1

☎220 517 274; www.bella-vista.cz

It doesn't take a genius to figure out that the reason people come here is the *bella vista* (pretty view). The restaurant's wooden tables have some of the best panoramic views of the city, and the prices have been set accordingly. If you want the view for cheap, order a beer or coffee; if you want the view for free, walk down one level to the area full of tourists.

▶ 🚊 The restaurant is below Strahov Monastery. Facing the monastery, turn left and continue until you reach a sloping path leading to the restaurant. Ⓢ Czech specials 255Kč. Desserts 120-135Kč. Small beer 65-69Kč. 🕗 Open daily 11am-midnight.

Klášterní Pivovar and St. Norbert Restaurant   CZECH $$$
Strahovské nádvoří 301

☎233 353 155; www.klasterni-pivovar.cz

Turns out Strahov has not only a restaurant, but also a microbrewery with its own signature beer—named after a saint with the somewhat uncommon name, "Norbert." The food isn't necessarily the best thing to happen since St. Norbert was around, but you can enjoy a cool glass of the beer right before going to see the saint's remains, also in glass, at the monastery's gallery. Oh boy!

▶ 🚊 Opposite the Strahov Monastery. *i* Book tours of the brewery in advance. Ⓢ Appetizers 79Kč; entrees 150-390Kč. St. Norbert beer 35-64Kč. Brewery tours 120Kč; includes 3 small beers. 🕗 Open daily 10am-10pm.

ŽIŽKOV

U Sadu   CZECH $$
Škroupovo náměstí 5
☎222 727 072; www.usadu.cz

This may be one of Žižkov's best-known restaurants. Choose between the patio seating or the dining room, where an entire antique shop dangles from the ceiling. But the coolest part of the restaurant is U Sadu's smoky cellar: behind the gambling machines, a spiral staircase leads to a foosball table and several small rooms filled with young people. Some of the most popular dishes are fried ribs with mustard and horseradish (155Kč) or roasted pork knee (195Kč).

▶ ♯ A: Jiřího z Poděbrad. From the Metro, cross diagonally through the park (pass in front of the church) and then walk north on Laubova. U Sadu is at the northern side of the square with the roundabout. ⓢ Snacks 55-95Kč. Meat entrees 125-195Kč. Beer 28-33Kč. ⏰ Open M-W 9am-2am, Th-Sa 9am-4am, Su 9am-2am. Kitchen open until 2am.

U Vystrelenýho Voka   PUB $
U Božích bojovníků 3
☎222 540 465; www.uvoka.cz

The title of this place means "at the shot-out eye" and over the last 19 years it has become something of a cult establishment. The menu is the opposite of fussy—the only two categories you can choose from are "cold food" and "warm food." Try the inexpensive Danube sausage (35Kč), or, if you want to splurge, the fried cheese (80Kč). The cascading terraces above the pub actually belong to a different establishment, **Kavárna U Voka** (ⓢ Beer 26-33Kč ⏰ Open M-F 3-10pm, Sa-Su 2-10pm), which is an equally great place to grab a drink. Oh, and if you ask the staff what the name means, you'll get a 30min. lecture on the history of Žižkov. Short answer: it refers to the one-eyed Jan Žižka, the famous Hussite general.

▶ ♯ Tram 5, 9, or 26: Husinecká. Walk uphill on Seifertova, then turn left on Blahníkova and continue as it turns into Jeronýmova. When you reach Husitská, take a right and then the 1st left into a little alley marked U Božích bojovníků. ⓢ Cold food 30-44Kč. Hot food 35-89Kč. ⏰ Open daily 4:30pm-1am.

Food

Amores Perros

MEXICAN $$

Kubelíkova 33

☎222 733 980; www.amoresperros.cz

The chefs may be Czech and the interior overcompensates (think sombreros and cactuses), but Amores Perros is still known as one of the better Mexican places in Prague (and the only one in Žižkov). Sizzling enchiladas (109Kč) smothered in heart-stopping sauce are the way to go. Come here for lunch, as the menu deals (79Kč) are filling and superb.

▶ 🚏 Tram 5, 9, or 26: Olšanské náměstí. From the stop, walk 2 blocks west on Kubelíkova. $ Salads 84-114Kč. Burritos 164-199Kč. ⏰ Open M-Th 11am-midnight, F 11am-1am, Sa 11am-midnight, Su 12:30pm-midnight.

U Mariánskeho Obrazu

CZECH $$

Kubelíkova 26

☎222 722 007; www.umarianskehoobrazu.cz

This down-to-earth Czech restaurant serves Pilsner from the tank and offers steaks from young cows, along with other, more traditional fare. If you haven't yet, try the Slovak specialty *bryndzové halušky* (115Kč)—the rough translation is sheep's cheese dumplings with bacon, but there's no precise translation for the goodness they entail.

▶ 🚏 A: Jiřího z Poděbrad. From the Metro, cross diagonally through the park and then take Milešovská; Kubelíkova is on the other side of the Žižkov tower park. $ Meals 115-155Kč. Steaks 210-360Kč. Beer 19-35Kč. Cash only. ⏰ Open daily 11am-midnight.

Zelená kuchyně

VEGETARIAN $$

Milíčova 5

☎222 220 114; www.zelenakuchyne.cz

Clean, fresh, wholesome ingredients combine to make any vegetarian orgasm. Check out the grilled tomatoes with goat cheese

Sweet Dreams

If you're looking for an after-dinner treat but want something a bit more exotic than a hot fudge sundae, try the Czech bakery favorite: honey cake. The delectable creation combines the sweetness of honey with multiple layers of cake-and-cream-filled paradise. Just one taste may be enough to convince you to move to Prague permanently.

and blackberry dressing...you should really get a room. Top off the pleasurable experience with a little dessert: savor cinnamon pancakes made from oatmeal and apples and topped with ice cream and blueberry sauce.

▸ 🚏 Trams 5, 9, or 26: Lipanská. From the stop, walk west on Seifertova and turn right at Milíčova. The restaurant is on the left. $ Menus from 90Kč. Entrees 110-290Kč. Cash only. ⏰ Open M-F 11am-8pm.

VINOHRADY

Almost every street in Vinohrady has a small restaurant or hidden cafe known and frequented by locals; the opportunities for exploration are unlimited. For groceries, there's a **Tesco** near I.P. Pavlova (Vocelova 11 ☎222 212 645 ⏰ Open daily 6am-10pm.) and an **Albert** near Jiřího z Poděbrad. (Vinohradská 50 ☎800 402 402 ⏰ Open daily 8am-9pm.)

👍 Vinárna U Palečka CZECH $$

Nitranská 22

☎224 250 626; www.vinarnaupalecka.cz

The rustic interior may look unassuming, but if you're after some great traditional Czech cuisine, this is the place. The menu is longer and more varied than in most Czech restaurants—it even makes a few attempts at Mexican cuisine—but we suggest sticking to the tried and true. The *svíčková* (beef in sour cream sauce; 139Kč) comes with whipped cream and cranberry jam. The lunch menu items are a steal at just 75Kč.

▸ 🚏 A: Jiřího z Poděbrad. From the station, head south on Nitranská; the restaurant is on the left. $ Entrees 80-230Kč. Beer 25-35Kč. Cash only. ⏰ Open daily 11am-midnight. Lunch menu 11am-4pm.

Café Šlágr CAFE $

Francouzská 72

☎607 277 688; www.kavarnaslagr.cz

True to the spirit of the First Czechoslovak Republic (1918-38), a sign on the wall of this traditional cafe prohibits "all left-wing political discussions." So skip the politics and enjoy the desserts: they are homemade and beautiful. If you're unfamiliar with Czech sweets, the overflowing *větrník* (29Kč) is a good place to start, or perhaps you'd like the cream-filled *kremrole* (15Kč). Coffee (42-75Kč) comes with cow-shaped vessels for milk and is a great complement to the desserts.

▸ 🚏 A: Náměstí Míru, or tram 4 or 22: Krymská. From the station, walk southeast along Francouzská. The cafe is on the right. $ Baked goods 17-40Kč. Breakfast 49-79Kč. Cash only. ⏰ Open M-F 8am-10pm, Sa-Su 10am-10pm. Breakfast served 8am-2pm.

Las Adelitas
MEXICAN $$

Americká 8

☎222 542 031; www.lasadelitas.cz

There are several would-be Mexican restaurants in Prague, but Las Adelitas is on top of the food chain when it comes to authenticity. The chefs and owners are from Mexico, and the music is Mexican. Try the *sopa Azteca* (49Kč), a soup with croutons, cheese, sour cream sauce, chili, and avocado; you can be sure you won't get this thing anywhere else around here. Thirsty *amigos* might appreciate a Corona (72Kč); frugal *amigos* will probably stick with a Staropramen (18Kč).

▶ ⚇ A: Náměstí Míru. From the station, walk down Americká. The restaurant is on the left, past the square with the dinosaur fountain. $ Burritos 145Kč. Enchiladas 169-179Kč. Beer 18-39Kč. Cash only. ⏰ Open M-F 11am-11pm, Sa-Su 2-11pm. Kitchen open until 10pm.

Mamacoffee
COFFEE $

Londýnska 49

☎773 263 333; www.mamacoffee.cz

Find more Mamacoffee outposts at Korunní 46 (Náměstí Míru) or Vodičkova 6 (Charles Square).

Coffee lovers, beware: these people take coffee even more seriously than you do. A staunch adherent of fair trade, organic coffee, Mamacoffee even has its own fair trade roasting facility. There are around 10 kinds of coffee waiting for you to try, and

Student Munchies

If you crave pizza, but want to save money and have an ISIC, we have a nearby alternative for you: **Pizzeria Einstein** (Rumunská 25; www.pizza-einstein.cz $ Pizza 106-159Kč ⏰ Open 11am-11pm). The ambience might not be up to par with nearby Grosseto's, but if you present your ISIC card in advance and order a pizza, you can get a second for **free** (just be careful not to get ripped off on drinks). Few foreigners know about this trick, as the special red menu that advertises the deal is in Czech.

Food

they can be made in all kinds of ways. The only gripe one might have is that there's no Wi-Fi, but this isn't the kind of place where you loaf around all day writing your long-postponed novel anyway.

▶ � A: Náměstí Míru. From the station, walk down Rumunská, then take a left at Londýnska. The cafe is on the right. Ⓢ Desserts 15-35Kč. Coffee 29-67Kč. Cash only. 🕐 Open M-F 8:30am-8pm, Sa-Su 10:30am-8pm.

Pizzeria Grosseto   ITALIAN $$
Francouzská 2
☎224 252 778; www.grosseto.cz

Popular with locals and tourists, this Italian chain brings a degree of style to Czech pizzerias, which otherwise tend to be rather unassuming. Made from predominantly Italian ingredients, Grosseto's pizzas are generous, and there are almost 30 kinds to choose from. If you snag a table upstairs, you'll be able to eat with a good view of the St. Ludmila Church.

▶ ✚ A: Náměstí Míru. Grosseto is directly across the street from the Metro exit. Ⓢ Pizza 125-219Kč. Desserts 85-95Kč. 🕐 Open daily 11:30am-11pm.

Radost FX   VEGETARIAN $$
Bělehradská 120
☎603 19 37 11; www.radostfx.cz

Before the club downstairs starts thrumming, head to Radost FX for their vegetarian specialties. You can eat in either the quieter, artsier cafe or the lounge, where mirror tiles, poison-green chandeliers, and red sofas combine for a slight hallucinogenic effect. A menu staple is the heavy "Popeye Burger" (180Kč), which replaces meat with—you guessed it—spinach! But there are many more culinary experiments to try, including the "White Trash Hot Artichoke Dip" (155Kč) and the "Crack Slaw Salad" (90Kč).

▶ ✚ C: I.P. Pavlova. From the station, walk east on Jugoslávská. Take a left on Bělehradská. The cafe is on the right. Ⓢ Entrées 130-210Kč. Cash only. 🕐 Open M-Th 11am-midnight, F-Sa 11am-1am, Su 10:30am-midnight.

Sokolovna   CZECH $$
Slezská 22
☎222 524 525; www.restaurantsokolovna.cz

Sokolovna is a notch above your traditional Czech restaurant: it's cleaner, more spacious, and the staff is less grumpy. The walls of this former *sokolovna* (gym) are almost completely covered by old newspapers, but the decoration remains understated. The locals keep coming back for the tank beer and hearty meals. The tourists haven't caught on yet; be a good hipster and get in before it gets mainstream.

▶ A: Náměstí Míru. From the station, head down Slezská. The restaurant is on the right. $ Entrees 139-265Kč. Desserts 77-115Kč. Beer 22-37Kč. ⏰ Open daily 11am-midnight.

Kavárna Zanzibar

CAFE $

Americká 15

☎222 520 315; www.kavarnazanzibar.cz

The wicker chairs outside this cafe make for very relaxed seating; it's no wonder this place has become a local hangout. But there's food too! In addition to breakfast sets (79-149Kč), which are served all day, there's a sizeable selection of croque monsieurs, crepes, omelettes, burritos, and more. The local specialty is the "beer cocktail," a mixtures of beer and either Coke, Sprite, or fruit syrup. Yikes.

▶ A: Náměstí Míru. From the station, walk down Americká. The cafe is on the right at the square with the dinosaur fountain. $ Croques monsieur 65-95Kč. Coffee 36-76Kč. Beer 26-45Kč. ⏰ Open M-Th 8am-11pm, F 8am-late, Sa 10am-late, Su 10am-11pm. Kitchen closes at 10pm.

Banditos

MEXICAN $$

Melounová 2

☎224 941 096; www.banditosrestaurant.cz

Nominally Mexican, Banditos seems to be more concerned with appealing to American expats and tourists than nailing the whole Mexico thing. That's not necessarily a bad thing—in addition to tacos, you also get sandwiches and burgers (including "Coronary Bypass" with fried egg, bacon, cheese, and mayo; 255Kč). The best time to come is the happy hour, which offers some really good deals: tacos for 30Kč, nachos for 50Kč, or ribs for 50Kč.

▶ C: I.P. Pavlova. From the station, head left down Ječná. Fork left at Kateřinská, then take the 1st right onto Melounová. *i* Free Wi-Fi. $ Sandwiches and burgers 170-215Kč. Mexican dishes 165-270Kč. ⏰ Open daily 9am-1am. Happy hour 4:30-6:30pm.

U Bulínů

CZECH $$

Budečská 2

☎224 254 676; www.ubulinu.cz

Following the quintessentially Czech tradition of fabricated history, this restaurant has a story of its own. The gist is that the original owners made a deal with Satan to be able to make devilishly good food, after which they grew horns. If you're not in the mood for local food, try the popular cheeseburger, made from Uruguay beef (169Kč). There's also very little smoke in this place: it's one of the few restaurants in Prague that has banned smoking.

▸ A: Náměstí Míru. From the station, walk southeast down Francouzská. The restaurant is 3 blocks down on the corner. $ Czech entrees 130-250Kč. Lunch menu 89Kč. ⏰ Open daily 11am-11pm.

HOLEŠOVICE

There are no big supermarkets in Holešovice, but there's a grocery on every other corner. For cheap Vietnamese food, try the **Prague Market**.

Ouky Douky

CAFE $

Janovského 14

☎266 711 531; www.oukydouky.cz

A favorite of expats, Ouky Douky is a one-stop shop—restaurant, used book store, internet cafe, and Cuban cigars (20-300Kč). Sit down and get one of their crunchy baguettes, or just browse through the English-language section (it's no Barnes & Noble, but there might be one or two good finds).

▸ C: Vltavská. From the Metro, take tram 1 or 25 or walk along the tracks on Bubenské for 1 stop to Strossmayerovo náměstí. Facing the church, take a left onto Janovského. The cafe is to the right. $ Breakfast 98-148Kč. Sandwiches 86-126Kč. Coffee 29-39Kč. Internet 65Kč per hr. Cash only. ⏰ Open daily 8am-midnight.

La Crêperie

CREPERIE $

Janovského 4

☎220 878 040; www.lacreperie.cz

Many cafes in Prague will fix you a crepe, but they are the specialty at this French-owned joint. Come for almost 50 kinds of savory galettes and sweet crepes, or design your own crepe-monster from the list of ingredients. French music plays in its underground rooms and the walls are covered with black and white photos, but La Crêperie is cozy and unpretentious.

▸ C: Vltavská. From the Metro, take tram 1 or 25 or walk along the tracks for 1 stop, to Strossmayerovo náměstí. Turn left just past St. Antonín

Church and walk past the tea shop. La Crêperie will be to the left. [$] Crepes 35-85Kč. Galettes 40-100Kč. Cash only. ⏰ Open daily 9am-11pm.

Zlatá Kovadlina

CZECH, BOWLING $$

Komunardů 36

☎246 005 313; www.zlatakovadlina.com

Bowling and eating, two pastimes of the wise and lazy man, are ingeniously combined in this underground restaurant. The cuisine is traditional Czech, so you can nibble on your pork fillet or whatnot while taking advantage of one of the four bowling lanes. If you don't plan on bowling, another traditional Czech restaurant, friendly **Korbel,** is just a few meters down the street. (Komunardů 30 ☎222 986 095; www.restauracekorbel.cz).

▶ 🚏 C: Vltavská. From the station, take tram 1, 3, 5, or 25 or walk along the tram tracks for 3 stops to Dělnická. Continue for 1½ blocks; the restaurant is on the right. [$] Entrees 79-199Kč. Beer 17-32Kč. Bowling 260-360Kč per person per hr. ⏰ Open M-Th 11am-11pm, F 11am-midnight, Sa noon-midnight, Su noon-10pm. Lanes open daily 2pm-midnight.

Long Tale Café

CAFE $

Osadní 35

☎266 310 701; www.longtalecafe.cz

A frequent haunt of architects and people returning from DOX (see **Sights**), this cafe manages to hover somewhere on the border between industrial and domestic. Housed in a building that used to be a ham factory (we couldn't make this stuff up), Long Tale now serves mostly bagels, baguettes, and panini, but you can also try their homemade ginger lemonade (55Kč). If you're coming from DOX and you're not tired of art, check out either of the two galleries that share the courtyard with Long Tale.

▶ 🚏 C: Vltavská. From the station, take tram 1, 3, 5, or 25 or walk along the tram tracks for 3 stops to Dělnická. Take a left onto Dělnická and a right at Osadní. The cafe is inside the courtyard to the left. [$] Breakfast 35-55Kč. Baguettes and panini 70-79Kč. Coffee 35-50Kč. Cash only. ⏰ Open M-F 9am-6pm.

Molo 22

INTERNATIONAL $$

U Průhonu 22

☎220 563 348; www.molo22.cz

One of the classier joints in this part of town, Molo 22 has a menu that might surprise: you'll probably see something pedestrian like *svíčková na smotaně* (sirloin in cream) alongside such exotic dishes as jumbo tiger prawns. The offerings change every three months, and the restaurant does not commit to any particular cuisine, so when it comes to the menu during your visit, your guess is as good as ours. The interior is chic, and it's a good place to enjoy a glass of wine.

▶ C: Vltavská. From the station, take tram 1, 3, 5, or 25 or walk along the tram tracks for 3 stops to Dělnická. Continue down Komunardů, then turn left on U Průhonu; the restaurant is on the left. $ Entrees 159-297Kč. Desserts 79-95Kč. Cocktails 99-145Kč. ⏰ Open M-F 8am-midnight, Sa-Su 9am-midnight.

Lucky Luciano II — ITALIAN $$

Dělnická 28

☎220 875 900; www.luckyluciano.cz

Named after the father of modern organized crime, this Czech-owned pizzeria is a solid joint geared toward the locals. On a sunny day, not a soul sits in Lucky Luciano—they're all outside under the giant covered patio. Pizzas are large enough for two but delicious enough for more, so keep leftovers close enough that you can slap away would-be scavengers. If you come during the happy hour (3-5pm), you can take advantage of the 30% discount on all pizzas. Lucky Luciano also offers some heavy-weight steaks.

▶ C: Vltavská. From the station, take tram 1, 3, 5, or 25 or walk along the tram tracks for 3 stops to Dělnická. Turn left onto Dělnická, the pizzeria is to the left. $ Pizza 105-150Kč. Pasta 115-145Kč. Beer 23-35Kč. ⏰ Open M-F 11am-11pm, Sa-Su 11:30am-11pm. Garden open M-F 11am-10pm, Sa-Su 11:30am-10pm.

DEJVICE

Even though it's not very touristy, Dejvice has its share of Western fast-food chains and exotic restaurants. Don't expect rural prices, but there are a few good deals that can't be found closer to the center.

Kulaťák — CZECH $$

Vítězné náměstí 12

☎773 973 037; www.kulatak.cz

This young restaurant has already managed to earn the affection of Czech superman Václav Havel, who has a table reserved in the back of the non-smoking section. We recommend the cheap lunch menus (75-99Kč) and the tank beer.

▶ ⚑ A: Dejvická. The restaurant is on the eastern side of the large round-about. Ⓢ Entrees 149-249Kč. Desserts 65-89Kč. Beer 24-39Kč. ⌚ Open daily 11am-midnight.

Café Technika
CAFE $

Technická 6

☎777 568 658; www.cafe-technika.cz

Housed in the futuristic National Technical Library, this university cafe has an industrial, modern feel. When you come here, take advantage of the cheap Kofola (24Kč), the socialist replacement for Coca Cola that's outrageously overpriced in most restaurants in Prague today. Indian lunches, Mamacoffee coffee, and outdoor seating make this a student favorite.

▶ ⚑ A: Dejvická. From the roundabout, walk northwest through the park that's opposite Dejvická. Continue up Technická until you reach the National Technical Library. *i* DJs and live music Th-Sa. Ⓢ Lunch 80-115Kč. Coffee 29-61Kč. Beer 21-34Kč. ⌚ Open daily 9am-11pm.

Vegetka
VEGETARIAN, ASIAN $

Kafkova 16

☎773 588 518

Vegetka is a Buddhist vegetarian restaurant that serves Chinese, Vietnamese, and Thai dishes (this last category proved too spicy for Czech customers and had to be watered down). It'll be hard not to like tofu after you've eaten here. The "special soup" is especially noteworthy and stocked with noodles, mushrooms, and coriander, along with some secret ingredients.

▶ ⚑ A: Dejvická. From the roundabout, walk southeast on Dejvická, take the 1st right onto Kafkova, then take the 1st left. The restaurant is on the left. Ⓢ Entrees 60-140Kč. Cash only. ⌚ Open M-F 10:30am-9pm, Sa 11am-9pm.

Dejvická Čajovna
TEA, HOOKAH $

V.P. Čkalova 12

☎776 792 701; www.dejvicka-cajovna.cz

Since you're already so far off the tourist track, we'll have you do something that only locals tend to do—go to a tea room. A favorite among young people who don't need alcohol to have fun, Dejvická Čajovna has candlelit rooms, soft cushions, and teas from around the world. The menu is only in Czech, but the staff will help you choose. The interior tries to look oriental but still has a bit of the socialist, run-down thing going on—the best way to get over it is to become absorbed in a long conversation with friends.

Food

▶ ✠ A: Dejvická. From the roundabout, walk southeast on Dejvická, then take the 3rd left onto V.P. Čkalova. The tea room is on the right. Ⓢ Tea 55-115Kč. Hookah 89-139Kč. Cash only. ⏰ Open M-F noon-11:30pm, Sa-Su noon-2am.

Perpetuum   DUCK $$$
Na Hutích 9

☎233 323 429; www.restauraceperpetuum.cz

As the duck statues scattered around the interior indicate, this high-end restaurant serves only dishes made from home-bred duck. (Desserts, thankfully, are an exception.) Specialties include foie gras (250Kč) and duck stuffed with pomegranate paste (310Kč). If you came to enjoy duck meat in Czech Republic and have some spending power, Perpetuum is an interesting place to go.

▶ ✠ A: Dejvická. From the roundabout, walk on Dejvická and turn left onto Na Hutích. Ⓢ Appetizers 130-250Kč; entrees 230-390Kč. ⏰ Open daily 11:30am-11pm.

Nightlife

Although Prague has one of the greatest clubs in Europe (Cross Club) and a few genuinely amazing bars, most of the nightlife centers on the *hospoda* (pub) scene. On a typical night, locals head out for dinner at a pub or a cafe bar and just stay there the entire night, drinking beer and chain smoking. Pubs stay open late (W until midnight, Th-Sa until 2-4am, Su until midnight), while clubs stay open until 4am or later. All outdoor terraces have to close at 10pm, after which most guests head indoors. In general, nights out start earlier than in the US, and it's not uncommon for everything to be over by midnight. This doesn't apply to clubbing, which doesn't usually get started before 11pm.

Don't leave Prague without trying the local fire waters: Fernet tastes like a less-syrupy Jagermeister, Becherovka tastes like Christmas in your mouth, and plum vodka tastes—well, the taste isn't the point with plum vodka. There's also the mythical absinthe, a green mouth-burner with a 70% alcohol content.

Alcohol in Prague is cheaper than what most Westerners are used to. On some nights, you can come home completely wasted having spent under 200Kč. But drink responsibly—drunk foreigners are an easy target for pickpockets and a nuisance for everyone else.

Budget Nightlife

Nightlife in Prague is diverse, but any traveler should make at least one trip to the major clubs: **Cross Club, Chapeau Rouge, SaSaZu,** and their ilk. If you want to do so without paying covers that can reach up to 270Kč, take our advice: go early. Even on nights when cover is charged (Friday, Saturday), if you get there before around 10pm, you should be able to make it in for less than 50Kč. When visiting jazz clubs, such as **Reduta Jazz** and **Jazz Dock,** make sure to ask about a student cover price.

NOVÉ MĚSTO

Most tourists head to Staré Město for nightlife, but Nové Město can get pretty lively, too, especially around **Národní třída** and **Wenceslas Square.** Speaking of "nightlife," Nové Město is also one of Prague's seedier districts at night, with some dubious establishments sprinkled around Wenceslas and Charles Squares.

▨ O2 Bar   BAR
Karlovo náměstí
☎608 144 344; www.o2bar.cz

Located in a former public toilet, the inside of this bar fits only three tables. Quarters are so tight that DJs set up their equipment on top of a foosball table. Even the disco ball above the counter is tiny. The crowds tend to spill out into the park and onto the terrace, which offers a surreal view of the lit-up New Town Hall. Since they also somehow managed to find space to store food (yikes), you can enjoy something called "ethno-sandwiches" (53Kč), which are inspired by Afghani, Armenian, Iranian, and Georgian cuisines. O2 bar is currently waging a war against the city authorities, which are planning to shut the place down and reconstruct the entire square. Sign the online petition if you want, and, while you're at it, check out the live webcam stream from inside the bar.

▶ ⚘ B: Karlovo náměstí, on the northwestern edge of the square. Ⓢ Beer 19-34Kč. Vodka 45-85Kč. ⌚ Open daily noon-2am.

U Sudu BAR

Vodičkova 10

☎222 232 207; www.usudu.cz

From the street, U Sudu might look pretty tame—four tables and a bar. But head inside and you'll become Alice in Wonderland, at least for a while. The stairs lead down into a large underground room, and then a tunnel to a different room, rinse, repeat: U Sudu's cellar is a labyrinth of drinking spaces, all with a slightly different ambience. There's a room for watching sports and one for foosball and still another with live DJs. Aside from regular drinks, U Sudu also has the 18-proof Master beer on tap.

▶ ♯ B: Karlovo náměstí. From the Metro, head north on Vodičkova past New Town Hall. The bar is on the right. *i* DJs play W-Sa 10pm-close. Ⓢ Snacks 10-55Kč. Beer 23-38Kč. Cash only. ☒ Open M-Th 9am-4am, F 9am-5am, Sa 10am-5am, Su 10am-3am.

Rock Café CLUB, MUSIC VENUE

Národní 20

☎224 933 947; www.rockcafe.cz

Loud and raw, with about equal amounts of beer in the plastic cups and on the floor, Rock Café remains one of Prague's best known music venues. Aside from live music, Rock Café also hosts film screenings and plays. Tuesdays are "Free Zone," which means you get a concert and 15min. of free internet use. (Oh boy!) The bands that play here tend to have weird, unfamiliar names, so if you feel like listening to something you actually know, head across the street to **Vagon** (Národní třída 25 ☎733 737 301; www.vagon.cz), another popular music club, which hosts revival bands every Friday and Saturday.

▶ ♯ B: Národní třída. From the Metro, walk north on Spálená and then turn left on Národní. The music club is on the left. Ⓢ Cover 50-150Kč; Tu free. Beer 27-33Kč. Liquor 30-50Kč. Cash only. ☒ M-F 10am-3am, Sa 5pm-3am, Su 5pm-1am.

Jáma (The Hollow) PUB

V Jámě 7

☎224 222 383; www.jamapub.cz

Whether you buy its self-styled Americanness or not, Jáma's lively atmosphere makes it a great place to grab a beer in the evening. Pick one of the 11 kinds on offer, and take it to the leafy garden, or to a wooden table inside. The walls are covered with a hodgepodge of posters from American pop culture, but it seems to work—Jáma is quite popular with English-speaking foreigners.

▶ Metro: A or B: Můstek. From the Metro, walk down Wenceslas Sq. and then turn right onto Vodičkova. Take the 1st left on V jámě; the pub is on the left. $ Tex-Mex meals 99-265Kč. Beer 29-45Kč. ⏰ Open daily 11am-1am.

K*Star Karaoke KARAOKE BAR

Legerova 78

☎720 365 044; kstarkaraoke.com

The first bar to bring Asian-style karaoke to Prague (that is, it's got private karaoke rooms, as opposed to a karaoke stage), K*Star works like this—you come in with your crew, rent a room, and then embarrass yourselves with help from adult beverages. The rooms are elegant and high-tech (you can even order drinks with a touchscreen). Come between 6 and 8pm to get half off the room rental.

▶ Metro: C: I.P. Pavlova. From the station, head north on Legerova. The club is on the right. *i* 10 languages. Reserve ahead F-Su. $ 800-1500Kč per hr. Bottled beer 45Kč. Cocktails 90Kč. ⏰ Open M-Th 6pm-2am, F-Sa 6pm-5am.

Reduta Jazz Club JAZZ CLUB

Národní 20

☎224 933 487; www.redutajazzclub.cz

Founded in 1958, Prague's first jazz club has jazz on the menu every night. Hosting almost exclusively Czech jazz musicians, Reduta nevertheless has quite a reputation—even Bill Clinton visited (twice!). On one of his visits, Clinton hopped on stage and jammed with the band, an event that was recorded and released on CD. What a guy. Check out the "saxophone bar" downstairs, where tap beer is pumped out of a saxophone-shaped spigot. We leave the ensuing Clinton innuendo here to you.

▶ Metro: B: Národní třída. From the Metro, walk north on Spálená and turn left onto Národní. Reduta is on the left. $ Cover 285Kč, students 185Kč. Beer 30-50Kč. Wine 50Kč. Liquor 50-100Kč. ⏰ Open 7pm-midnight. Music 9:30pm-midnight.

Lucerna MUSIC BAR

Vodičkova 36

☎224 215 957; www.musicbar.cz

Lucerna is one of the most well-attended music venues in Nové Město. Two or three concerts happen here every week, but on

Fridays and Saturdays live music gives way to famous '80s- and '90s-themed dance parties (Cover 100Kč). On your way out, check out the David Černý sculpture hanging inside the Lucerna complex.

▶ A or B: Můstek. From the Metro, walk up Wenceslas Sq. toward the statue of St. Wenceslas and turn right onto Vodičkova. Lucerna is on the left. $ Cover 100-700Kč. Beer 24-40Kč. Shots 40-95Kč. Cash only. ⏰ Ticket office open daily 10am-7pm. Bar open daily 8pm-3am. Concerts 9pm.

Rocky O'Reillys

IRISH PUB

Štěpánská 32

☎222 231 060; www.rockyoreillys.cz

If you're the kind of person who'd go to an Irish pub in Prague—such people must exist—then you might enjoy visiting Rocky O'Reillys. Expect steep prices, rabid decor, and big screens tuned to sports. Perhaps the most interesting aspect of the pub is the hanging poster of "Rocky's Ten Commandments," which aims to educate travelers on the basics of not getting their wallet stolen or themselves arrested. The takeaway? Prague is full of small girls who are after your wallet. Also, if somebody says he is a "currency inspector" and wants to see your money, walk away.

▶ A or B: Můstek. From the Metro, walk down Wenceslas Sq. and take a right onto Štěpánská. The pub is on the left. $ Entrees 245-295Kč. Beer 40-100Kč. ⏰ Bar open daily 10am-1am. Kitchen open 10am-11pm.

STARÉ MĚSTO

At night, Staré Město is besieged with stag partiers, pub crawlers, and all sorts of revelers. Most places here are geared toward tourists, but it doesn't hurt to try them out before heading to hipper pastures in other neighborhoods.

Chapeau Rouge

BAR, CLUB

Jakubská 2

☎222 316 328; www.chapeaurouge.cz

For a place established in 1919, Chapeau Rouge is young at heart: the interior decoration tends to be edgy and dark. It's a tourist trap par excellence, but it's still worth the experience. The bar on the street level still maintains some decorum, while the underground dance floor is smokier, darker, and louder. Some people say that this could be a place to go if you're in the market for some weed, but remember that buying drugs in touristy places is generally a bad idea.

▶ B: Náměstí Republiky. From Old Town Sq., walk toward Church of Our Lady Before Týn and pass it on the right. Bear left on Štupartská and take a left on Malá Štupartská. $ Downstairs is often free; if not, cover may be 50-100Kč 10pm-2am. Beer 28-40Kč. Shots 60-90Kč. Cash only. ⏰ Open M-F noon-3am, Sa-Su 4pm-4am. Dance club open M-Th 9pm-4am, F-Sa 9pm-6am, Su 9pm-4am.

Propaganda Pub (aka Iron Curtain) PUB

Michalská 12

☎776 858 333; www.propagandapub.cz

Brought to you by the entrepreneurial mind who also created Bohemia Bagel and the Museum of Communism, Propaganda Pub is one of the newer additions to Prague's nightlife scene. With over 200 original artifacts from the Communist era, Propaganda feels almost like a fun museum that serves drinks. Local bands provide live music four times per week and there's a DJ twice a week, but this underground place is large and can easily accommodate a quiet conversation (especially in the Red Library, a cozy section with a collection of socialist literature). If you're hungry, walk over to the restaurant section and order something from the grill. Oh, and is it a Monday? The first 100 beers are just 12Kč.

▶ A or B: Můstek. From Old Town Sq., pass the Astronomical Clock and go south on Melantrichova. Take the 1st right and continue until

Sobering Up

So you've had a few too many drinks at one of the local bars and you're not sure whether you should head back to your hostel and sleep it off or get some help. Well, Prague has the perfect place for you: a sobering-up station. In the United States, if you're intoxicated in public, the police will take you into custody; in the Czech Republic they'll take you to one of these venues.

Staffed by nurses and doctors, the facilities allow inebriated locals and travelers to sleep off a night of binge drinking under the careful supervision of a medical team. In the morning, when you're sober, you're free to leave. With all of the beer, travelers certainly take advantage of this service.

the street becomes Michalská. *i* Not to be confused with Propaganda Café on Pštrossova 29. $ Beer 25-35Kč. Grilled Hermelín 85Kč. ⏰ Open daily 6pm-late.

Roxy

CLUB

Dlouhá 33

www.roxy.cz

Something of a local institution, Roxy is enormous and has a vaguely industrial feel. Locals come here for the concerts (both Czech and international performers; Mondays are free and feature new local bands) and the nightly dance parties. Chill-out sections on the side let you awkwardly watch the revelers below, while the shining circular bars supply reasonably priced drinks.

▶ ♯ B: Náměstí Republiky. From Old Town Sq., pass the Jan Hus statue and continue north on Dlouhá. $ No cover, but concerts are ticketed. Beer 39Kč. Shots 39-70Kč. Cocktails 85-189Kč. Cash only. ⏰ Open M-Sa 10pm-late.

K4 Klub & Galerie

BAR

Celetná 20

☎224 491 930; www.k4klub.org

This underground art space is almost exclusively a student hangout, run by and for students from Charles University. Events like concerts, screenings, and gallery openings take place almost every day, and the walls are always covered with art. There's little to do on the weekends; the space is at its liveliest during the week when students are in town. Drinks come at rock-bottom student-friendly prices. This might not be a place to visit if you're in town for only five days, but if you're here for five months, definitely check it out.

▶ ♯ B: Náměstí Republiky. From Old Town Sq., pass the Týn church on the right as you walk down Celetná. At Celetná 20 turn right inside the courtyard, then head down a flight of stairs. $ Beer 19-23Kč. Coffee 26-39Kč. Cuba Libre 39Kč. Cash only. ⏰ Open M-F 10am-midnight, Sa-Su 4pm-midnight.

Buddha Bar

BAR

Jakubská 8

☎221 776 300; www.buddhabarhotelprague.com

Pricey and classy, this concept club can be affordable if you keep yourself in check. If you don't, you may end up paying 1600Kč for the set dinner menu. The upper floor is all cozy red sofas and intimate nooks, where you can exchange winks with

What Would You Do?

Wandering Prague's Karlova Street is the ghost of the Mad Barber — or so says a Czech legend. Under Rudolph II, the Barber was successful, but wanted more money. He turned to magical alchemy to make gold at home, but it was never enough. Despite his family's warnings, he let his greed destroy him and spent his family's fortune. After that he sold his house, his three daughters were forced into prostitution, and his wife committed suicide. The Barber was so crazed by his poverty that he began slashing the throats of passersby on the street — Johnny Depp-style — until one night a group of soldiers beat him to death. Now his ghost roams the streets, waiting to be set free. Brave enough to help? Allow him to give you a shave, and his spirit will finally be able to move on.

Western and Eastern influences, but this isn't where people come to dance—it's more of a pregame destination.

▶ ♯ B: Náměstí Republiky. From Old Town Sq., pass the Týn church on the left and go straight through the underpass. Continue as Týn becomes Jakubská; the bar is on the right. Ⓢ Beer 80Kč. Cocktails 160-190Kč. Sushi 95-125Kč per piece. ⏰ Open daily 6pm-late.

Karlovy Lázně   CLUB

Smetanovo nábřeží 198

☎222 220 502; www.karlovylazne.cz

A colossal five-story club with some impressive lighting and dance floor effects, Karlovy Lázně can be hit-or-miss. Either you spend the night dancing away, fascinated by the design choices (there's a torso that shoots lasers, a neon cage containing a half-naked dancer, a kaleidoscope room), or you get a depressive episode induced by the place's overall ugliness and all the men with popped collars (on some nights, Karlovy Lázně would make for a wonderful gay club, given the gender ratio). Each floor plays a different kind of music: disco, oldies, dance, chill-out, and something called "black music." Most pub crawls end here.

▶ ♯ A: Staroměstskà. From the station, head toward the river then south on Křižovnické. Club is directly past the Charles Bridge, through the tunnel of tourist shops. *i* No dress code. Free computers on the 1st floor. Ⓢ Cover 120Kč. Beer 45Kč. Cash only. ⏰ Open daily 9pm-5am.

MALÁ STRANA

Malá Strana has some vigorous nightlife, with many smaller music venues and artsy dive bars. In addition, many cafes and restaurants serve double duty as bars, staying open past midnight.

▨ Jazz Dock   JAZZ CLUB
Janáčkovo nábřeží 2
☎774 058 838; www.jazzdock.cz

This new jazz club has been making waves—and not just because it's on the water. Jazz Dock swings hard during live performances every night of the week. The gig here is serious; there are double shows five days per week, children's theater on Saturday, and a Dixieland program on Sunday. Due to its genius design, live music can play until 4am without prompting noise complaints.

▶ ⚲ B: Anděl. From the Metro, head toward the river on Lidická. At the river, take a left and continue for 6 blocks. Jazz Dock is down some stairs on the right. *i* Jam session Sa 1am. Guests who visit the club 3 times are entitled to a 10% discount on future club transactions. Ⓢ Cover 120-450Kč, under 25 or over 65 90Kč. Beer 23-43Kč. Cocktails 135-155Kč. Meals 125-225Kč. ☾ Open M-Th 3pm-4am, F-Sa 1pm-4am, Su 1pm-2am. Concerts daily Jan-June 7, 10pm; Jul-Aug 10pm; Sept-Dec 7, 10pm.

Klub Újezd   BAR
Újezd 18
☎251 510 873; www.klubujezd.cz

The only thing wilder than Klub Újezd's guests is its decor: bathroom doors show monsters doing their business and a giant leviathan snaps above the bar. The clientele isn't exactly monstrous, but the three floors cater to three very different scenes. The upstairs cafe is secluded and smoky, the basement is dungeon-like with a DJ spinning on a mini-stage for the 20 people who can squeeze in, and the main bar is filled with artists—or people who wish they were.

▶ ⚲ A: Malostranská. From the Metro, walk south or take tram 12, 20, or 22 to Újezd. Ⓢ Beer 20-39Kč. Cocktails 59-149Kč. Cash only. ☾ Bar open daily 2pm-4am. Cafe open daily 6pm-4am. Club open daily 8pm-4am.

Blue Light Bar   BAR
Josefská 1
☎257 533 126; www.bluelightbar.cz

There might not be a better place to go stargazing in Prague than this intimate bar. It's a well-known hangout for Czech politicians, artists, and singers, and it's a frequent location for film crews' wrap parties. If Czech heavyweights don't impress you, check out Daniel Craig's signature right above the bar. While the odds that you'll brush shoulders with Johnny Depp are slim, you can still pretend your life is glamorous.

▶ A: Malostranská. From the Metro, head down Letenská toward Malostranské náměstí. Turn left into Josefská before you reach the square. The bar is on the right. $ Beer 35-85Kč. Cocktails 105-175Kč. Coffee 55-100Kč. Cash only. ⏰ Open daily 6pm-3am.

U Malého Glena Jazz and Blues Club — JAZZ CLUB

Karmelitská 23

☎257 531 717; www.malyglen.cz

This tiny jazz spot brings in big talent for small audiences—the pleasurably cramped space has an underground-New-York vibe. The American food here and in the pub upstairs deserves special mention—this is one of the few places in town with chili fries (150Kč). There's Guinness on tap and Staropramen's Velvet. Every Saturday there's a jam session, so if you happen to be a jazz enthusiast and are carrying your instrument around, it may be time to unleash the beast.

▶ A: Malostranská. From the Metro, walk to Malostranské náměstí and continue south on Karmelitská, which becomes Újezd. The club is on the right. $ Cover 100-200Kč. Beer 30-70Kč. Food 65-189Kč. Cocktails 79-129Kč. ⏰ Club open daily 8pm-2am. Jazz 9:30pm-12:30am. Pub open daily 11am-2am.

PopoCafePetl Music Club — MUSIC CLUB

Újezd 19

☎739 110 021; popocafepetl.cz

This small music club in a brick cellar captures the essence of cool. PopoCafePetl hosts live music concerts almost every night. Genres vary wildly, with jazz concerts on some nights, art folk on others, and even some hip hop. On Fridays, a DJ spins from the colorfully lit stage. Hoegaarden on tap also comes as a relief to those who've had enough Pilsner.

▶ A: Malostranská. From the Metro, walk or take tram 12, 20, or 22 to Hellichova and continue south on Újezd; the club is on the right. $ Cover 30-100Kč; some nights free. Beer 24-45Kč. Cocktails 70-110Kč. Cash only. ⏰ Open daily 6pm-2am.

Divadlo Na Prádle

CAFE, THEATER

Besední 3

☎257 320 42; www.napradle.cz

During the summer, this cafe is merely a hangout for artsy winos, but it gets livelier during the regular season, when all kinds of plays enliven the performance space upstairs. The theater has been around since 1863 and is still a landmark. We recommend the wine, but there's also Bernard beer on tap.

▶ 🚇 A: Malostranská. From the Metro, walk south or take tram 12, 20, or 22 to Újezd. Backtrack up Újezd, take the 1st right at Říční, and then a left onto Besední. $ Wine 28Kč. Beer 18-35Kč. Student discounts available for plays. Cash only. ⏰ Open M-F 11:30am-midnight, Sa-Su 3pm-midnight.

ŽIŽKOV

The nightlife in Žižkov is very lively and, for the most part, tourist-free. Go forth and party, brave *Let's Go* reader.

👍 Big Lebowski

BAR

Slavíkova 16

☎774 722 276; www.biglebowski.cz

There aren't many places in the world where you can come in, order a drink, and then pay whatever price you want. This is such a place. Mr. Lebowski (no relation), the owner and sole employee of this unique bar, decided to dispose with price tags because he "likes freedom." The bar seems small at first, but this is deceptive—there's a surprisingly spacious upper level with walls covered in snapshots from cult films. Oh, and if you're in the mood for chess, there's one more reason to come by—Mr. L will play with anyone who expresses the slightest interest in the chessboard resting on his bar.

▶ 🚇 A: Jiřího z Poděbrad. From the Metro, walk north on Slavíkova. The bar is to the right. $ It's all up to you. ⏰ Open M-F 6-11pm (or later).

Bukowski's

BAR

Bořivojova 86

Famous for having some of the best cocktails in Žižkov, Bukowski's is a designer bar popular with intellectuals and expats. It may take some time for you to realize what's strange about this bar, so we'll help you—it's the carpeting! The floor is fully carpeted. Anyway, in true spirit of its patron saint/writer/drunkard, the bar adds a literary flourish here and there (with cocktails like The Dorian Gray and Tthe Naked Lunch), while retaining a certain blunt edge (bathrooms are marked in an unprintable way).

▶ ☎ Trams 5, 9, or 26: Husinecká. From the tram, take Seifertova east, make a right onto Víta Nejedlého, and another right onto Bořivojova. $ Beer 30-45Kč. Cocktails 85-130Kč. Cash only. ⏰ Open daily 7pm-3am.

Palác Akropolis
CAFE, CLUB

Kubelíková 27

☎296 330 912; www.palacakropolis.cz

Situated in a pre-WWII theater, Palác Akropolis has become something of a Žižkov landmark. The complex consists of a restaurant, a cafe, a theater, and two downstairs bars with nightly DJs.

▶ A: Jiřího z Poděbrad. From the Metro, cross diagonally through the park and then take Milešovská. Kubelíkova is on the other side of the Žižkov tower park. $ Cover F-Sa 30-60Kč. Some concerts cost more; check online before you go. Beer 18-30Kč. Cash only. ⏰ Cafe open daily 10am-midnight. Club open daily 7pm-5am.

Bunkr Parukářka
CLUB, MUSIC VENUE

Parukářka Park

☎774 451 091; www.parukarka.eu

Now here's a novelty for you: a concert venue inside an underground nuclear bunker. It takes a while to descend down the long spiraling staircase, but, once you get there, you're not only ready to listen to some alternative music, you're also 100% safe in the event of nuclear war. The place is rough around the edges, with primitive drawings on its walls and all sorts of decay in the interior, but that only makes a concert here all the more enjoyable. There is no regular events schedule, so check online before you go.

▶ Trams 5, 9, or 26: Olšanské náměstí. From the square, walk up on Prokopova (toward the overpass) on the right side of the street. Walk past the RIAPS building and up a flight of stairs toward the park. Bunkr is the door to the right. *i* Wheelchair-accessible through the cargo entrance. $ Beer 20-26Kč. Shots 30-60Kč. Cash only. ⏰ Open only for shows, usually 8pm-late.

Matrix
CLUB, MUSIC VENUE

Koněvova 13

☎777 254 959; www.matrixklub.cz

This black-and-green-themed dance club has the privilege of playing music as loud as it wants for as long as it wants, since

Sweet Becherovka

Absinthe may pack a serious alcoholic punch, but the well-known green fairy is so last *fin-de-siècle*. Becherovka, though, is nearly as potent, has medicinal properties (allegedly), and is brewed just outside Prague. The herbal liqueur, concocted in the hot-spring-rich town of Karlovy Vary, is known as the nearby spa city's "13th spring." The closely guarded recipe involves some 35 herbs and spices—putting it two dozen ahead of KFC—and its alcohol content is 38%.

it's acoustically isolated from its upstairs neighbors. It's open to all sorts of music events but is best known for its underground concerts and Techno Fridays. Those disinclined to dance may enjoy playing on one of the many foosball tables (the rare kind designed for only two players).

▶ ⚇ Tram 5, 9, or 26: Lipanská. Turn onto Chlumova and walk all the way to Husitská, then take a right. The club is on the left, through a courtyard and above a bowling alley. ⓢ Beer 29-39Kč. Shots 35-75Kč. Cash only. ⏰ Hours depend on concerts, usually 8pm-late.

VINOHRADY

Vinohrady is full of small bars and clubs and is home to Prague's gay nightlife.

Radost FX   CLUB
Bělehradská 120
☎224 254 776; www.radostfx.cz

The painted Coke bottles seem symbolic: Radost FX opened in 1992 and was among the first to bring Western-style clubbing to the newly democratic country. Not that you care; you're here to dance. Needless to say, you're in the right place. Zebra-print couches and weird chandeliers add up to an edgy atmosphere (to stay fresh, the interior design in Radost FX changes every year), and one of the more advanced light rigs in Prague takes care of the dance floor. When you tire of dancing, head upstairs to the lounge and soak up the alcohol with pricey vegetarian food. You must try one of the following drinks: Cosmic Granny, Lesbian Joy, or Sex with an Alien (just don't combine them).

▶ ⚇ C: I.P. Pavlova. From the station, head east on Jugoslávská for a little more than 1 block. When you reach Bělehradská, the club is on the left.

i Hip hop Th. House F. R and B Sa. Ⓢ Cover 100-150Kč; women free 10pm-midnight. Beer 35-95Kč. Cocktails 110-145Kč. 🕗 Open Th-Sa 10pm-5am.

ON
CLUB, GLBT

Vinohradská 40

☎222 520 630; www.club-valentino.cz

Formerly "Valentino," ON is the largest gay club in Prague. On weekends, the caterpillar blooms into a butterfly, and the club adds two additional dance floors to its bar and disco in the basement.

▶ 🚇 A: Náměstí Míru. From the station, walk east on Korunní, then turn left onto Sázavská and left onto Vinohradská. *i* Women are regularly in attendance; straight gentlemen, not so much. Ⓢ Beer 22-35Kč. Shots 45-75Kč. 🕗 Cafe open daily 11am-5am. Disco open daily 9pm-5am. Dance club open Th-Sa 11pm-6am.

SoKool
BAR

Polská 1

☎222 210 528; www.sokool.cz

Housed in an amusingly ugly Communist-era building, the bar's name actually comes from the *sokolovna* (gym) next door. One can tell just by looking that SoKool is a place beloved by young locals: it's got plenty of wooden benches, it serves beer in 1L glasses *(tupláky)*, and it's right next to Riegrovy sady (a popular student hangout—grab a plastic cup of beer and sit on the grassy slope that overlooks the city). Don't expect any dancing; SoKool is more about drinking and bonding.

▶ 🚇 A: Náměstí Míru. From the station, walk east on Korunní and turn left onto Budečská. Continue to the end and up the stairs. Ⓢ Beer 17-64Kč. Shots 30-60Kč. Cash only. 🕗 Open M-F 11am-midnight, Sa noon-midnight, Su noon-11pm.

Piano Bar
BAR, GLBT

Milešovská 10

☎775 727 496; www.pianobar.sweb.cz

This low-key gay bar is unlike other local bars. There's no dance floor and no light rigs—just a jukebox. Also, if you play the piano, you might end up being "live music" for the night. The prices are very friendly, and there are two old computers for patrons to use at no cost.

▶ 🚇 A: Jiřího z Poděbrad. From the station, head east on Vinohradská and take a left onto Milešovská. Ⓢ Beer 19-30Kč. Shots 37-57Kč. Cash only. 🕗 Open daily 5pm-5am.

Vinárna Vínečko

WINE BAR

Londynská 29

☎222 511 035; www.vineckopraha.cz

A local wine bar that errs on the side of adult, Vinárna Vínečko is the perfect place to spend a relaxed evening discussing how delightfully well your houseplants have been doing lately. The front garden, with its metal chairs and small hedge, isn't the coziest place ever, but ordering a delicious dessert may solve the problem. If you're lucky enough to be spending the evening with yourself, bring your laptop for the free Wi-Fi and treat yourself to a nice glass of *víno.* No buts—you deserve this.

▶ A: Náměstí Míru. From the station, head west down Rumunská, then take a left down Londynská. The bar is actually to the right on Bruselská where it meets Lodynská. $ Wine 30-38Kč. Beer 23-35Kč. Desserts 35-64Kč. ⏰ Open M-F noon-midnight, Sa 2pm-midnight, Su 2-10:30pm.

Latimerie Club

BAR

Slezská 74

☎224 252 049; www.latimerieclub.cz

This vaguely nautical gay bar brings together a group of hip locals and fun foreigners. There's a small dance floor and some minor colorful lights flashing, but that's apparently enough to please. This is not to say that the club doesn't get wild—no printed closing time means that party goes as late as you can stand.

▶ A: Jiřího z Poděbrad. From the station, head south down Nidranská. Slezská will be on your left. $ Beer 30-50Kč. Mixed drinks 50-180Kč. Cash only. ⏰ Open M-F 4pm-late, Sa-Su 6pm-late.

HOLEŠOVICE

Holešovice's clubs and bars tend to be huge and far apart. They are among the city's best.

👍 Cross Club

CLUB

Plynární 23

☎736 535 010; www.crossclub.cz

This is about the coolest club you'll ever set foot in. Affectionately dubbed "Optimus Prime's ass" by some, the place is decorated with the most amazing assortment of neon-lit industrial steel you'll find anywhere outside a junk yard, or, well, anywhere at all. Cross exists on five levels, with a three-floor outdoor patio and a maze of a rooms downstairs. There are two sections: the upstairs cafe and patio are free for everyone, while access to the underground club may require a cover. The descent into the club is surreal, as each room has its own quirks: one is only tall enough to sit in, while another has lamps made from car engines. The upstairs cafe hosts cultural events, such as free film screenings on Wednesdays that showcase works by young Czech filmmakers as well as established directors.

▶ ✦ C: Nádraží Holešovice. From the Metro, walk east on Plynární, past the bus bay and parallel to the tram tracks. Cross Club is the tall yellow building with metal sculptures out front. Ⓢ Cover 40-270Kč. Beer 19-37Kč. Cash only. 🕐 Cafe open daily 2pm-2am. Club open 6pm-late.

SaSaZu
CLUB, RESTAURANT

Bubenské nábřeží 306

☎284 097 444; www.sasazu.com

One of the newest and hottest additions to Prague's nightlife scene, SaSaZu has an enormous dance floor flanked by six bars. The DJ's saucer-shaped outpost hovers—sometimes quite literally—over the dancing crowds. Housed in a former slaughterhouse, SaSaZu also contains an über-stylish restaurant that serves Southeast Asian cuisine. Wait for a good event and then pounce—this place is worth checking out at least once.

▶ ✦ C: Vltavská. From the Metro, take tram 1, 3, 5, or 25 or walk along the tracks on Bubenské nábřeží for 1 stop to Pražská Tržnice (Prague Market), and enter the Prague Market grounds. SaSaZu is to the left, in front of a big parking lot. 𝑖 No open-toed shoes for men. Ⓢ Cover 100-200Kč; no cover for women before midnight. Cocktails 145-185Kč. Beer 49-75Kč. Entrees 130-485Kč. 🕐 Restaurant open daily noon-midnight. Club hours depend on events; check the website.

Club Mecca
CLUB

U Průhonu 3

☎602 711 225; www.mecca.cz

If a club's quality can be judged by the number of disco balls hanging above its dance floor, then Mecca's score is around 40. Open only three nights per week, Mecca has hosted some big names and continues to do so twice per month, when it invites well-known international performers. You may appreciate the fact that there's no cover on Wednesdays and that vodka shots cost 39Kč, but if you have money to burn, consider getting a VIP ticket to the upstairs lounge, which will cost either a drinks tab of 1000Kč per person, or the purchase of one bottle per two people. If you want to take a break from house music, there's a chill-out lounge downstairs.

▶ ✈ C: Vltavská. From the station, take tram 1, 3, 5, or 25 or walk along the tram tracks for 3 stops to Dělnická. Continue down Komunardů, then turn left on U Průhonu. The club is on the right. *i* No shorts or sandals. Ⓢ Cover F-Sa 190-290Kč. Small beer 39-47Kč. Cocktails 109-219Kč. 🕑 Open W 11-5am F-Sa 11pm-5am (or later).

Fraktal   BAR, RESTAURANT
Šmeralova 1
☎777 794 094; www.fraktalbar.cz

At night, Fraktal, a favorite local restaurant, functions as one of the more colorful local bars. The cavernous underground features childlike drawings and eccentric seating (one table in the corner is clearly meant for hobbits). Come for drunk food, such as burgers, nachos, or quesadillas, and for the opportunity to peek inside the kitchen through a poster's cut-out eyes.

▶ ✈ C: Vltavská. From the station, take tram 25 or walk along the tram tracks on Milady Horákové for 3 stops to Letenské náměstí. The bar is on the right. *i* Wheelchair-accessible on patio only. Ⓢ Beer 22-37Kč. Nachos 80-120Kč. Burgers 185-250Kč. Cash only. 🕑 Open daily 11am-midnight. Kitchen open M-Th 11am-11pm, F-Su 4-11pm.

Arts and Culture

While Prague has incredible shows, art, and concerts, there are also tons of God-awful tourist shows that cost inexcusable sums. Use this rule of thumb: if it costs more than 200Kč after a student discount, it's probably not worth the money. Some of the best art can be had for little money: Prague's opera is available to students for the cost of a sausage from a street vendor. The same thing applies to classical music at the Rudolfinum. Prague has at least three world-class symphony orchestras and three opera stages as well as a number of private galleries all around the city.

Travelers interested in seeing English-language theater should visit www.expats.cz or the "English Theatre in Prague" Facebook group for extensive listings. Prague Playhouse (www.pragueplayhouse.cz) has been producing English-language plays since 2003, while Blood, Love, and Rhetoric (www.blrtheatre.com) is an up-and-coming company. The Prague Shakespeare Festival (www.pragueshakespeare.org) puts on several Shakespeare plays each year.

Daily film listings at movie theaters can be found at www.prague.tv. The artsy Kino Světozor (www.kinosvetozor.cz) off Wenceslas Sq. shows three or four films every day, many of them indie favorites. Palace Cinemas (www.palacecinemas.cz) and CineStar Anděl (www.cinestar.cz) are two multiplexes across the street from each other in Smíchov that show Hollywood's latest.

Budget Culture

Like most things in Prague, getting your daily dose of culture doesn't have to be expensive. Just about every listing in *Let's Go* can be accessed at the cost of a few beers—but hey, we're not saying that choice is mutually exclusive. Check the **State Opera** or the **Rudolfinum** to pretend you're much snootier than your budget suggests.

OPERA AND THEATER

National Theater (Národní divadlo) NOVÉ MĚSTO

Národní třída 4

☎224 901 638; www.narodni-divadlo.cz

Producing a program of ballet, opera, and Czech-language drama, the National Theater is considered one of the most important cultural institutions in the Czech Republic. The theater opened in 1881, though various fires and other setbacks have caused alterations since then. The venue closes for the summer, but smaller, open-air productions often grace its inner courtyard.

▶ Ⓜ B: Národní třída. From the station, walk north to Národní třída and turn left toward the river. $ Tickets 300-1200Kč. ⏰ Open M-F 9am-6pm, Sa-Su 10am-6pm. Evening box office opens 45min. before curtain.

State Opera (Státní Opera Praha) NOVÉ MĚSTO

Legerova 75

☎296 117 111; www.opera.cz

Thanks to the State Opera's student-rush program, travelers can see a fully staged opera for less than the price of a sausage at the nearby Wenceslas Sq. Presenting more than a dozen operas every month, the State Opera sticks with favorites; works by Tchaikovsky, Mozart, Puccini, and Verdi are most frequently produced, with some other names occasionally mixed in.

▶ Ⓜ A or C: Muzeum. From the station, head past the National Museum. *i* Operas have Czech and English supertitles. Formal attire encouraged. $ Tickets 100-1500Kč. Up to 50% student discounts. ⏰ Open M-F 10am-5:30pm, Sa-Su 10am-noon and 1-5:30pm. Evening box office opens 1hr. before curtain.

Some Strings Attached

Puppet theater dates back 600 years in the Czech capital, beginning with Biblical plays and progressing to satirical allegories about Hitler and Nazi occupation—what better way to make fun of Europe's puppet master than through marionettes, right? After the Iron Curtain came tumblin' down, puppet culture declined in scope, although you can still find plays performed in this classic form.

But it's the puppets themselves that make the plays more interesting — and maybe a little bit creepy, too. The puppets are traditionally carved from lime wood, and woodcarvers strive to achieve contradictory goals: they want them to look as human as possible, but strive to craft them with overly neutral expressions. This results in miniature, jagged-featured people who stare blankly into the distance as strings manipulate their otherwise lifeless arms and legs. You might think it's impossible to make puppets seem real, but once you've seen one performing an aria from *Don Giovanni* at the **National Marionette Theatre,** you'll start to forget that he's made of wood.

Estates Theater — STARÉ MĚSTO

Železná 11

☎224 228 503; www.stavovskedivadlo.cz

If it's not enough for you to walk by the famous theater where Mozart premiered *Don Giovanni,* buy a ticket to one of the performances. These days, the tourist-friendly Estates puts on a few plays as well as operatic hits like *Carmen, The Marriage of Figaro,* and—you guessed it—*Don Giovanni.*

▶ 🚇 A or B: Můstek. From Old Town Sq., walk south on Železná; the theater is on the left. $ Tickets 300-1200Kč. ⏰ Open M-F 10am-5:30pm, Sa-Su 10am-12:30pm and 1-5:30pm. Evening box office opens 1hr. before curtain. Performances usually at 7pm.

MUSIC

Rudolfinum — JOSEFOV

Alšovo nábřeži 12

☎227 059 227; www.ceskafilharmonie.cz

Home of the Czech Philharmonic Orchestra since 1896,

Rudolfinum is Prague's premiere venue for classical music. The first concert in this building was conducted by none other than the composer Antonín Dvořák, who was the Orchestra's first conductor. The matinees and afternoon concerts tend to be cheaper than those in the evening, and with a student discount on top of that, hearing the Czech Republic's top symphony orchestra will cost practically nothing.

► B: Staroměstská. From the Metro, walk toward the river. Rudolfinum is the big building to the right. The box office is on the side facing away from the river. $ Tickets 110-600Kč. 50% student discount. ⏰ Box office open M-F 10am-6pm. Closed in summer.

Municipal House (Obecní Dům) NOVÉ MĚSTO

Náměstí Republiky 5

☎222 002 101; www.obecni-dum.cz

Home to the Czech National Symphony Orchestra (est. 1993), Municipal House is more tourist-oriented than Rudolfinum—it stays open during the summer and ticket prices tend to be higher. On the upside, many interesting music festivals take place here, so check the schedule online.

► B: Náměstí Republiky. From Old Town Sq., walk east on Celetná all the way to Náměstí Republiky; Municipal House is on the left. $ Tickets 500-1000Kč. ⏰ Box office open daily 10am-7pm.

FESTIVALS

There's always some kind of festival happening in Prague. We've listed a few here, but the tourist information website (www.praguewelcome.cz) also has a solid list of festivals and cultural events.

Febiofest CITYWIDE

Růžová 13

☎221 101 111; www.febiofest.cz

It may not be as high-profile as the festival in Karlovy Vary, but Febiofest is Central Europe's largest film event, screening over 4000 films of all genres. During the festival, Prague comes alive with film, and screenings take place in other Czech towns and in Slovakia as well.

► $ Ticket prices vary. ⏰ Mar. Check website for specific dates.

Prague Writers' Festival CITYWIDE

Revoluční 28

☎224 241 312; www.pwf.cz

An exciting five-day celebration of writers from around the world, the Prague Writers' Festival prides itself on bringing in the best of the craft. In 2011, the festival hosted such names as Don DeLillo, Junot Díaz, and the Iraqi poet Saadi Yousef. Events include readings, signings, galas, and question-and-answer sessions.

▶ Ⓢ Tickets 100-300Kč. 50% student discount. ⏰ Mid-Apr. Check website for specific dates.

Prague Biennale OUTSKIRTS

Československého exilu 4

☎244 401 894; www.praguebiennale.org

Prague's Biennale, which takes place on odd-numbered years, is the city's biggest and baddest showcase of international contem-

Moviegoer Mecca

For film lovers traveling in the Czech Republic in March, **Febiofest** is an event not to be missed. No, it's not a weekend devoted to worshipping the muscular model. Febiofest is a week-long extravaganza that combines the best films and documentaries of the past year, drawing attention from movie buffs worldwide. Started in 1993, the event began as a small gathering for some film-loving friends. Today the festival screens films from nearly 60 countries at 12 locations, including three theaters in Prague. In fact, Febiofest is so big that the country can't handle it on its own: once the Czech event ends, Febiofest moves to neighboring Slovakia for another trip around the world through film.

Think it couldn't get any cooler? When the sun sets, Febiofest turns into the **Febiofest Music Festival,** bringing the night to life with music from around the globe. Jazz, blues, rock, you name it: bands of all genres flock to Febiofest to showcase their world-class talent. In 2010 there was even an Open Stage for groups that didn't make the cut, turning into a "Battle of the Bands" to become the next crowd favorite. To top it off, the music performances are free, and the bands rock on 'til the wee hours of the morning. High cinematic art by day, moshpits by night: Febiofest has it all.

porary art. If you're lucky enough to be in town during the three days that the exhibition is on, you have to go.

▶ $ 150Kč, students 75Kč. ⏰ May. Check website for specific dates. Next festival scheduled for summer 2013.

Prague Spring Music Festival (Pražské Jaro) CITYWIDE

Hellichova 18

☎257 312 547; www.festival.cz

The enormous, month-long festival features some 50 performances by the world's top soloists, small ensembles, symphony orchestras, and conductors. The festival helps launch the careers of talented musicians by hosting soloist competitions in different instrument categories.

▶ ℹ Check website for specific dates. $ Ticket prices range from free to exorbitant. 20% student discount on most concerts. ⏰ From early May to early June.

Karlovy Vary International Film Festival OUTSIDE THE CITY

Karlovy Vary

☎359 001 111; www.kviff.com

Some 130km west of Prague, Karlovy Vary hosts the country's most prestigious film festival. Screening over 180 feature films, this Czech Cannes has been a launching pad for many European hits, including *Amélie, Ma Vie En Rose,* and *The Chorus.* It's a bit of a ride from Prague, but it's a must-see for film enthusiasts who happen to be around in July. The ticket prices are much more reasonable than those at big festivals in Western Europe.

▶ 🚆 From Prague's Main Train Station (Hlavní nádraží), trains to Karlovy Vary take just over 3hr. and cost 600Kč. $ Tickets 60Kč, students 50Kč. 1-day pass 200Kč, students 150Kč; 3-day 500/350Kč. ⏰ Early July. Check website for specific dates.

Shopping

Prague may not exactly be a shopping destination, but rare items and great deals await. Staré Město is a bastion of touristy shops selling overpriced Bohemian crystal, marionettes, and all sorts of souvenirs. This is where you can pick up one of those cheesy "Czech Drinking Team" T-shirts, the obligatory uniform of many a foreign tourist. Wenceslas Sq. is home to huge international chain stores, while Pařížská, which connects Josefov and Staré Město, is the most expensive street in Prague, famous for its high-end designer shops. Handmade clothes and accessories from Czech designers can be found in a few stores around the center, while some of the more residential areas hold rare communist artifacts and other antiques. There's a handful of Western-style malls; the closest ones are in Staré Město and Smíchov. There are also plenty of good bookstores, and even the lesser-known ones tend to be well stocked with English-language classics from big-name Czech authors like Hašek, Hrabal, Kafka, and Kundera. Then there are the quirky places, like a witch store near Náměstí Míru or the hat shop in Malá Strana. And let's not forget about the Prague Market in Holešovice, the city's largest marketplace, where you can get everything from cheap clothes to swords.

Budget Shopping

As in any city, bargain-hunting in Prague centers around secondhand stores and markets where prices can be negotiated. The best of all these can be found in **Holešovická Tržnice** (Prague Market) in Holešovice. You can get literally anything here, though recognize that as an English-language bargainer, you will have to haggle down vendors who think you have no idea how much anything is worth. If you go in with a strong idea of prices and an iron will, however, you should come out with great deals.

CLOTHING

Parazit — STARÉ MĚSTO

Karlova 25

☎603 561 776; www.parazit.cz

An amazing find in any city, Parazit has more outrageous, one-of-a-kind wardrobe pieces than a Tim Burton nightmare. Every item is handmade by Czech and Slovak designers and design students. There are definitely more options for women, but men can find a few original T-shirts. If you don't want to spend much, take a look at the huge selection of accessories, diaries, and other bric-a-brac that are sold alongside the clothes.

▶ 🚏 A: Staroměstská. From Old Town Sq., head toward Charles Bridge on Karlova. The shop is in a courtyard on the right. $ Shirts 420-1000Kč. Dresses from 1500Kč. Bags from 500Kč. Cash only. ⏰ Open M-Sa 11am-8pm.

Julius Fashion — NOVÉ MĚSTO

Ostrovní 20

☎731 419 953; www.juliusfashion.com

Julius is very similar to Parazit in that it sells original handmade items by local designers, but the wares here tend to be a bit less crazy and more conventionally elegant. Nevertheless, you'll still find a few outlandish items (handbags made from LPs, for instance). Check out the store's online shop to get a sense of its wares.

▶ 🚏 B: Národní třída. Walk on Ostrovní toward the river. The shop is on the left. $ Accessories 100-500Kč. T-shirts 500-690Kč. Dresses 700-3000Kč. ⏰ Open M-F 11am-7pm, Sa 11am-6pm.

Palladium   STARÉ MĚSTO
Náměstí Republiky 1
☎225 770 250; www.palladiumpraha.cz

Enter this enormous Western-style mall, and you're not in Old Town anymore—you could be anywhere. There's a food court and plenty of stores selling clothing, books, electronics, beauty products, eyeglasses, and everything else you'd expect from a mall.

▶ ⌗ B: Náměstí Republiky. The mall is near the Metro exit. 🕙 Shops open M-W 9am-9pm, Th-Sa 9am-10pm, Su 9am-9pm. Supermarket open M-F 7am-10pm, Sa-Su 8am-10pm.

Obchodní Centrum Nový Smíchov   SMÍCHOV
Plzeňská 8
☎251 101 061; www.novysmichov.eu

This giant mall boasts a Tesco, a Palace Cinemas multiplex (☎840 200 240; www.palacecinemas.cz), several coffee shops, clothing stores, a sporting-goods shop, and a food court. Much of downtown Smíchov is organized around this area. The mall may be a bit out of the way, but it's very popular with locals.

▶ ⌗ C: Anděl. 1 block north of the Metro. To get here from Malá Strana, walk or take tram 12 or 20. 🕙 Shops open daily 9am-9pm. Tesco open daily 7am-midnight.

Šatna (The Cloakroom)   STARÉ MĚSTO
Konviktská 13
☎777 030 415

Šatna is a tiny boutique with a large supply of secondhand leather jackets and men's jeans in good condition as well as a few men's shirts, shoes, and some blouses. It may not be exactly a bargain (especially for a secondhand store), but Šatna is definitely the pick of the litter.

▶ ⌗ B: Národní třída. From the station, head north on Spálená and continue as it becomes Na Perštýně. Curve around to the left and move onto Konviktská. Ⓢ Shirts 100-300Kč. Pants 200-500Kč. Jackets 300-400Kč. Cash only. 🕙 Open M-F 11am-7pm, Sa 11am-6pm.

BOOKS

📗 Shakespeare & Sons   MALÁ STRANA
U lužického semináře 10
☎257 531 894; www.shakes.cz

Shakespeare & Sons is our favorite bookstore in Prague, and

Shopping (side tab)

not just because it sells *Let's Go.* The bookstore boasts an impressive collection of fiction, comics, and social science books (mostly in English), as well as a cozy downstairs cellar that's perfect for browsing, and tons of cheap used books. If you're searching for your obligatory Kundera paperback, start here.

▶ ⚡ A: Malostranská. From the Metro, walk south parallel to the river and bear right on U lužického semináře. The store is on the right. ⏰ Open daily 11am-7pm.

🏪 Globe Bookstore   NOVÉ MĚSTO
Pštrossova 6

☎224 934 203; www.globebookstore.cz

Attached to a cafe with the same name, the Globe caters specifically to American and British expats looking for literary enlightenment in Prague. The store features an expansive collection of English-language literature, travel guides, and general-interest books, while the cafe hosts cultural events, such as readings or film screenings.

▶ ⚡ B: Karlovo náměstí. From the Metro, take Resslova toward the river and then turn right on Na Zderaze, which becomes Pštrossova; the cafe is on the right. ⏰ Open daily 9:30am-11pm.

Big Ben Bookstore   STARÉ MĚSTO
Malá Štupartská 5

☎224 826 559; www.bigbenbookshop.com

This cute little bookshop, located across from St. James Cathedral, offers travelers a solid literary outlet in the middle of the Old Town. Despite its small size, Big Ben has enough literature and travel guides to warrant a look. Stop by in June during the Prague Writers' Festival (see **Arts and Culture: Festivals**) for book signings by visiting authors.

▶ ⚡ From Old Town Sq., take Týnska east, continuing straight through the courtyard as it turns into Týn. Take a left when the courtyard lets out at Malá Štupartská. ⏰ Open M-Sa 9:30am-8pm, Su 11am-7pm.

ANTIQUES

Bazar   HOLEŠOVICE
Přístavní 18

Antique shopping in Prague isn't the expensive hipster affair that it is in the States, but there are a bunch of places where you

Shopping

can pick up your First Republic-era bottle opener or Communist-era hat. Bazar is a great place to start your hunt for such objects—the one large room has enough objects to satisfy your inner hoarder. The wares here include war knives, old pocket watches, Art Deco relics, and much more. Look carefully in the store window too—some of the best stuff is not visible from inside the store.

▶ 🪧 C: Vltavská. From the Metro, take tram 1, 3, 5, or 25 or walk along the tram tracks 3 stops to Dělnická. After 1 more block, Bazar will be on the corner to the left. $ Prices negotiable. Cash only. ⏰ Open M-F 11am-12:30pm and 1:30-4:30pm.

Vetešnictví — MALÁ STRANA

Vítězná 16

☎257 310 611

Walking around Vetešnictví feels like snooping through somebody's attic, with many strangely personal, flimsy, and useless objects, but here and there you'll discover an actual hidden gem. Even if you don't intend to buy anything, take a few minutes to wander around—it's strangely educational.

▶ 🪧 A: Malostranská. From the Metro, walk or take tram 12, 20, or 22 to Újezd. Walk toward the river on Vítězná. $ Antiques 10-10,000Kč. Cash only. ⏰ Open M-F 10am-6pm, Sa 10am-noon.

MARKETS

👍 Holešovická Tržnice (Prague Market) — HOLEŠOVICE

Bubenské nábřeží

☎220 800 592; www.holesovickatrznice.cz

Dozens of clothes vendors, furniture salesmen, food peddlers, and other entrepreneurial-minded gentlemen and women call this market home. Housed in a warehouse complex on the bank of the Vltava, Prague Market is the largest market in town and the perfect place to hunt for bargains on manufactured goods. A sampling of what's for sale: clothes, bags, toys, smokeless cigarettes, swords, ice cream. Bargaining languages are Czech, English, and Vietnamese.

▶ 🪧 C: Vltavská. From the station, take tram 1, 3, 5, or 25 or walk along the tracks on Bubenské nábřeží for 1 stop to Pražská Tržnice (Prague Market). $ Prices negotiable. ⏰ Hours vary by vendor, roughly 7am-9pm.

'Tis the Season

In the last weeks of November, the people of Prague begin to bask in festivity and holiday cheer as the annual Christmas markets roll in. The markets are open from morning until late evening, seven days a week. Don't expect any extraordinary seasonal products, though: there are some nifty stocking stuffers like candles, toys, and ornaments, but those can be bought year-round. The tradition is more about the atmosphere than the actual shopping. If you visit Old Town Sq. or Wenceslas Sq. in the city center, a dazzling spectacle of dozens of street shops, glimmering Christmas lights, and a bustling crowd will surely get you into the holiday spirit. Throw in some traditional Czech cuisine and a glass of mulled wine *(svařené víno)* and you'll want to spend every Christmas in Prague.

Farmers' Markets
NOVÉ MĚSTO, JOSEFOV

Locations vary

www.farmarsketrziste.cz

On most days of the week, there's a farmers' market happening in some part of Prague, selling not only local fruits and vegetables, but also fish, smoked meat, mushrooms, baskets, ceramics, flowers, beer, wine, and more. Some of the locations are a bit out of the way, but two are located on embankments not far from tourist areas—on Saturdays, there are markets at Rašínovo nábřeží (near the bridge connecting New Town with Smíchov), and on Thursdays, there are markets in Josefov, on the river bank between Hotel Intercontinental and a hospital. The markets are a great place to discover what the Czech countryside has to offer.

▶ 🚊 To get to Kubánské náměstí, take trams 6, 7, 19, 22, or 24: Kubánské náměstí. To get to Náměstí Jířího z Poděbrad, take Metro A or trams 10 or 16: Náměstí Jířího z Poděbrad. To get to Rašínovo nábřeží, take Metro B to Karlovo náměstí and walk toward the river. Dvořákovo nábřeží is just above Hotel Intercontinental in Josefov. 🕐 Kubánské náměstí market open Tu 8am-6pm, Th 8am-6pm, Sa 8am-2pm. Náměstí Jířího z Poděbrad market open W 8am-6pm, Sa 8am-2pm. Rašínovo nábřeží market open Sa 8am-2pm. Dvořákovo nábřeží market open Th 8am-6pm.

Havelské Tržiště   STARÉ MĚSTO
Havelská

Just in case you haven't noticed yet, there's an open-air market in the city center, between Wenceslas and Old Town Squares. It sells fresh produce and, along with the much bigger Pražská Tržnice, is one of the only permanent marketplaces around central Prague.

▶ ⚑ A or B: Můstek. From Wenceslas Sq. walk on Na Můstku as it becomes Melantrichova. 🕐 Generally open daily 7am-7pm.

Excursions

There are several small trips to be made from Prague; we've listed three very different ones here. **Karlštejn,** the first, is a 14th-century castle easily visited as a daytrip from Prague. There, you'll find the main attraction, a real live castle on top of a mountain, to be just about all the sights you need. Look into the variety of tour options and schedule one before you go. The second trip, **Terezín,** is of an entirely different flavor: though it was not constructed as such, it was used as a concentration camp for victims of WWII. Therefore, anticipate the melancholy reverence of the trip and the weight of the experience. Finally, there's **Kutná Hora,** a small village just 90min. away from Prague. Here you'll find churches made of bones, churches not made of bones, and everything in between. If you're in Prague for any kind of extended period, we recommend checking out at least one of these places to diversify your Czech Republic experience.

KARLŠTEJN

Karlštejn Castle was built by Charles IV in 1348 to guard the crown jewels, and unlike its counterpart in Prague, this sucker's a full-on castle. We're talking a big-ass wall perched on a mountaintop with the cutest little support town you've ever seen. The schlep to and from Prague can be done in half a day, and the experience of seeing the fairytale castle suddenly pop into view is quite worth it. If you're thinking of going, you should reserve tickets ASAP for the Tour II (available May-October), which takes you inside the castle's tower and shows you the Chapel of the Sacred Heart, the stunning room where crown jewels and holy relics were stored. Unfortunately, English-language tours are infrequent and capped at a certain number of visitors, so they often get booked quickly. You can't buy tickets at the gate for the second tour—they must be reserved or purchased in advance. Most daytrippers come just for the castle, which is perhaps the biggest tourist destination in the Czech Republic outside of Prague. If you have time, though, hike through the jurassically overgrown woods in the nature reserve surrounding Karlštejn.

Orientation

Karlštejn is a tiny one-street village leading up to the castle. That one street's name seems to be **"Sri Chinmoy,"** which is puzzling, to say the least. The train station is located across the **Berunka river** in Karlštejn II, several minutes away by foot. A few kilometers

Excursions

to the north of the castle, **Lom Velká Amerika** (an old limestone quarry) is a popular hiking destination.

Sights

Karlštejn Castle

The Karlštejn Castle (reservations ☎274 008 154; www.hradkarl-stejn.cz) offers four tours. We've covered I and II below; Tour III (60Kč, students 30Kč) includes a photo op at the top of the castle tower and Tour IV (30Kč, students free) includes the upper castle exterior. We highly recommend buying tickets online instead of just reserving them—it saves you the hassle of paying twice (first for the reservation and then for the ticket). Printed tickets must be validated at the ticket register (bear in mind it closes for lunch July-August noon-12:30pm, September-June noon-1pm). There's no overlap between tours, so if you want to see the Chapel of the Sacred Heart, you'll have to book Tour II.

Castle Tour I

The 1hr. tour of Karlštejn Castle takes you through Charles IV's bedroom, his throne chambers, and other rooms in the palace. One of the more interesting parts is the King's collection of holy relics, which contains the head of the 🐉**dragon** famously killed by St. George. (Guess what: it's a crocodile skull.) Also check out the statue of St. Nicholas, which was carved by Charles IV himself; he took up woodcarving upon suggestion from his doctors, who believed it would help cure his arthritis. The women's quarters are closed to visitors, but watch for the small staircase that connected the king's bedroom to the queen's—the door had a handle on only one side, so he could visit her whenever he wanted, but she couldn't do the same (it's sort of like being invisible on GChat). He also liked being invisible when receiving visitors; the throne was positioned right next to two bright windows, so that the king's face was hidden in shadow. The real crown jewels are no longer located in Karlštejn, but the tour includes some polished copies. Overall, the first tour is perhaps less impressive than the second, but it offers a more intimate look at the life of this legendary Czech figure.

▶ Ⓢ 270Kč, students 180Kč. ⌚ Tours July-Aug daily 9am-7pm; Sept Tu-Su 9am-6pm; Oct Tu-Su 9am-5pm; Nov-Feb Tu-Su 9am-3pm; Mar Tu-Su 9am-4pm; Apr Tu-Su 9am-5pm; May-June Tu-Su 9am-6pm.

Castle Tour II

This tour takes you to the heart of Karlštejn Castle, including the Great Tower, which has never been conquered—not even when the Swedes seized the fortification during the 30 Years' War. The tour ends with a visit to the **Chapel of the Sacred Heart,** which was used to store the crown jewels. Best of all, the tour is limited to 15 guests, so you can tap the tour guides' knowledge—they're holding onto stories they won't tell unprompted. One example: while most castles used wells for water (in case of a siege), Karlštejn couldn't tap its well and had to dig a secret water main from the nearby brook. If anyone found that out, they could easily poison the brook and take the castle. Charles IV, problem-solver that he was, allegedly had all the workers who built the duct killed so they wouldn't tell anyone. Another highlight of the tour is the **Church of Our Lady,** which has an original biblical apocalypse scene splayed on its walls in all its violent glory. Though some of the mural has been destroyed in various sieges, there are still enough nine-headed dragons, ghouls made of fire, and skeletons on horseback to let you glimpse the horror of the medieval imagination. The **Chapel of the Holy Cross,** the final stop on the trek, houses 129 portraits of Bohemian kings and saints and is covered with the country's largest collection of semi-precious stones. But the ceiling is what rocks. It's covered in thousands of glass plates that try (and mostly succeed) to look like a starry sky.

▶ *i* Advanced reservations required; no tickets sold at the gate. ⓢ 300Kč, students 200Kč. ⏰ Open Tu-Su May-June 9am-6pm; July-Aug 9am-7pm; Sept 9am-6pm; Oct 9am-5pm.

Food

A dozen or so restaurants fill this little village, and they're all more or less fine.

Restaurace pod Dračí skálou   CZECH $$
Karlštejn 130
☎311 681 177; www.poddraciskalou.eu

This maverick of a restaurant isn't located on Karlštejn's only street, oh no—it's in the middle of a forest, 10min. from the castle by foot. You'll often see tour buses parked outside, but the restaurant manages to avoid being a tourist trap, serving huge, reasonably priced portions. Aside from the traditional

Czech fare, there are some more unusual options, like buttered asparagus (59Kč). Sit outside if it's sunny, but do check out the interior, which is packed with taxidermied animals, ranging from an enormous boar's head to all sorts of birds of prey. The menu is only in Czech, but you'll manage.

▶ ⚑ From the castle, turn left after the 2nd gate (the restaurant's sign will direct you into the woods). Follow the path downhill, and continue right when you reach a road. From the village, proceed toward the castle and take the only major left there is, opposite the Nativity Museum. When in doubt, follow the small stream—it leads to the restaurant. The restaurant will be on the right—look for the statue of a dragon. The walk takes about 10min. Ⓢ Entrees 69-230Kč. Beer 15-35Kč. ⚏ Open M-Sa 11am-11pm, Su 11am-8pm.

Essentials

Practicalities

- **TOURIST OFFICES:** The **Information Center** has some info and brochures on sightseeing and hiking in the region. (Karlštejn parking lot ☎311 681 370; www.karlstejnsko.cz ⚏ Open daily 8am-8pm.)

Emergency

- **EMERGENCY NUMBER:** ☎112.

Getting There

Trains from Prague to Karlštejn leave frequently from both Hlavní nádraží (93Kč) and Smíchovské nádraží (83Kč). Take the **Beroun train** and get off at Karlštejn train station. If you're confused about the platform and time of departure in Prague, the large boards overhead have up-to-date departure information. The Karlštejn train station is not well marked, but it's small and easy to navigate. The last trains back to Prague leave around 11pm, but, if you end up stranded or decide to spend the night, your return ticket will still be valid the next day.

Getting Around

Karlštejn is easily navigable by foot. To get to the castle after getting off the train, exit the station and turn right. Walk straight along the train tracks until the rail crossing, turn left, and cross the Berunka river bridge. At every intersection there are signs directing you to the castle—follow the ones that say "Hrad." The walk from the train station to the village should take around 10-15min., and it's another 10-15min. uphill to the castle. The tourist office is located near the big parking lot at the base of the hill, but you can probably manage without it.

TEREZÍN

Grassy, decrepit, and almost abandoned, Terezín belongs to ghosts. Built at the end of the 18th century, it was originally a strategic stronghold against invaders from the east. It quickly became apparent that Terezín was ineffective as a defensive structure, and it was adapted to serve as a prison, home to such famous inmates as the assassins of Archduke Ferdinand. Its most infamous era was during WWII when it was the site of a prison camp for victims of the Third Reich. Initially Terezín was used as a prison for political prisoners of the SS, but it was slowly converted into a concentration and transit camp for Jews, Roma, Communists, and homosexuals. However, Terezín was unique in its designation as a prison for high-profile prisoners. The abundance of artists, writers, and intellectuals kept in Terezín would produce some of the war's most striking and stark images of life in a concentration camp. By the time of the liberation, 155,000 men, women, and children had passed through Terezín; 35,000 died at the camp, while 87,000 moved on to extermination camps in the east. Only a fraction of the prisoners to pass through Terezín survived the war.

Orientation

Terezín is located some 60km north of Prague. The grounds are defined by two star-shaped sets of fortifications separated by the river **Ohře**—the larger star to the west is the former **Jewish ghetto,** while the smaller star to the east is the former **prison.** All distances can be easily covered on foot.

Sights

Terezín's major sights are administered by a centralized organization, **Terezín Memorial.** A universal ticket can be purchased at any of the sites (200Kč, students 150Kč), or tickets can be purchased separately for each (160Kč/130Kč). When planning your visit, keep in mind that on Saturdays the crematorium is closed and buses run less frequently. If you're short on time, go straight to the former prison camp, Small Fortress. Otherwise start with the **Ghetto Museum,** which gives a good introduction to Terezín's history.

Small Fortress — MEMORIAL, CEMETERY

Malá Pevnost

☎416 782 225; www.pamatnik-terezin.cz

Although the information center provides explanatory maps of the small fortress grounds, try to get a guided tour. If you're traveling solo or with few companions, join somebody else's tour—there are up to 10 English tours per day. The Nazis used Terezín for various purposes, including imprisonment, extermination, and propaganda. A guide will explain to you that the sinks in the main cell block didn't actually work and were just built for show. Before a visit from the Red Cross, they built up the prison facilities to demonstrate humane treatment of prisoners. Swallows have long built mud nests here like the ones on the light fixtures—they were a symbol of hope for the winter-frozen prisoners. During the 1hr. tour, you'll see the large holding cells, the solitary confinement cells, the showers and delousing stations, and the various execution grounds. After the tour, travelers can see exhibits on the WWI and WWII history of the fortress or view documentaries and propaganda films that are shown in a former Nazi cinema. A relaxed visit to the small fortress can easily take 2hr.

▶ 🚏 From the bus stop, head east away from town, crossing the bridge that the bus passed on the way in. At the cemetery memorial, take the left fork. $ 160Kč, students 130Kč. Combined 200Kč, students 150Kč. Cash only. ⏰ Open daily Apr-Oct 8am-6pm; Nov-Mar 8am-4:30pm.

Ghetto Museum — MUSEUM

Komenského ulice

☎416 782 225; www.pamatnik-terezin.cz

The Ghetto Museum contains a permanent exhibit on the Nazi's "Final Solution" and on life in Terezín during WWII. Not only does the museum put this tragedy in context, but it also contains one of the most moving exhibits of the entire compound: hundreds of drawings by children who were briefly allowed to attend school during the occupation of the ghetto. The museum also screens a documentary about the memorial and the various events that contributed to the tragedy.

▶ ⚐ Next to the info center, to the north. 𝒊 Cafe in the basement sells lunch and snacks. Ⓢ 160Kč, students 130Kč. Combined 200Kč, students 150Kč. Cash only. ⏰ Open daily Apr-Oct 9am-6pm; Nov-Mar 9am-5:30pm.

Crematorium   CEMETERY
Krematorium a židovský hřbitov
☎416 782 225; www.pamatnik-terezin.cz

The crematorium, where the remains of prisoners were burned, suffered heavy damage in the flooding of 2004. The facilities have since been restored, almost to the point where they look functional. From the outside, the unassuming building looks like a small synagogue in the middle of a Jewish graveyard, where a giant stone menorah and various urns and other monuments commemorate the murdered Jews of the "Final Solution." On the way to the crematorium, just outside the ghetto fortifications, the **Central Mortuary** and **Columbarium** contain coffins and boxes that once held prisoners' ashes.

▶ ⚐ From the bus stop, head across the square to the southwest corner of the Terezín. Continue walking 5min. out of town, following the signs that say "Krematorium." 𝒊 Men should cover their heads before entering the grounds. Ⓢ 160Kč, students 130Kč. Combined 200Kč, students 150Kč. Yarmulkes 20Kč. ⏰ Open daily Apr-Oct 10am-6pm, Nov-Mar 10am-4pm.

Madgeburg Barracks   MUSEUM
Komenského ulice
☎416 782 225; www.pamatnik-terezin.cz

The Madgeburg Barracks house a collection of paintings, drawings, and manuscripts produced by Terezín's unusually large population of artists, performers, and writers during their time in the ghetto. While these images were created in secret and intended to alert the outside world of the atrocities being committed at Terezín, attempts to transmit them were discovered and the perpetrators brutally punished, and most of the works were not recovered until after the war. The barracks additionally hold the various manuscripts, set pieces, and costumes from the performances that prisoners were forced to put on for the Red Cross workers.

▶ ⚐ From the bus station head across the square along Komenského. The barracks are to the left at the end of the street. ⓢ 160Kč, students 130Kč. Combined 200Kč, students 150Kč. ⏰ Open daily Apr-Oct 9am-6pm, Nov-Mar 9am-5:30pm.

Food

Restaurace Na Hradbách   CZECH $
Bohušovická brána 335
☎723 287 738

Technically located outside of the ghetto area, Na Hradbách offers a brief escape from the dreary buildings within. Sit on the terrace with a beer or a snack (try the sunny-side up egg on toast; 25Kč) and watch goats graze on the grassy fortifications. The restaurant offers a small selection of cheap Czech dishes too.

▶ ⚑ Head to the southwest corner of the garrison. The restaurant is just outside town proper on the way to the Crematorium. ⓢ Entrees 72-97Kč. Cash only. ⏰ Open M-F noon-10pm, Sa-Su noon-8pm.

Essentials

Practicalities

- **TOURIST OFFICES: Information Center.** (Náměstí ČSA 179 ☎416 782 616; www.terezin.cz ⏰ Open M-Th 8am-5pm, F 8am-1:30pm, Su 9am-3pm.)

Emergency

- **EMERGENCY NUMBER:** ☎112.

- **POLICE:** Náměstí ČSA 179 ☎416 782 333 or ☎158.

Getting There

Buses leave regularly from Prague's Nádraží Holešovice on Metro line C. Nádraží Holešovice can be difficult to navigate for first-timers—your best bet is to find the platform number online before you go (www.jizdniradys.idnes.cz). At Holešovice, follow the "Buses" signs to get to the platform. Tickets (one-way;

80Kč) are purchased on the bus. The ride is about 1hr., with stops at Ohře (near the Small Fortress) and directly in front of the Terezín tourist office, inside the former ghetto. Check the tourist office's door for a schedule of return buses. Be warned: the last bus leaves Terezín for Prague around 6pm on most days and at 4pm on Saturdays. In case you miss the last bus, it's also possible to walk 3km to the nearby village of Nové Kopisty, which has a train to Prague every hour.

KUTNÁ HORA

The peaceful village of Kutná Hora is perfect for a daytrip from Prague—so perfect, in fact, that the tourism industry here has launched an entire campaign that aims to get people to stay overnight. We still think that one day is pretty much enough. That doesn't mean the sights aren't incredibly interesting—from a church decorated with the bones of some 40,000 dead people to one of the most beautiful Gothic cathedrals in Central Europe to the experience of absolute darkness inside a silver mine, Kutná Hora has much to offer.

Orientation

The center of Kutná Hora is fairly small and easy enough to navigate. If you arrive by bus, walk past the Billa supermarket and up the hill for 10min. to reach the town center. **Palackého náměstí** is the town's biggest square—here you can get a free map from the tourist office. The Saint Barbara Church, the Czech Museum of Silver, and Saint James's Church are all a stone's throw from the square. The Bone Church and the Church of the Assumption of Our Lady are located 4km away in the village of **Sedlec**—you can get there by taking a local bus from the bus station. The train station that serves all trains to and from Prague is also in Sedlec, 10min. from the Bone Church. With a decidedly smaller English-speaking population, Kutná Hora can be a bit more difficult to navigate than Prague. The best advice is to look for signs, and remember that everything important is in the same basic area.

Sights

Saint Barbara Church CHURCH
Barborská 51
☎775 363 938; www.khfarnost.cz

From a distance, St. Barbara looms like an enormous circus tent; from close-up it's all spires and flying buttresses and gargoyles jutting willy-nilly. The church conspicuously resembles the St. Vitus Cathedral in Prague's Hradčany—it was conceived during Kutná Hora's better days, when the two cities still had a kind of rivalry. The construction had to be interrupted a number of times, and, even though its origins go back to the 14th century, the church wasn't completed until the early 20th century. If you look up, you'll see the crests of rich families floating on the ceiling. Don't miss the golden organ with its angel band stroking harps or the various exhibits in the arches behind the altar.

▶ ⚓ From Palackého náměstí, head west on Husova, then take a left on Minciřská and a right onto Komenského náměstí. Then take a left onto Barborská. Follow it as it snakes uphill and ends at the church. Ⓢ 60Kč, students 40Kč. 🕐 Open daily Apr-Oct 9am-6pm, Nov-Mar 10am-4pm.

The Bone Church/Ossuary (Kostnice) CHURCH
Zámecká 127
☎326 551 049; www.kostnice.cz

There's a good reason why this place, officially known as "Cemetery Church of All Saints," is referred to by most people as the Bone Church: the interior is decorated with human bones. In the 13th century, the local cemetery became a huge hit with people in the market for burials after an abbot sprinkled it with some soil from the Holy Land. The cemetery also owes some of its success to the various plagues, which decimated Europe's population. There were so many people hoping to rest here that the cemetery had to be expanded, so, of course, they decided to dig up nearly 40,000 skeletons to decorate the ossuary. In 1870, the sculptor František Rint was commissioned to arrange the bones, and boy, did he go all out: inside the ossuary, you'll find a chandelier that contains every single bone of the human body and many other innovative designs. Notice Mr. Rint's signature on the wall, which is made of—you guessed it—bones.

▶ ⚓ From the Kutná Hora bus station, take a local bus to Sedlec. Once at the bus stop, cross the road and walk up the street. Ⓢ 60Kč, students 40Kč. Joint ticket with the cathedral 80Kč, students 50Kč. 🕐 Open daily Apr-Sept 8am-6pm; Oct 9am-5pm; Nov-Feb 9am-4pm; Mar 9am-5pm.

Excursions

Czech Museum of Silver (Hrádek) MUSEUM

Barborská 28

☎327 512 159; www.cms-kh.cz

The next contestant on Kutná Hora's search for most haunted sight, this tour of an abandoned silver mine arms you with a lab coat and a helmet, before leading you 35m below the surface of the Earth. The experience is gritty: ground water streams under the rocks around you and, in some parts of the tour, visitors must duck and squeeze through the rock. The 1½ hr. tour also covers the history of mining in the city and a lot of other information that seems weak-sauce compared to the mine itself. The visit helps you appreciate the difficulties of a miner's life—they would spend 2-3hr. just climbing out of the mine, and then another hour sitting together in a dark room, slowly adjusting their eyes to daylight.

▶ From Palackého náměstí, head west on Husova, take a left on Mincířská, a right onto Komenského náměstí, and a left onto Barborská. *i* Not recommended for overweight visitors or people with even mild claustrophobia, cardiac disease, breathing problems, or motion or eyesight problems. It's better to book the tour in advance. $ Tour 120Kč, students 80Kč. Museum-only tour 70Kč, students 40Kč. ⏰ Open May-Jun daily 9am-6pm, July-Aug daily 10am-6pm, Sept daily 9am-6pm, Oct daily 9am-5pm, Nov Sa-Su 10am-4pm, Apr daily 9am-5pm.

Cathedral of the Assumption of our Lady CHURCH

Vítězná 1

☎326 551 049; www.sedlec.info

In another town, the Cathedral of the Assumption of our Lady would be a very interesting church. It exhibits, among other things, the skulls of Cistercian monks who were tortured to death after defending the place from the Hussites. After a visit to the Bone Church, though, this may not seem that impressive. Don't miss the second floor, where you can wander around the cathedral's attic. The Hussites burned the cathedral during the war, but it was rebuilt in the Baroque style in the 18th century. According to legend, Jan Žižka forbade his soldiers to burn the church, but one disobeyed. To identify the guilty soldier, Žižka promised "enough gold and silver for the rest of his life" to the person who did it. When the culprit showed up with witnesses, Žižka fulfilled the promise: he had gold and silver melted and poured into the man's mouth.

▶ From the bus station, take a local bus to Sedlec. The cathedral is at the bus stop. $ 30Kč, students 20Kč. Joint ticket with the Bone Church 80Kč, students 50Kč. 🕑 Open Apr-Oct M-Sa 9am-5pm, Su noon-5pm; Nov-Mar daily 11am-3pm.

Food

There's quite a range of food options in Kutná Hora, from tourist spots with hefty price tags to tiny local dives that we'd recommend only to the most hard-core seekers of the local experience. To roll American-style, get a coffee to go at **Kofeinlove.** (Palackého náměstí Ⓢ Coffee 29-59Kč. 🕑 Open M-F 8:30am-9:30pm, Sa 9am-midnight, Su 10:30am-7pm.)

🖼 V Ruthardce   CZECH $$

Dačického náměstí 15

☎607 286 298; www.v-ruthardce.cz

Hidden from sight on a small street behind the Museum of Silver, this is the perfect place to lunch in Kutná Hora. If it's sunny, snag one of the tables in the grassy courtyard and order the grilled Hermelin cheese with spicy cranberry sauce and fries (110Kč). If you're feeling adventurous, try the snails with herb butter (130Kč).

▶ 🚶 Facing away from the gate of the Czech Museum of Silver, walk straight and take the 1st right onto a small sloping street. The entrance is on the left. Ⓢ Grilled entrees 50-185Kč. Desserts 30-65Kč. 🕑 Open M-Th noon-11pm, F-Sa noon-1am, Su noon-11pm.

Essentials

Practicalities

- **TOURIST OFFICE:** Palackého náměstí 377 ☎327 512 378; www.guide.kh.cz Ⓢ Computer use 60Kč per hr. 🕑 Open Apr-Oct daily 9am-6pm; Nov-Mar M-F 9am-5pm, Sa-Su 10am-4pm.

Emergency

- **EMERGENCY NUMBER:** ☎112.

- **POLICE: Local police.** (Kremnická 54, 284 01, ☎327 515 808 or ☎156.)

- **RESCUE SERVICE: Rescue and emergency service Kutná Hora.** (Vojtěšská 687, 284 01, ☎155 or ☎327 514 033.)

Getting There

This may seem weird, but Kutná Hora is best reached by bus and best left by train (just trust us on this—buses arrive closer to the center, but they stop running earlier in the day). Buses to Kutná Hora leave infrequently from **Florenc** bus station. (Metro B, C. Ⓢ 166Kč. 🕑 1½hr.) For a full day in Kutná Hora, it's best to be at Florenc before 10am. A visit to Kutná Hora takes about 5hr., not including travel. From the bus station in Kutná Hora, it's a short walk uphill to Palackého náměstí. To reach the Bone Church, take a local bus to **Sedlec** from the bus station. (Bus stop 1B. *i* Take bus #1 M-F, bus #7 Sa-Su. Ⓢ 12Kč. 🕑 15min.) The **train station** is a 10min. walk from the Bone Church. (www. jizdnirady.idnes.cz Ⓢ 194Kč. 🕑 55min., every 2hr.)

Essentials

You don't have to be a rocket scientist to plan a good trip. (It might help, but it's not required.) You do, however, need to be well prepared, and that's what we can do for you. Essentials is the chapter that gives you all the nitty-gritty you need to know for your trip: the hard information gleaned from 50 years of collective wisdom and several months of furious fact-checking. Passports? Check. Where to find Wi-Fi? Check. The dirt on public transportation? Check. We've also thrown in communications info, safety tips, and a phrasebook, just for good measure. Plus, for overall trip-planning advice, from what to pack (money and as little underwear as possible) to how to take a good passport photo (it's physically impossible; consider airbrushing), you can also check out the Essentials section of www.letsgo.com.

So, flip through this chapter before you leave so you know what documents to bring, while you're on the plane so you know how you'll be getting from the airport to your accommodation, and when you're on the ground so you can find a laundromat when you run out of underwear. This chapter may not be the most scintillating, but it just might save your life.

RED TAPE

Documents and Formalities

We're going to fill you in on visas and residence permits, but don't forget the most important ID of all: your **passport.** We repeat: don't forget your passport!

Entrance Requirements

- **PASSPORT:** Required for all non-EU travelers and must be valid for at least 90 days after the end of your stay.
- **VISA:** Required for citizens of Australia, Canada, New Zealand, or the US who plan to stay 90 days or more.
- **WORK PERMIT:** Required for all foreigners planning to work in the Czech Republic.

Visas

Those lucky enough to be EU citizens do not need a visa to travel through the Czech Republic. Citizens of Australia, Canada, New Zealand, the US, and other non-EU countries do not need a visa for stays of up to 90 days, but this three-month period begins upon entry into any of the countries that belong to the EU's **freedom of movement** zone. For more information, see **One Europe.** Those staying longer than 90 days may apply for a long-term visa; consult an embassy or consulate for more information. Double-check entrance requirements at the nearest Czech embassy or consulate for up-to-date information before departure. US citizens can also consult **http://travel.state. gov.** Studying in the Czech Republic requires a special visa. Entry into the Czech Republic as a traveler does not include the right to work, which is authorized only by a **work permit.** For more information on student visas and work permits, see **Beyond Tourism.**

One Europe

The EU's policy of **freedom of movement** means that most border controls have been abolished and visa policies harmonized. Under this treaty, formally known as the Schengen Agreement, you're still required to carry a passport (or government-issued ID card for EU citizens) when crossing an internal border, but, once you've been admitted into one country, you're free to travel to other participating states. Most EU states (the UK is a notable exception) are already members of Schengen, as are Iceland and Norway.

In recent times, debate over immigration has led to calls for suspension of the freedom of movement policy. Border controls are being strengthened, but this shouldn't affect casual travelers.

Embassies and Consulates

At Home

- **CZECH EMBASSY IN AUSTRALIA:** 8 Culgoa Circuit, O'Malley, Canberra, ACT 2606 ☎+61 2 6290 1386; www.mzv.cz/canberra

- **CZECH EMBASSY IN CANADA:** 251 Cooper St., Ottawa, ON K2P 0G2 ☎+1-613-562-3875; www.mzv.cz/ottawa/en/index.html ☒ Open M-Th 8am-5pm, F 8am-2:30pm.

- **CZECH EMBASSY IN IRELAND:** 57 Northumberland Rd., Ballsbridge, Dublin ☎+353 16 68 11 35; www.mzv.cz/dublin ☒ Open Tu 9:30-noon and 1:30-4pm, Th 9:30-noon, 1:30-4pm.

- **CZECH CONSULATE IN NEW ZEALAND:** Level 1, 110 Customs St. W, Auckland P.O. Box 106-740 1010 auckland@honorary.mvz.cz

- **CZECH EMBASSY IN UK:** 26-30 Kensington Palace Gardens, London, W8 4QY ☎+44 20 7243 1115; www.mzv.cz/london ☒ Open by appointment only.

Essentials

- **CZECH EMBASSY IN US:** 3900 Spring of Freedom St. NW, Washington, D.C. 20008 ☎+1-202-274-9100; www.mzv.cz/washington ⏰ Open M-Th 9am-5pm; F 9am-3:30pm.

In Prague

- **AUSTRALIAN CONSULATE:** Solitaire Building, 6th fl. Klimentská ul. 10 ☎221 729 260; www.dfat.gov.au/missions/countries/cz.html ⏰ Open M-Th 8:30am-5pm, F 8:30am-2pm.

- **CANADIAN EMBASSY:** Muchova 240/6 ☎272 101 800; www.czechrepublic.gc.ca ⏰ Open M-F 8:30am-12:30pm and 1:30-4:30pm. Consular office open M-F 8:20am-12:30pm.

- **IRISH EMBASSY:** Tržiště 13 ☎257 530 061; www.embassyofireland.cz/home ⏰ Open M-F 9:30am-12:30pm and 2:30-4:30pm.

- **NEW ZEALAND CONSULATE:** Dykova 19 ☎222 514 672; egermayer@nzconsul.cz ⏰ Open M-Th 9:30am-1pm and 2-5:30pm.

- **UK EMBASSY:** Thunovská 14 ☎257 402 370; www.ukinczechrepublic.fco.gov.uk ⏰ Open M-F 8:30am-5pm.

- **US EMBASSY:** Tržiště 15 ☎257 022 000; http://prague.usembassy.gov ⏰ Open M-Th 1-4pm.

MONEY

Getting Money from Home

Stuff happens. When stuff happens, you might need some money. When you need some money, the easiest and cheapest solution is to have someone back home make a deposit to your bank account. Otherwise, consider one of the following options.

Wiring Money

Arranging a **bank money transfer** means asking a bank back home to wire money to a bank in Prague. This is the cheapest way to transfer cash, but it's also the slowest and most agonizing, usually taking several days or more. Note that some banks may only release your funds in local currency, potentially sticking you with a poor exchange rate; inquire about this in advance.

Money transfer services like **Western Union** are faster and more convenient than bank transfers—but also much pricier. Western Union has many locations worldwide. To find one, visit www.westernunion.com or call: in Australia }1800 173 833, in Canada }800-235-0000, in the UK }0808 234 9168, in the US }800-325-6000, or in the Czech Republic }0224 948 252. Money transfer services are also available to **American Express** cardholders and at selected **Thomas Cook** offices.

US State Department (US Citizens Only)

In serious emergencies only, the US State Department will help your family or friends forward money within hours to the nearest consular office, which will then disburse it according to instructions for a US$30 fee. If you wish to use this service, you must contact the **Overseas Citizens Services** division of the US State Department (☎+1-202-501-4444, from US 888-407-4747).

Withdrawing Money

To use a debit or credit card to withdraw money from a **cash machine** (ATM) in Europe, you must have a four-digit Personal Identification Number (PIN). If your PIN is longer than four digits, ask your bank whether you can just use the first four or whether you'll need a new one. Credit cards don't usually come with PINs, so if you intend to hit up ATMs in Europe with a credit card, call your credit card company before leaving to request one.

ATMs aren't difficult to locate in Prague. Exchange rates and fees vary. Check with your bank before leaving to determine how they will be charging you for conversion from your home currency into Czech **korunas.**

Tipping and Bargaining

Like most European cities, Prague's policy on tipping is pretty relaxed: most locals will just round up. Aim for around **5-10%** if you're satisfied with your service. Touristy restaurants in the center of town will expect a 15-20% tip, but it's best to avoid those places anyway. Bargaining is only done in open-air markets or antique shops.

Taxes

Many goods in Prague are subject to a **value-added tax** (VAT) which can be refunded to non-EU citizens. In order to qualify for a refund, a traveler must have spend over 2000Kč in one shop, and the shop must carry a tax-free shopping logo. To collect your refund, ask the cashier for a receipt and a tax refund form, to be validated at the border or at the airport by the Czech Customs Office. If you travel by train you must ask for a Customs officer. Finally, in order to qualify, the purchased goods must leave the country within three months after the purchase date.

GETTING THERE

By Plane

Ruzyně Airport (☎220 111 888; www.prg.aero) is some 10km west of the city center. The cheapest way to get to the center is to take bus **#119** to Ⓜ Dejvická (Ⓢ 26Kč. ☒ 24min.) or **#110** to Ⓜ Zličín (Ⓢ 26Kč. ☒ 18min.) and then change to the Metro. **Airport Express** buses go directly to the main train station. (Hlavní nádraží. Ⓢ 50Kč. ☒ 35min., every 30min. 6:30am-10pm.) **Student Agency** goes to Florenc bus station. (☎841 101 101; www.studentagency.cz Ⓢ 60Kč. ☒ Every hr. 6am-9pm.)

By Train

Prague has three major train stations: the main one is **Hlavní nádraží** in Prague 2; the others are **Smíchovské nádraží** in Smíchov and **Nádraží Holešovice** in Holešovice. Trains are operated by **Česká Doprava** (☎840 112 113; www.cd.cz). International destinations include: Berlin, DEU (Ⓢ 1425Kč. ☒ 5hr., 8 per day.); Bratislava, SLK (Ⓢ 643Kč. ☒ 4hr., 8 per day.);

Budapest, HUN (**ⓢ** 1430Kč. 🕐 7hr., 6 per day.); Krakow, POL (**ⓢ** 1025Kč. 🕐 8hr., 3 per day.); Moscow, RUS (**ⓢ** 3628Kč. 🕐 33hr., 1 per day.); Munich, DEU (**ⓢ** 1385Kč. 🕐 6hr., 4 per day.); Vienna, AUS (**ⓢ** 1010Kč. 🕐 5hr., 8 per day.); Warsaw, POL. (**ⓢ** 1300Kč. 🕐 9-12hr., 3 per day.)

By Bus

Florenc ÚAN (☎900 144 444) is Prague's main bus terminal. To search bus schedules, visit www.jizdnirady.idnes.cz/autobusy/spojeni. **Eurolines** (☎245 005 245; www.eurolines.cz) runs international buses to some 20 European countries and a few domestic destinations. **Student Agency** (☎841 101 101; www.studentagency.cz) runs domestic and international buses with discounted prices for ISIC holders and travelers under 26.

GETTING AROUND

By Public Transportation

Prague's tram system alone could sufficiently serve this pocket-sized city, but Prague also has a Metro, a bus system, a horde of taxis, a funicular, and some ferries. **Dopravní Podnik Prahy** (☎296 191 817; www.dpp.cz) runs the public transportation system. Tickets can be used for trams, the Metro, buses, the funicular, and some ferries. The **limited ticket** (18Kč) is valid for 20min. or five metro stations, while the **basic ticket** (26Kč) is valid for 75min. and unlimited transfers. One-, three-, and five-day tickets are also available (100/330/500Kč), while a **monthly pass** (670Kč) can be purchased only at certain DPP centers. Tickets are available at ticket machines and convenience stores, and must be validated when you enter a vehicle or the Metro platform; unstamped tickets are not valid. **Ticket inspections** are more frequent in the Metro than on trams and buses; the fine for not having a validated ticket is 800Kč. There are three metro lines (A is green, B is yellow, C is

Walk It Out

Let's Go recommends **walking.** It's healthy. Plus, Prague is small enough to be conquered on foot.

Essentials

red); they run Monday through Thursday from 5am to midnight, Friday and Saturday from 5am to 1am, and Sunday from 5am to midnight. Aside from walking, trams are probably the best way to get around the city. **Tram #22** connects some of the most important parts of Prague. Travelers should beware of pickpockets on crowded vehicles. It is customary to let seniors sit in your seat if there are no empty seats. Locals are nearly silent on public transportation—don't make an ass of yourself.

PRACTICALITIES

For all the hostels, cafes, museums, and bars we list, some of the most important places you'll visit during your trip may be more mundane. Whether it's a tourist office, internet cafe, or post office, these practicalities are vital to a successful trip, and you'll find all you need right here.

- **TOURIST OFFICES: Prague Information Service.** (Staroměstské náměstí 1 ☎221 714 444; www.praguewelcome.cz ⚓ On the ground floor of Old Town Hall, to the left of the Astronomical Clock. ⏰ Open daily Apr-Oct 9am-8pm; Nov-Mar 9am-7pm.) Other branches: Rytířská 31, Malostranská mostecká věž (Malá Strana Bridge Tower), Hlavní nádraží (main train station), and Letiště Praha Ruzyně (Prague airport, terminal 2).

- **TOURS: New Europe Tours** offers free tours of the city center. (www.newpraguetours.com ⚓ Tours depart the Starbucks in Old Town Sq. ⏰ 3hr.; 11am, 2pm.) **Prague Royal Walk** (www.discover-prague.com *i* Offers walking tours of the city center. Ⓢ Free. ⏰ 2½hr.; 11am, 2pm.)

- **LUGGAGE STORAGE:** At the **main train station** (Hlavní nádraží) in either self-service lockers (☎777 082 226 *i* Max. 24hr. Ⓢ 60-90Kč per day ⏰ Open daily 3:10am-12:50am) or in the storage room. (*i* Max. 30 days. Ⓢ 60-100Kč per day ⏰ Open daily 6am-11pm.) **Florenc bus station.** (Ⓢ 35Kč per day. ⏰ Open daily 5am-midnight.)

- **INTERNET CAFES:** Many cafes and restaurants offer free Wi-Fi. Computer use in internet cafes usually costs around 60Kč per hr. **Bohemia Bagel.** (Masná 2 ☎224 812 560 Ⓢ Internet 2Kč per min. ⏰ Open daily 8am-9:30pm.)

Emergency

Hopefully, you'll never need any of these things, but if you do, it's best to be prepared.

- **EMERGENCY NUMBERS:** ☎112 (operators speak Czech, English, and German). **Medical Emergencies:** ☎155. **Fire:** ☎150.

- **PHARMACIES: Lékárna Palackého.** (Palackého 5 ☎224 946 982 ⚕ Ⓜ Můstek. Ⓩ Open 24hr.) **Lékárna u Svaté Ludmily.** (Belgická 37 ☎222 519 731 ⚕ Ⓜ Náměstí Míru. Ⓩ Open 24hr.)

- **MEDICAL SERVICES: Na Homolce.** (Roentgenova 2 ☎257 272 144; www.homolka.cz. ⚕ Tram 22 or 36: Vypich. Ⓩ Emergency room open 24hr. Foreign department open M-F 7:30am-4:30pm, but foreigners can get help any time.) **Doctor Health Centre Prague.** (Vodičkova 28 ☎603 433 833; www.doctor-prague.cz ⚕ Ⓜ Můstek. Ⓩ Open M-F 8am-4:30pm. Hotline 24hr.)

- **POST OFFICE:** Jindřišská 14. ☎221 131 111; www.ceska-posta.cz. ⚕ Ⓜ Můstek. Ⓩ Open daily 7:30am-8pm.

- **POSTAL CODE:** 110 00.

SAFETY AND HEALTH

General Advice

In any type of crisis, the most important thing to do is **stay calm.** Your country's embassy abroad is usually your best resource in an emergency; registering with that embassy upon arrival in the country is a good idea. The government offices listed in **Travel Advisories** can provide information on the services they offer their citizens in case of emergencies abroad.

Local Laws and Police

Local police are usually a visible presence in Prague, though they may be unhelpful in situations of currency exchange scams; for this you should contact your local embassy or consulate.

Travel Advisories

The following government offices provide travel information and advisories:

- **AUSTRALIA: Department of Foreign Affairs and Trade.** (☎+61 2 6261 1111; www.smartraveller.gov.au)
- **CANADA: Department of Foreign Affairs and International Trade** Call or visit the website for the free booklet *Bon Voyage, But...* (☎+1-800-267-6788; www.international.gc.ca)
- **NEW ZEALAND: Ministry of Foreign Affairs and Trade.** (☎+64 4 439 8000; www.safetravel.govt.nz)
- **UK: Foreign and Commonwealth Office.** (☎+44 845 850 2829; www.fco.gov.uk)
- **US: Department of State.** (from the US ☎888-407-4747; outside the US +1-202-501-4444; www.travel.state.gov)

Drugs and Alcohol

Authorities are beginning to crack down on drinking in the open in Prague, so avoid public drunkenness; it will jeopardize your safety and earn you the disdain of locals. The **drinking age** in Prague is 18. Recreational drugs like marijuana are illegal and best avoided altogether, though possession of small amounts has been decriminalized. Embassies may be unwilling to help those arrested on drug charges.

Specific Concerns

Petty Crime and Scams

Scams and petty theft are unfortunately common in Prague. An especially common scam in bars and nightclubs involves a local woman inviting a traveler to buy her drinks, which end up costing exorbitant prices; the proprietors of the establishment (in cahoots with the scam artist) may then use force to ensure that the bill is paid. Travelers should always check the prices of drinks before ordering. Another common scam involves a team of con artists posing as metro clerks and demanding that you pay large fines because your ticket is invalid. Credit card fraud is also common Eastern Europe. Travelers who have lost credit cards or fear that the security of their accounts has been compromised should contact their credit card companies immediately.

Con artists often work in groups and may involve children. Beware of certain classics: sob stories that require money, rolls of bills "found" on the street, mustard spilled (or saliva spit) onto your shoulder to distract you while they snatch your bag. **Never let your passport or your bags out of your sight.** Hostel workers will sometimes stand at bus and train arrival points to recruit tired and disoriented travelers to their hostel; never believe strangers who tell you that theirs is the only hostel open. Beware of **pickpockets** in large crowds, especially on public transportation.

Visitors to Prague should never enter a taxicab containing anyone in addition to the driver and should never split rides with strangers. While traveling by train, it may be preferable to travel in cheaper "cattle-car" type seating arrangements; the large number of witnesses makes such carriages safer than seating in individual compartments. Travelers should avoid riding on night buses or trains, where the risk of robbery or assault is particularly high. *Let's Go* discourages hitchhiking and picking up hitchhikers.

Pre-Departure Health

Matching a prescription to a foreign equivalent is not always easy, safe, or possible, so if you take **prescription drugs,** carry up-to-date prescriptions or a statement from your doctor stating the medications' trade names, manufacturers, chemical names, and dosages. Be sure to keep all medication with you in your carry-on luggage. It is also a good idea to look up the Czech names of drugs you may need during your trip.

Immunizations and Precautions

Travelers over two years old should make sure that the following vaccines are up to date: MMR (for measles, mumps, and rubella); DTaP or Td (for diphtheria, tetanus, and pertussis); IPV (for polio); Hib (for *Haemophilus influenzae* B); and HepB (for Hepatitis B). For recommendations on immunizations and prophylaxis, check with a doctor and consult the **Centers for Disease Control and Prevention (CDC)** in the US (☎+1-800-232-4636; www.cdc. gov/travel) or the equivalent in your home country.

Essentials

KEEPING IN TOUCH

By Email and Internet

Hello and welcome to the 21st century, where you're rarely more than a 5min. walk from the nearest **Wi-Fi hot spot,** even if sometimes you'll have to pay a few bucks or buy a drink for the privilege of using it. **Internet cafes** and free internet terminals are listed in **Practicalities**. For lists of additional cybercafes in Prague, check out **www.hotspot-locations.com.**

Wireless hot spots make internet access possible in public and remote places. Unfortunately, they also pose security risks. Hot spots are open, public networks that use unencrypted, insecure connections. They are susceptible to hacks and "packet sniffing"—the theft of passwords and other private information. To prevent these breaches, disable "ad hoc" mode, turn off file sharing and network discovery, encrypt your email, turn on your firewall, beware of phony networks, and watch for over-the-shoulder creeps.

By Telephone

Calling Home from Prague

If you have internet access, your best—i.e., cheapest, most convenient, and most tech-savvy—means of calling home is probably our good friend **Skype** (www.skype.com). You can even videochat if you have a webcam. Calls to other Skype users are free; calls to landlines and mobiles worldwide start at US$0.023 per minute, depending on where you're calling.

For those still stuck in the 20th century, **prepaid phone cards** are a common and relatively inexpensive means of calling abroad. Each one comes with a Personal Identification Number (PIN) and a toll-free access number. You call the access number and then follow the directions for dialing your PIN. To purchase prepaid phone cards, check online for the best rates; **www.call-ingcards.com** is a good place to start. Online providers generally send your access number and PIN via email, with no actual "card" involved. You can also call home with prepaid phone cards purchased in Prague.

Another option is a **calling card,** linked to a major national telecommunications service in your home country. Calls are billed collect or to your account. Cards generally come with instructions for dialing both domestically and internationally.

Placing a **collect call** through an international operator can be expensive but may be necessary in case of an emergency. You can frequently call collect without even possessing a company's calling card just by calling its access number and following the instructions.

Cellular Phones

The international standard for cell phones is **Global System for Mobile Communication (GSM).** To make and receive calls in the Czech Republic you will need a GSM-compatible phone and a **SIM (Subscriber Identity Module) card,** a country-specific, thumbnail-size chip that gives you a local phone number and plugs you into the local network. Many SIM cards are prepaid, and incoming calls are frequently free. You can buy additional cards or vouchers (usually available at convenience stores) to "top up" your phone. For more information on GSM phones, check out **www.telestial.com.** Companies like **Cellular Abroad** (www.cellularabroad.com) and **OneSimCard** (www.onesimcard.com) rent cell phones and SIM cards that work in destinations around the world.

International Calls

To call the Czech Republic from home or to call home from the Czech Republic, dial:

- **THE INTERNATIONAL DIALING PREFIX.** To call from the Czech Republic, dial ☎00, from **Australia,** ☎0011; **Canada** or the **US,** ☎011; and from **Ireland, New Zealand,** or the **UK,** ☎00.

- **THE COUNTRY CODE OF THE COUNTRY YOU WANT TO CALL.** To call the Czech Republic, dial ☎420; for **Australia,** ☎61; **Canada** or the **US,** ☎1; **Ireland,** ☎353; **New Zealand,** ☎64; and for the **UK,** ☎44.

- **THE LOCAL NUMBER.** If the area code begins with a zero, you can omit that number when dialing from abroad.

By Snail Mail

Sending Mail Home from Prague

Airmail is the best way to send mail home from Prague. Write "airmail," *"par avion,"* or *"letecká pošta"* on the front. For simple letters or postcards, airmail tends to be surprisingly cheap, but the price will go up sharply for weighty packages. Surface mail is by far the cheapest, slowest, and most antiquated way to send mail. It takes one to two months to cross the Atlantic and one to three to cross the Pacific—good for heavy items you won't need for a while, like souvenirs that you've acquired along the way.

Receiving Mail in Prague

There are several ways to receive mail in Prague, even if you do not have an address of your own. Mail can be sent via **Poste Restante** (General Delivery) to Prague and it is pretty reliable. Address Poste Restante letters like so:

> Václav Havel
> Poste Restante
> Prague, Czech Republic 110 00

The mail will go to a special desk in the central post office at **Jindřišská 14, Prague 1,** unless you specify a local post office by street address or postal code. It's best to use the largest post office, since mail may be sent there regardless. Bring your passport (or other photo ID) for pickup; there may be a small fee. If the clerks insist that there is nothing for you, ask them to check under your first name as well. It's usually safer and quicker, though more expensive, to send mail express or registered. If you don't want to deal with Poste Restante, consider asking your hostel or accommodation if you can have things mailed to you there. Of course, if you have your own mailing address or a reliable friend to receive mail for you, that may be the easiest solution.

TIME DIFFERENCES

Prague is 1hr. ahead of Greenwich Mean Time (GMT) and observes Daylight Saving Time. This means that it is 9hr. ahead of Los Angeles, 6hr. ahead of New York City, 1hr. ahead of the British Isles, 8hr. behind Sydney, and 10hr. behind New Zealand.

CLIMATE

Prague's climate could be called diverse, if we were writing a college brochure. Since we aren't, we'll just say that it has pretty hot summers and freaking cold winters.

MONTH	AVG. HIGH TEMP.		AVG. LOW TEMP.		AVG. RAINFALL		AVG. NUMBER OF WET DAYS
January	0°C	32°F	-5°C	23°F	18mm	0.7 in.	13
February	1°C	34°F	-4°C	25°F	18mm	0.7 in.	11
March	7°C	45°F	-1°C	30°F	18mm	0.7 in.	10
April	12°C	54°F	3°C	37°F	27mm	1.1 in.	11
May	18°C	64°F	8°C	46°F	48mm	1.9 in.	13
June	21°C	70°F	11°C	52°F	54mm	2.1 in.	12
July	23°C	73°F	13°C	55°F	68mm	2.7 in.	13
August	22°C	72°F	13°C	55°F	55mm	2.2 in.	12
September	18°C	64°F	9°C	48°F	31mm	1.2 in.	10
October	12°C	54°F	5°C	41°F	33mm	1.3 in.	13
November	5°C	41°F	1°C	34°F	20mm	0.8 in.	12
December	1°C	34°F	-3°C	26°F	21mm	0.8 in.	13

To convert from degrees Fahrenheit to degrees Celsius, subtract 32 and multiply by 5/9. To convert from Celsius to Fahrenheit, multiply by 9/5 and add 32. The mathematically challenged may use this handy chart:

°CELSIUS	-5	0	5	10	15	20	25	30	35	40
°FAHRENHEIT	23	32	41	50	59	68	77	86	95	104

MEASUREMENTS

Like the rest of the rational world, the Czech Republic uses the metric system. The basic unit of length is the meter (m), which is divided into 100 centimeters (cm) or 1000 millimeters (mm). One thousand meters make up one kilometer (km). Fluids are measured in liters (L), each divided into 1000 milliliters (mL). A liter of pure water weighs one kilogram (kg), the unit of mass that is divided into 1000 grams (g). One metric ton is 1000kg.

MEASUREMENT CONVERSIONS	
1 inch (in.) = 25.4mm	1 millimeter (mm) = 0.039 in.
1 foot (ft.) = 0.305m	1 meter (m) = 3.28 ft.
1 yard (yd.) = 0.914m	1 meter (m) = 1.094 yd.
1 mile (mi.) = 1.609km	1 kilometer (km) = 0.621 mi.
1 ounce (oz.) = 28.35g	1 gram (g) = 0.035 oz.
1 pound (lb.) = 0.454kg	1 kilogram (kg) = 2.205 lb.
1 fluid ounce (fl. oz.) = 29.57mL	1 milliliter (mL) = 0.034 fl. oz.
1 gallon (gal.) = 3.785L	1 liter (L) = 0.264 gal.

LANGUAGE

Cha-cha-cha-czech It Out

Cut from the same cloth as many Slavic languages (though thankfully severing the ties to the Cyrilic alphabet), **Czech** (Česky) is the official language of the Czech Republic and you will likely encounter it on your journey to Prague. Elementary Czech could take years of practice, but don't despair—a basic understanding of the pronunciation, some beginners' phrases, and a healthy dose of courage will get you from A to B.

Pronunciation

There are no two ways about it: Czech pronunciation is tough for the average English speaker. If a word appears vowel-less, try not to panic. In Czech, the stress falls on the first syllable, though an accent (á, é, í, ó, or ú) lengthens a vowel. The table below covers the basics of Czech pronunciation.

PHONETIC UNIT	PRONUNCIATION	PHONETIC UNIT	PRONUNCIATION
c	TS, as in "gets"	ř	ZH, close to the -ge sound in "luggage"
ě	YE, close to "yet"	w	V, as in "very" or "Vaclav"
j	Y, as in "young"	Milan Kundera; Václav Havel	MEE-lahn KOON-dehr-ah; VAHTS-lahv HAH-vel

Phrasebook

ENGLISH	CZECH	PRONUNCIATION
Hello	Dobrý den (formal)	DOH-bree dehn
Yes/No	Ano/ne	AH-noh/neh
Please	Prosím	PROH-seem
Thank You	Děkuji	DYEH-koo-yee
Goodbye	Nashledanou	NAS-kleh-dah-noh
Good morning	Dobré ráno	DOH-breh RAH-noh
Good evening	Dobrý večer	DOH-breh VEH-chehr
Good night	Dobrou noc	DOH-broh NOHTS
Sorry/excuse me	Promiňte	PROH-meen-teh

Do you speak English?	Mluvíte anglicky?	MLOO-veet-eh ahng-GLEET-skee
I don't speak Czech.	Nemluvím Česky.	NEH-mloo-veem CHESS-kee
I don't understand.	Nerozumím.	NEH-rohz-oo-meem
Please write it down.	Prosím, napište to dolů.	PROH-seem nah-PEESH-teh toh dohl-oo
When?	Kdy?	gdee

TRAVELING		
Where is...?	Kde je...?	gdeh yeh
...the bathroom?	...koupelna?	KOH-pehl-nah
...the nearest telephone booth?	...nejbližší telefonní budka?	NEY-bleezh-shee TEH-leh-foh-nee BOOT-kah
...the center of town?	...v centru města?	VTSEN-troo MYEHST-stah
toilet	W.C.	VEE-TSEE
left	vlevo	VLEH-voh
right	vpravo	VPRAH-voh
straight ahead	přímo	PRZHEE-moh
Do you have a room?	Máte pokoj?	MAH-teh POH-koy
I'd like a room.	Chtěl bych pokoj.	khtyel bikh PO-koy
single room	jednolůžkový pokoj	YEHD-noh-loozh-koh-vee POH-koy
double room	dvoulůžkový pokoj	DVOH-loozh-ko-vee POH-koy
reservation	rezervace	REH-zer-vah-tseh
luggage	zavadla	ZAH-vahd-lah
station	nádraží	NAH-drah-zhee
train	vlak	vlahk
bus	autobus	OW-toh-boos
bus station	autobusové nádraže	OW-toh-boo-sohv-eh NAH-drazh-eh
airport	letiště	LEH-teesh-tyeh
I want a ticket to...	Chtěl bych jízdenku do...	khtyel bikh YEEZ-den-koo DOH
ticket	lístek	LEES-tek
round-trip	zpáteční	SPAH-tehch-nyee
one-way	jednosměrný	YED-noh SMNYER-nee
How much does this cost?	Kolik to stojí?	KOH-leek toh STOH-yee
How long does the trip take?	Jak dlouho trvá cesta se?	yahk DLOH-ho tra-VAH TSE-stah seh
departure	odjezd	OHD-yehzd
arrival	příjezd	PZHEE-yehzd
square	náměstí	NAH-myeh-stee
passport	cestovní pas	TSEH-stohv-nee pahs
bank	banka	BAHN-kah
currency exchange	směnárna	smyeh-NAHR-nah
post office	pošta	POSH-tah
stamp	známka	ZNAHM-kah
airmail	letecky	LEH-tehts-kee

Essentials

DAYS OF THE WEEK		
Monday	pondělí	POHN-dyeh-lee
Tuesday	úterý	OO-teh-ree
Wednesday	středa	STRZHEH-dah
Thursday	čtvrtek	CHTVER-tehk
Friday	pátek	PAH-tehk
Saturday	sobota	SOH-boh-tah
Sunday	neděle	NEH-dyeh-leh
today	dnes	dnehs
tomorrow	zítra	ZEE-trah
day	den	dehn
week	týden	tee-dehn
morning	ráno	RAH-noh
afternoon	odpoledne	OHD-pohl-ehd-neh
evening	večer	VEH-chehr

OUT TO LUNCH		
breakfast	snídaně	SNEE-dahn-yeh
lunch	oběd	OHB-yed
dinner	večeře	VEH-cher-zheh
market	trh	terh
grocery	potraviny	POH-trah-vee-nee
menu	menu	meh-noo
I would like...	Chtěl bych	khtyel bikh
bread	chléb	khlep
vegetables	zelenina	ZEH-leh-nee-nah
meat	maso	MAH-soh
coffee	káva	KAH-vah
milk	mléko	MLEH-koh
hot	horký	HOR-kee
cold	studený	STOO-deh-nee
beer	pivo	PEE-voh
Cheers!	Na zdraví!	nahz-DRAH-vee
I don't eat...	Nejím...	NEH-yeem
I'm allergic.	Jsem alergický.	ysehm AH-lehr-gits-kee
Check, please.	Paragon, prosím.	PAH-rah-gohn proh-SEEM

EMERGENCY		
Help!	Pomoc!	POH-mots
Please leave.	Prosím odejděte.	pro-SEEM ODEH-dyeh-teh
police	policie	POH-leets-ee-yeh
doctor	doktor	DOHK-tohr
hospital	nemocnice	NEH-mots-nee-tseh

THE UNIVERSAL LANGUAGE		
I love you.	Mám tě rád	MAHM tyeh RAHD

CARDINAL NUMBERS		
one	jedna	YEHD-na
two	dva	dvah
three	tři	trzhee
four	čtyři	CHTEER-zhee
five	pět	pyet
six	šest	shest
seven	sedm	SEH-dom
eight	osm	OH-suhm
nine	devět	DE-vyet
ten	deset	DE-set

Let's Go Online

Plan your next trip on our spiffy website, **www.letsgo.com.**
It features full book content, the latest travel info on your
favorite destinations, and tons of interactive features: make
your own itinerary, read blogs from our trusty Researcher-
Writers, browse our photo library, watch exclusive videos,
check out our newsletter, find travel deals, follow us on
Facebook, and buy new guides. Plus, if this Essentials wasn't
enough for you, we've got even more online. We're always
updating and adding new features, so check back often!

Prague 101

Many visitors come to Prague for two things: the architecture and the beer. But there's more to Prague than cheap pints of Pilsner and ancient castles and cathedrals. There's a huge student culture, contemporary art, a well-established music scene, and enough history to satisfy even your dweebiest of travel companions. Invaded by Catholics, communists, and crowds of tourists, Prague has been through a lot and it shows. But neither the heavy history (Soviets, anyone?) nor the heavy food has been enough to weigh down the artists, the revolutionaries, and the musicians who make this city one to Czech out.

Facts and Figures

- **LONGEST CONSTRUCTION TIME ON A SINGLE BUILD-ING:** 585 years on St. Vitus Cathedral.

- **MOST MUSICAL FOUNTAIN:** the Singing Fountain's water drops onto a bronze plate. Squat below the basin to take a listen.

- **NUMBER OF NEW TREES PLANTED IN PRAGUE IN UNDER FOUR YEARS:** 555,000

- **PINTS OF BEER CONSUMED PER PERSON PER YEAR:** 287

- **NUMBER OF SURVEILLANCE CAMERAS IN THE CITY TO CATCH THOSE NASTY PICKPOCKETS:** 550

- **MOST EXPENSIVE VIOLIN IN PRAGUE (OR EVER):** $27,000

HISTORY

From Spade to Trade (500 BCE-1300 CE)

Prague might not technically be the "mother of cities," as the nickname goes, but it certainly has been around long enough. The Celts settled the **Vltava River** basin around 200 BCE, but legend has it that the city was actually founded in the eighth century CE by a Slavic power couple named **Libuse and Přemysl.** This semi-mythical pair founded the Přemyslid dynasty, which ruled the city until 1306. The oldest evidence of the Přemyslids is **Prague Castle,** built on a hill overlooking the Vltava around 870. Prague soon became the seat of the Kings of Bohemia, a region of the Holy Roman Empire. The city kept growing thanks to the trade routes that crossed it. A busy market settlement turned into **Old Town** (Stare Město) on one side of the river, while the other bank saw **Lesser Town** (Malá Strana) grow out of the foot of Prague Castle.

Prague's big break came in the 14th century, when the Bohemian king and Holy Roman Emperor **Charles IV** made it his capital. His reign laid the foundations for **"New" Town** (Nové Město), the aptly named **Charles University** (the first of its kind in Central Europe), and a major bridge over the Vltava, which was then named—you guessed it—Charles.

Defenestration: The New Reformation (1402-1700)

Prague's prosperity was wounded by the viral Reformation bug spreading across Europe in 1402. The passionate sermons of scholar **Jan Hus** turned Czech parishioners against Catholicism, until the church fought back with fire...and burned Hus at the stake. In response, his followers took the whole "overthrow the Church" thing a bit literally and threw several city councilors out the window in the **First Defenestration** (spoiler: there's another one coming up).

Riding on popular sentiment, Prague and the rest of Bohemia became peacefully Protestant and remained so for the next 200 years. But the rise of the Catholic **Hapsburg Dynasty** to the head of the Holy Roman Empire brought new enemies to Protestantism. Returning to tried and true methods, Praguers sent the Catholic-friendly regents of Bohemia flying out the window in the **Second Defenestration** of 1618. Despite the effort, the Protestant Czechs fell to the Hapsburgs and saw Prague lose its prestige and status as a capital city. Smelling fresh blood (and closed windows), Saxons, Swedes, and two bouts of the plague all invaded Prague by the end of the 17th century.

Nationalism (1784-1945)

Perhaps tired of remembering four names for one city, Emperor Joseph II united Prague's four sections (Old, New, and Lesser Towns, and the Castle District) into a single provincial capital. Later, the Industrial Revolution brought Prague its first suburb, its first railway, and its first replica of the Eiffel Tower **(Petřín Lookout Tower)**. In 1848, workers and students took to the streets against their Austrian overlords. In the next decades, Prague fought off Imperialism with liberal politics and cultural cachet, creating the **National Theatre** (Národní divadlo), the **Czech Philharmonic,** and the **National Museum** (Národní muzeum). This Nationalism peaked when Prague became capital of the newly independent Czechoslovakia in 1918. Hungry for more land, the city gobbled up nearby neighborhoods and villages to become a metropolis just shy of one million inhabitants.

Nazi Germany cut this growth short, first by stripping land from Czechoslovakia in the **Munich Agreement** and then by invading the region and the city in 1939. Prague fought back hard. Czech assassins bombed and shot the Nazi Reichsprotektor

Reinhard Heydrich in 1942, and the national resistance, with the help of the Soviet Red Army, evicted the Germans and restored the fomer Czechoslovak president in the 1945 **Prague Uprising.**

Velvet Underground (1948-90)

Riding on popular support for the Soviet Union, the Communist Party came to power and imposed Stalinism in 1948. Economic troubles and student riots, however, pressured the party to adopt the more liberal **Prague Spring** reforms in 1968. Feeling threatened, the Soviet Union led Warsaw Pact countries in a military invasion. Despite the best efforts of city dwellers, who tore down street signs so that the invaders would get lost, Prague was dragged back to Moscow-friendly politics for another 20 years.

In 1989, democratic reformers faced off against the Communist apparatchiks in the **Velvet Revolution.** Half a million people held strikes and marched through Prague, giving Party leaders such a headache that they resigned before the end of the year.

You're Up, Europe (1990-today)

After Czechoslovakia split in 1993, Prague became the capital city of the Czech Republic (Slovakia had dibs on Bratislava). And while it increasingly embraces Western European culture, the city still remembers its history, building memorials to the victims of Communism (such as the one in Malá Strana). The international community honored the city's more distant past, making its medieval center a UNESCO World Heritage Site and later naming Prague a European City of Culture, four years before the Czechs joined the European Union in 2004.

CUSTOMS AND ETIQUETTE

Czechs aren't exactly known for their generous warmth toward foreigners, but you probably wouldn't be either if your city was a favorite of stag parties and tourists looking for cheap beer (yes, we're looking at you). Czechs tend to smile only when genuinely pleased, so don't be surprised at their indifference to your witticisms. Keep in mind that a serious demeanor is a show of respect. It's polite to say hello *(dobrý den)* and goodbye *(na shledanou)* to people you meet, even complete strangers. If you find yourself invited to someone's home, remember to remove your shoes.

Finally, shouting, drunkenly singing, or even just speaking to your friends on the subway or tram is a surefire way to identify yourself as a foreigner: you'll notice that natives are positively silent on their commutes.

Hospoda-Hopping

Pivo (beer) is basically a national treasure. Patrons are expected to sit next to strangers at the **hospoda** (pub). A standard drink is a half liter (16 oz.), which may, for some, require a couple weeks of preseason training. Always finish your beer, and never mix it with anything else, even the leftover beer from a previous drink. It's just rude. **Víno** (wine), on the other hand, is fine to dilute (in the summer try *strik*, a 50-50 mix of white wine and soda). In late summer and early fall, wine shops and pubs throughout the city peddle **burčák,** a partially fermented "young wine" that tastes something like adult Orangina and is best enjoyed in the out of doors. When you're out *hospoda*-hopping, remember that tips aren't expected, and neither is buying rounds for the table.

FOOD AND DRINK

Although Czech writer Pavel Eisner once described his country's food as "quite deleterious to the soul," Prague's heavy **meat and potatoes** diet is a good way to line your stomach for a night of *pivo.* For Czechs, *oběd* (lunch) is traditionally the main meal of the day. In urban Prague they're more likely to go for a quick fix of *klobása* (smoked sausage), from stands such as those that line Wenceslas Sq.

Variations on a Theme of Dumplings

Vepřo-knedlo-zelo, pork-dumpling-cabbage goes the refrain, and you'll easily find these Czech staples around the city. For those with carnivorous urges, menus are conveniently organized by category of meat. Pork, the most popular, comes in sausages, goulash, and, for the more adventurous, pig offal. As for vegetarians, the joke goes that there are two vegetarian options—green cabbage and red cabbage. Although somewhat of an exaggeration (there's often frozen spinach!), traditional non-meat dishes extend little beyond *salat* (salad), *smažený sýr* (fried cheese), and *bramboráky* (potato pancakes). Filling *knedlíky* (dumplings) come as side dishes or desserts, in an uninspiring set of flavors: potato, fruit, and yes, even bread. (If visions of pierogi or Chinese dumplings are dancing in your head, think again: these guys are more like matzah meal rolled into a loaf and sliced.)

Drinkin' Beerz, Beerz, Beerz

If you don't immediately take to Czech cuisine, fear not: almost everything tastes better with beer (or at least after you've had a few). Czechs are some of the world's heaviest beer drinkers, with each person knocking back five half liters in an average sitting, which computes to a stunning average of 287 pints per person per year. Even under Communist rule, beer was subsidized. The Czechs recognize only two types of beer: **světlé** (light) and **černé** (dark). Darker beers are rich and taste like cake. The local degree system tells you how much malt extract was used in brewing: the higher the degree, the more malt and the greater the alcohol content. Twelve-degree beer is about four- to five-percent alcohol, and most taverns serve 10- or 12-degree beer. The most common Czech beer is **Pilsner,** named after the town Plzen outside of Prague.

If beer is too tame for you, absinthe and clove-flavored **Becherovka** pack a heavier punch. And if you prefer to stay sober and watch your friends make fools of themselves, power through the night with Turkish coffee (hot water poured directly onto the grounds). Don't expect a to-go cup, though, because they don't exist. Only the silliest of tourists totes a $5 Starbucks through Old Town.

ARTS AND ARCHITECTURE

With museums and galleries galore and 2000 officially registered monuments it's hard to miss all the art and architecture in Prague. If it's Modern and contemporary art you're after, head to **Museum Kampa** or **DOX.** Even the National Gallery, preserver of all things historic, sponsors the **NG333 competition,** for the best and brightest in young Czech art. Perhaps the best—and certainly the cheapest—way to experience the history of Czech art and architecture is just to walk around and look up.

Building Excitement

Prague first became know for its **Romanesque** churches and monasteries, with huge rotundas, single-aisle churches, and triple-aisle basilicas. As the power of the Catholic Church rose higher, so did the religious buildings, with the twin spires of St. Vitus Cathedral eventually reaching 318 ft. (a big step in the 1300s!). The cathedral was heralded in the **High Gothic** period, which dressed up Charles University, several churches, and the entire New Town, and gave Prague Castle a 14th-century makeover.

The Hapsburgs brought the bigger-than-life **Baroque** trend, and the Czechs turned to bigger palaces, supersized church buildings, and gaudy interior design. Emperor Joseph II, an ardent Catholic, bulldozed old Protestant churches and buildings to make way for these projects. Meanwhile, Prague Castle was reconstructed (again).

Not content with just waging revolution and forming political parties, Czech Nationalism took up the Neo-Renaissance style in a construction boom that brought the National Theatre and other national treasures. In the 20th century, Czechs looked to Vienna to find the curves of the **Art Nouveau** movement. After WWII, Communism sadly squashed architectural innovation for its own bland brand of Socialist Realism. After the Velvet Revolution, Prague regained architectural freedom and did a celebratory jig in the form of the **Dancing House.**

MUSIC

Prague's music history dates back to the 19th-century Nationalist movement, when Czech composers did their part to help carve out a Czech identity. **Classical** music buffs should check out the **Prague Spring International Music Festival** (☎257 312 547; www.prague-spring.net), which brings some of the best European artists and conductors to the city each year.

Jazz aficionados will be happy to know that the Communists considered jazz a peaceful (read: non-rebellious) type of music and allowed its survival under their regime. These days, festivals like **Strings of Autumn** (}224 901 247; www.strunypodzimu.cz) let jazz artists jam alongside avant-garde and classical performers from around the world.

The city also has a soft spot for **hard rock.** Under Communism, censors blacklisted Frank Zappa's album *Absolutely Free.* That didn't stop smugglers from bringing the sounds of America to oppressed city dwellers, and Zappa quickly became the hottest thing to hit Prague since Nationalist drinking songs. When the Communist regime collapsed, president Vaclav Havel personally invited Zappa to Prague and even made him a "special ambassador." Although noise regulations have pushed most rock clubs out to the suburbs, you can still catch Zappa's legacy at places like **Rock Café** or **Bunkr Parukářka.**

HOLIDAYS AND FESTIVALS

Czechs are rather secular compared to other Europeans, but no one turns down an excuse to take the day off and take a swig—or several—of beer. Although public services and banks close on national holidays, restaurants and tourist attractions are usually open. Public transportation also runs on a limited schedule during some holidays and festivals.

HOLIDAY OR FESTIVAL	DESCRIPTION	DATE
New Year's Day and Czech Independence Day	The creation of the independent Czech Republic and an excuse to start the year off tipsy.	January 1
Masopust (Czech Mardi Gras)	Revelers pig out, cramming in as much booze, dance, and pork as they can before the start of Lent.	40 days before Ash Wednesday
Easter Monday	Chocolate, liquor, and whips—what could possibly go wrong?	late March or early April
May Day / Labor Day	Not feeling the anarcho-socialist vibe? Take your date to Petřín Hill for a traditional kiss instead.	May 1
Feast Day of St. Cyril and St. Methodius; Jan Hus Day	The unofficial start to summer means locals head out of the city to vacation.	July 5 and 6
Foundation of the Czechoslovak State	The most important secular holiday celebrates the creation of Czechoslovakia in 1918.	October 28
Christmas	Families start baking holiday cookies in mid-November but fast until dinner on Christmas Day. Some would call this a form of torture.	December 25

Beyond Tourism

If you are reading this, then you are a member of an elite group—and we don't mean "the literate." You're a student preparing for a semester abroad. You're taking a gap year to save the trees, the whales, or the dates. You're an 80-year-old woman who has devoted her life to egg-laying platypuses and what the hell is up with that. In short, you're a traveler, not a tourist; like any good spy, you don't just observe your surroundings—you become an active part of them.

Your mission, should you choose to accept it, is to study, volunteer, or work abroad as laid out in the dossier—er, chapter—below. We leave the rest (when to go, whom to bring, and how many changes of underwear to pack) in your hands. This message will Zself-destruct in five seconds. Good luck.

STUDYING

Between centuries-old Charles University, the newer Anglo-American University, and a variety of international programs, your biggest challenge will be choosing *where* to study. Those already fluent in the language can enroll directly with other Czech students in Prague's universities; if your Czech doesn't go much farther than politely ordering a Pilsner, there are plenty of language programs to bring you up to speed as well as a number of English-speaking study-abroad programs. Almost all programs provide accommodations, although not all are conveniently located to your classes. (Think waking up in Prague 12 for 9am Econ in Prague 2.)

Universities

Because few international students arrive in Prague with a background in Czech, most study-abroad programs are conducted in English. But if you dream of mingling with real live Czech students or even taking classes in Czech, don't despair: many programs allow you to cross-register at Charles and the Anglo-American University.

International Programs

American Insitute for Foreign Study (AIFS)

9 W. Broad St., Stamford, CT 06902, USA

☎+1-800-727-2437; www.aifsabroad.com

The AIFS Prague program is at the Collegium Carolinum (that's Charles University for those of you not fluent in Latin). The majority of courses cover Czech or Central European topics, with a particularly large literature selection. The program also includes local daytrips and excursions to Poland and Vienna.

▸ i Dorm housing, meal allowance, and airfare included. $ Semester $14,375-14,695 depending on USA departure city. 3-day excursions to Poland or Vienna $295.

Council on International Exchange (CIEE)

300 Fore St., Portland, ME 04101, USA

☎+1-207-553-4000; www.ciee.org

Dream of impressing a cute stranger by claiming to be a screenwriter or filmmaker? CIEE's program through the Prague Film and Television School of the Performing Arts (FAMU) let's students produce short films or write screenplays at one of Europe's oldest film schools (earning you extra points with the ladies/fellas for being a European-trained filmmaker no less).

▶ *i* Includes apartment or dormitory housing with CIEE participants and local students or a homestay. Meals not provided. Min. GPA 3.0. $ Semester $18,400.

Cultural Experiences Abroad (CEA)

2005 W. 14th St., Ste. 113, Tempe, AZ 85281, USA

☎+1-800-266-4441; www.gowithcea.com

If *"prominte, kde je toalety?"* ("excuse me, where is the bathroom?") is about as far as you get with Czech, then CEA's program at the Anglo-American University in Prague may be your perfect match. All courses are taught in English and students share apartments with other CEA participants. For those seeking more cultural immersion, CEA offers various volunteer and internship opportunities in the local community as well as numerous excursions within Central Europe.

▶ *i* Housing and excursions—but not meals—included. $ Semester $10,995, academic year $20,495; summer session $3,495-5,095 depending on course load.

Lexia International

4 W. Wheelock St., Ste. 8, Hanover, NH 03755, USA

☎+1-800-77-LEXIA; www.lexiaintl.org

Lexia's program with Charles University lets students engage in an independent research project. Other than intensive language courses, students are involved in seminars directly relating to their chosen topic. Frequent contact with professors means that your new drinking buddy could be a world-class expert on Czech literature.

▶ *i* Tuition includes room and board (either dorm or homestay). $ Semester $14,750; full year $25,550; summer $7250.

Czech Studies Programs

Is your most overused adjective "Kafkaesque"? Do your friends groan every time you drag them to yet another screening of *Closely Watched Trains*? Ditch them for a semester of Czech studies with other likeminded Czechophiles.

Visa Information

Travelers may spend up to 90 days total in any of the 25 Schengen countries (including the Czech Republic) without a visa. Those studying for a semester or longer will need a **student visa.** Apply through your local consulate. Student visas take at least 60 days to process, so it's a good idea to apply as soon as you've been accepted into a program. You will need two recent passport photographs, a valid passport (not a photocopy), a photocopy of the passport's data page (the one with your photo), a letter of acceptance from your study-abroad program, an affidavit confirming a clean criminal history, proof of income and accommodations in Prague and travel medical insurance, and a pre-paid, self-addressed envelope. Student visas cost $130. For the most update visa information, see the Czech embassy's webpage, www.mzv.cz/washington/en, where you will also find a list of consulates.

Council on International Exchange (CIEE)

300 Fore St., Portland, ME 04101, USA

☎+1-207-553-4000; www.ciee.org

CIEE's Czech Area Studies Program has courses in everything from Czech cinema, art, and literature to political science and history courses dealing with the Czech Republic and its neighbors. There's even a course entitled "Living and Learning in Prague," which teaches you to extract the maximum Czech-ness from your study abroad. Internships and volunteer positions with local organizations through CIEE are yet another way to immerse yourself in the culture. A two-week orientation with intensive language training gives students a chance to get their bearings before regular classes begin.

▶ *i* Tuition includes either homestay, dormitory, or apartment housing. Does not include all meals. Excursions within the Czech Republic included; optional excursions to Berlin, Krakow, and Vienna cost extra. $ Semester $14,000, full year $25,700; 3-week summer session $3150, 6 weeks $6200.

School for International Training (SIT)

PO Box 676, 1 Kipling Rd., Brattleboro, VT 05302, USA

☎+1-888-272-7881; www.sit.edu/studyabroad

Study abroad at SIT's Art and Social Change program and you'll spend the last four weeks of your semester working on an independent study project. Students spend eight weeks taking courses and living with Czech families before embarking on a 10-day tour of Central Europe to complete their projects.

▶ *i* Students are recommended to have taken courses in the desired field of enrollment, but it is only required of creative writing students. Ⓢ Semester $15,039. Homestay accommodations and board $3704.

Language Schools

As renowned novelist Gustave Flaubert once said, "Language is a cracked kettle on which we beat out tunes for bears to dance to." While we at Let's Go have absolutely no clue what he was talking about, we do know that the following are good resources for learning Czech.

Charles University Institute for Language

Albertov 7/3a, 128 00, Prague 2
☎224 918 775; www.ujop.cuni.cz

Charles University's language institute is especially convenient for study-abroaders already spending most of their class time on campus.

▶ Ⓢ Intensive class €610; evening €322; full semester €1785.

Czech for Foreigners

Dukelských hrdinů 21, 170 00, Prague 7
☎777 048 000; www.czechforforeigners.cz

Want to learn Czech, but too lazy to leave your boudoir? Czech for Foreigners also offers individual lessons in which the tutor comes to you for no extra charge in addition to large classroom lessons. Classes generally run three months and accommodate novices and advanced speakers alike.

▶ Ⓢ Group classes 5400 Kč. Individual lessons vary. Contact info@czech-forforeigners.cz for updated rates.

VOLUNTEERING

With one of the highest orphans-per-capita rates in the "developed" world, Prague has plenty of opportunities to work with its tiny and adorable citizens, although you'll have to inquire at specific orphanages upon arrival. If you're more of a green thumb, environmental work can be found just outside the city in the breathtaking Czech countryside. Otherwise, international organizations offer volunteer placements doing all kinds of work.

Environmental Conservation

Earthwatch
256 Banbury Rd., Oxford, OX2 7DE, UK
☎+44 1865 318 838; www.earthwatch.org

Looking for a (legal) acid trip to complete your European journey? Earthwatch operates in the Jizera Mountains just outside of Prague, working to reverse the damage caused by acid rains from Europe's coal plants. If collecting water samples and catching fish is a bit too outdoorsy for you, test and record the samples collected by fellow volunteers in Earthwatch's indoor lab. At the end of the day return to the 200-year-old farmhouse you all share for a three-course Czech meal.

▶ *i* Includes housing in a double room and meals. Ⓢ 15-day placement £1495.

Community and Cultural Outreach

Arda
Londýnská 30, 120 00 Prague 2
☎272 701 387; www.adra.cz

Help reunite orphaned children with their biological family members, distribute clothing to the poor, or assist those leaving prison to start their lives over. You'll also get the opportunity to mingle with the Czech volunteers who make up the majority of workers.

▶ *i* Must be somewhat fluent in Czech.

Concordia International Volunteers
19 North St., Portslade, Brighton, BN41 1DH, UK
☎+44 012 73 422 218; www.concordiavolunteers.org.uk

Concordia has the advantage of being a large enough non-profit (over 2000 projects worldwide) to provide volunteers with room and board in the Czech Republic as well as pre-departure and in-country support. Projects range from helping refugees and orphans to restoration of castles or setting up free music festivals.

▶ *i* Projects generally range 2-4 weeks. Room and board included. Ⓢ Registration fee £150.

Inex
Varšavská 30, 120 00 Prague 2
☎222 362 715; www.inexsda.cz

At these workcamps (somewhere between summer camp and an

actual job), volunteers clean up national forests, help out in local community centers, and document Czech historical sights. After-hours activities like campfires and group sing-alongs will fulfill all of your sleepaway camp fantasies.

▶ i Sessions last 2-3 weeks depending on project. Accommodations provided and include cabins with kitchen access to cook meals. Friendship bracelets optional.

WORKING

Finding a job in Prague used to be as easy as the ABCs—as long as you could recite them in English. Although English teachers are still in demand, travelers need a work visa and will compete with EU citizens who require far less hoop-jumping on the part of employers. For the most part, internships are the best bet for those looking for work, although if you're willing to do a little footwork upon arrival, businesses in tourist areas often love native English speakers.

Long-Term Work

If you can find yourself an employer willing to sponsor your visa, you're in luck. Otherwise expect competition from those with EU citizenship.

Teaching English

Jobs teaching English are some of the few you may be able to find on your own via online and bulletin board postings. TEFL certification nearly guarantees you a job with a school or business, but less formal teaching jobs (private lessons in a cafe or a home perhaps) can also be found for those without certification.

Caledonian School
Vltavská 24, 150 00 Prague 5
www.teflinprague.com

For those of you needy folks searching for both a TEFL certification and a job, look no further. The Caledonian School offers quick certification classes (less than four weeks long!) and guarantees a job teaching at their school to those who pass. They also offer free Czech lessons to students.

▶ $ Course €1200. Apartment accommodation with private bedroom and shared kitchen and bathroom facilities additional €350.

Bridge Tefl

915 S. Colorado Blvd., Denver, CO 80246 USA

☎+1-303-785-8864; www.bridgetefl.com

From full TEFL certification courses to basic English grammar review sessions, Bridge offers plenty for the savvy English teacher-to-be. Job placements are included in the cost of the full certification course. Bridge also offers headhunting services for those already certified.

▶ Ⓢ Courses range from $95-1995 for full certification. Job support and placement fees range

▶ from gratis to $1595 depending on previous course enrollment.

Spevacek Education Center

Namesti Miru 15, 120 00 Prague 2

☎222 517 869; www.spevacek.info

SPEVACEK sends English teachers to businesses around Prague. Classes are generally in the mornings and evenings, giving you lengthy lunch breaks to explore the city, do a bit of shopping, or recover from the previous evening's festivities. Spevacek also provides travel allowances and Czech lessons.

▶ *i* TEFL certification required. 1 year of teaching experience recommended.

Au Pair Work

Tell people you're a nanny and you're Fran Drescher. Tell them you're an au pair and you're living the life: an elegant pied-à-terre, beautiful children with European manners, and time left over to meet a handsome stranger. While we can't guarantee a movie deal—or even well-behaved children—working as an au pair in Prague definitely has its perks in the forms of compensation and picturesque surroundings.

Great Au Pair

1329 Highway 395, Ste. 10-333, Gardnerville, NV 89410 USA

☎+1-800-935-6303; www.greataupair.com

Great Au Pair is the au pair's craigslist: families post individual listings with information about their children, requirements for their au pair, even pictures of their families. So go ahead—find yourself the family with the cutest kids, most vacation time, or least amount of household chores.

Beyond Tourism

More Visa Information

Apply for a **work visa** at your local Czech consulate. Processing time for employment visas is 90-120 days, so be sure to submit your application well in advance. You will need two recent passport photographs, a valid passport (not a photocopy), a copy of the data page (the page with your photo), and a completed application for **a long stay visa.** You will also need a notarized copy of a work permit, confirmation that your employer applied for the work permit, and proof of accommodation using original documents either in Czech or with accompanying Czech translation. Finally, you will need an affidavit confirming a clean criminal history as well as proof of travel medical insurance, a visa application fee of $130 (cash or money order only), and a pre-paid, self-addressed envelope. For the most up to-date visa information, see the Embassy of the Czech Republic webpage at www.mzv.cz/washington, which also lists regional consulates.

Internships

If you're willing to pay, a variety of organizations will set you up with an unpaid internship in Prague. Some even provide accommodations for an additional cost. Many study abroad programs also have internship options for course credit, which can be convenient if you're already enrolled. Although pricey, such programs offer the security of a guaranteed job upon landing in the Czech Republic; to strike out on your own you'll probably have the best luck approaching businesses in person upon arrival.

Multicultural Center Prague

Vodičkova 36, 116 02 Prague 1

☎ 296 325 345; www.mkc.cz/en

Party planners wanted. Interns at the Multicultural Center in Prague help to design, set up, and execute cultural events all over the city. Both international and Czech students are hired by the organization, and internships range from a brief summer interlude to a year-long session.

▶ *i* Interns must be fluent in either English, German, or French. Accommodations not provided.

Panrimo

330 E. Maple Rd., Ste. 188, Birmingham, MI 48009 USA

☎+1-248-686-2225; www.panrimo.com

Panrimo's internship placements range from photojournalism to museum conservation work, all handpicked for you based on an initial interview. Interns then have a whole list of customizable add-ons, from airport pickups to hot spring excursions, that come at additional fees.

▶ [$] Placement fee $2490. 8-week shared apartment $1600, single apartments $2000.

World Education Group

☎+1-704-461-8480; www.worldeducationgroup.com

If American media has left something to be desired, why not try a bit of Bohemian broadcasting? World Education Group offers internships with various radio and TV stations in Prague, in addition to a variety of NGO and governmental organizations. Czech lessons are available, and all internships are considered "English-friendly."

▶ *i* Dorm or shared housing provided. Required 2½-week intensive Czech course. [$] Internship $3995.

Short-Term Work

Legal short-term work can be hard to come by. Employers often do not wish to petition for a work visa when another able EU candidate is available. English language skills will be your biggest asset; search for jobs in the tourism industry, particularly hostels, restaurants, and lower-end hotels that do not require experience. Use websites like www.expats.cz with job databases as jumping off points when looking for a job.

Tell the World

If your friends are tired of hearing about that time you saved a baby orangutan in Indonesia, there's clearly only one thing to do: get new friends. Find them at our website, www.letsgo.com, where you can post your study-, volunteer-, or work-abroad stories for other, more appreciative community members to read.

Index

Accommodations Index

Restaurants Index

Nightlife Index

Shopping Index

PRAGUE ACKNOWLEDGMENTS

DOROTHY THANKS: MPMP for being my favorite and doing more than her share of work. All of the RWs for surviving, and being undaunted by the seemingly endless things asked of them. Pod Sinai for being the best "do your f-ing work-themed" pod of all time. All of Masthead for being sweethearts, especially Sarah. Marykate for being calm and wise. Iya for guerrilla compliments. Grooveshark for being free. Tanjore Tuesdays and Bagel Fridays for providing me with essential nutrients. Finally, the best for last: thanks to the Oxford Commas, for being the harvestest; to Maine, for quickly becoming my favorite state; and to my family, for everything.

MARY THANKS: Thank you Dorothy, Graham, Mark, Michal, Patrick, Sarah, and everyone at HQ for all of your hard work.

ABOUT LET'S GO

The Student Travel Guide

Let's Go publishes the world's favorite student travel guides, written entirely by Harvard students. Armed with pens, notebooks, and a few changes of clothes stuffed into their backpacks, our student researchers go across continents, through time zones, and above expectations to seek out invaluable travel experiences for our readers. Because we are a completely student-run company, we have a unique perspective on how students travel, where they want to go, and what they're looking to do when they get there. If your dream is to grab a machete and forge through the jungles of Costa Rica, we can take you there. If you'd rather bask in the Riviera sun at a beachside cafe, we'll set you a table. In short, we write for readers who know that there's more to travel than tour buses. To keep up, visit our website, www.letsgo.com, where you can sign up to blog, post photos from your trips, and connect with the Let's Go community.

Traveling Beyond Tourism

We're on a mission to provide our readers with sharp, fresh coverage packed with socially responsible opportunities to go beyond tourism. Each guide's Beyond Tourism chapter shares ideas about responsible travel, study abroad, and how to give back to the places you visit while on the road. To help you gain a deeper connection with the places you travel, our fearless researchers scour the globe to give you the heads-up on both world-renowned and off-the-beaten-track opportunities. We've also opened our pages to respected writers and scholars to hear their takes on the countries and regions we cover, and asked travelers who have worked, studied, or volunteered abroad to contribute first-person accounts of their experiences.

Fifty-Two Years of Wisdom

Let's Go has been on the road for 52 years and counting. We've grown a lot since publishing our first 20-page pamphlet to Europe in 1960, but five decades and 60 titles later, our witty, candid guides are still researched and written entirely by students on shoestring budgets who know that train strikes, stolen luggage, food poisoning, and marriage proposals are all part of a day's work. Meanwhile, we're still bringing readers fresh new features, such as a student-life section with advice on how and where to meet students from around the world; a revamped, user-friendly layout for our listings; and greater emphasis on the experiences that make travel abroad a rite of passage for readers of all ages. And, of course, this year's 16 titles—including five brand-new guides—are still brimming with editorial honesty, a commitment to students, and our irreverent style.

The Let's Go Community

More than just a travel guide company, Let's Go is a community that reaches from our headquarters in Cambridge, MA, all across the globe. Our small staff of dedicated student editors, writers, and tech nerds comes together because of our shared passion for travel and our desire to help other travelers get the most out of their experience. We love it when our readers become part of the Let's Go community as well—when you travel, drop us a postcard (67 Mt. Auburn St., Cambridge, MA 02138, USA), send us an email (feedback@letsgo.com), or sign up on our website (www. letsgo.com) to tell us about your adventures and discoveries.

For more information, updated travel coverage, and news from our researcher team, visit us online at www.letsgo.com.

HELPING LET'S GO. If you want to share your discoveries, suggestions, or corrections, please drop us a line. We appreciate every piece of correspondence, whether a postcard, a 10-page email, or a coconut. Visit Let's Go at www.letsgo. com or send an email to:

feedback@letsgo.com, subject: "Let's Go Budget Prague"

Address mail to:

Let's Go Budget Prague, 67 Mount Auburn St., Cambridge, MA 02138, USA

In addition to the invaluable travel advice our readers share with us, many are kind enough to offer their services as researchers or editors. Unfortunately, our charter enables us to employ only currently enrolled Harvard students.
Maps © Let's Go and Avalon Travel
Interior design by Darren Alessi
Production by Amber Pirker
Photos © Let's Go, Michal Labik, Nelson Greaves and Vanda Gyuris, photographers

Distributed by Publishers Group West.
Printed in Canada by Friesens Corp.

ISBN-13: 978-1-61237-010-1
ISBN-10: 1-61237-010-1
First edition
10 9 8 7 6 5 4 3 2 1

Let's Go Budget Prague is written by Let's Go Publications, 67 Mt. Auburn St., Cambridge, MA 02138, USA.

Let's Go® and the LG logo are trademarks of Let's Go, Inc.

QUICK REFERENCE

YOUR GUIDE TO LET'S GO ICONS

[icon]	*Let's Go* recommends	☎	Phone numbers	[icon]	Directions
i	Other hard info	[$]	Prices	⏰	Hours

IMPORTANT PHONE NUMBERS

EMERGENCY: ☎112			
Amsterdam	☎911	London	☎999
Barcelona	☎092	Madrid	☎092
Berlin	☎110	Paris	☎17
Florence	☎113	Prague	☎158
Istanbul	☎155	Rome	☎113

TEMPERATURE CONVERSIONS

°CELSIUS	-5	0	5	10	15	20	25	30	35
°FAHRENHEIT	23	32	41	50	59	68	77	86	95

MEASUREMENT CONVERSIONS

1 inch (in.) = 25.4mm	1 millimeter (mm) = 0.039 in.
1 foot (ft.) = 0.305m	1 meter (m) = 3.28 ft.
1 mile (mi.) = 1.609km	1 kilometer (km) = 0.621 mi.
1 pound (lb.) = 0.454kg	1 kilogram (kg) = 2.205 lb.
1 gallon (gal.) = 3.785L	1 liter (L) = 0.264 gal.